MW01030310

Unshakeable Confidence
The Freedom to Be Our Authentic Selves
Mindfulness for Women

Unshakeable Confidence
The Freedom to Be Our Authentic Selves
Mindfulness for Women

Mare Chapman

Copyright © 2017 Mare Chapman
Mare Chapman, LLC
715 Hill Street Suite 200
Madison, WI 53705
USA
marechapman.com
Editor: Lisa Ruffolo
Production: Lillian Sizemore
Author photo: Kalleen Mortensen
Consultants: Kate Peyton and Pamela Porter

Books are available at special discounts in bulk purchase for fundraising, educational needs, and promotions.
Book excerpts can be created to fit specific needs.
For details, contact the website or write to the address above.

ALL RIGHTS RESERVED
This book, or parts thereof, may not be reproduced in any form without permission.

Grateful acknowledgement to Harriet Brown for permission to reprint the
"I Love My Body Pledge"
Copyright © 2007 by Harriet Brown/harrietbrown.com

- - -

Publisher's Cataloging-in-Publication data

Names: Chapman, Mare, author.
Title: Unshakeable confidence, the freedom to be our authentic selves:
mindfulness for women / Mare Chapman M.A.
Description: Includes bibliographical references. |
Madison, WI: Mare Chapman LLC, 2017.
Identifiers: ISBN 978-1537553412 | LCCN 2016915562
Subjects: LCSH Self actualization (Psychology). | Meditation--Therapeutic use. |
Women--Mental health. | Women--Psychology. | Buddhism--Psychology. | BISAC
SELF-HELP / Self-Management / General | SELF-HELP / Personal Growth / General |
SOCIAL SCIENCE / Women's Studies
Classification: LCC BF637.M4 C48 2017 | DDC 158.1/2/082--dc23

To my grandmother, my mother,
my daughter, and my granddaughter.

Contents

Guided Meditations

Preface

When I attended a meditation retreat a few years into learning the practice of mindfulness, the teacher mentioned that one characteristic of an enlightened being is unshakeable confidence. Unshakeable confidence! Those words startled and intrigued me. Developing unshakeable confidence through a spiritual practice? It seemed almost inappropriate to me at first. Then I thought, "I'm sure this isn't the egotistical, big-headed kind of confidence, like 'I am THE greatest of all.' Instead, it must mean a deep, stable, inner trust that you can handle whatever is happening in the present moment — the awful, hard, seemingly unbearable things in life, as well as the outrageously amazing and wonderful."

I was struck with how fantastic it would be to actually live that way, free from being trapped in the old fears that I'm not good enough, not smart enough, or not anything enough. It would mean freedom from the habits of judging and comparing myself to others. It would mean complete self-acceptance and self-respect. It would mean transparency, being completely open and vulnerable. I wouldn't need to be anything other than authentic, honest, and real in every circumstance. With such quiet and steadfast confidence, I would have no barriers in loving and connecting with others. I aspired in that moment to learn to live my life with the complete faith that I can respond wisely, skillfully, and compassionately to whatever arises. I vowed to live with unshakeable confidence!

Buddhist teachings say unshakeable confidence is our birthright. This way of being is a part of our natural, unconditioned mind that has always been here, is here in fact right now, but has become covered by the habits of our conditioning. Those habits keep us caught in perceptions, judgments, assumptions, and beliefs that imprison us in feeling small and afraid to be ourselves, afraid to truly know ourselves, afraid to risk our significance. Beyond these limiting views that seem so real to us is our authentic true nature, untarnished by the messiness, grime, and confusion of the mind's habits.

This book is dedicated to shining the transformative light of mindfulness on those of us women who are caught in the habit of losing track of ourselves in relationships and feel self-doubt, insecurity, and anxiety more often than we'd like to admit. It's for those of us who believe in gender equality, but still feel that we tend to sell ourselves short. It's for those of us who long for freedom from our inner critic, are sick and tired of her constant nattering about perfection, and pine for inner peace and self-acceptance. It's for those who hear a still small voice inside, maybe a whisper, saying something like, "I could be happier. I could learn to relax with myself and believe in myself. I could be free to be my true self. Really I could." This book is for those of us who yearn for the freedom to be our authentic selves and live with the steady power of unshakeable confidence.

Mare Chapman
October 30, 2016
Madison, Wisconsin

1

Introduction:
The Map
for the Journey

What other people think of you
is none of your business.
No one can make you feel inferior
without your consent.

Eleanor Roosevelt

The tart, wise advice from Eleanor Roosevelt, a brave and powerful woman rings true. Can we follow it? We'd love to be unaffected by others' opinions, but doing so is *extremely* hard for many of us. Because self-doubt and insecurity too often rule, especially when we're afraid others aren't happy with us, we try to shore up our sense of self by doing all we can to make sure they're content. In fact, we can become so focused on pleasing others that we lose connection with ourselves, sometimes unknowingly sacrificing our own health and well-being in the effort. We assume that when others are happy with us, we'll feel secure, and *then*, finally, we can relax.

The obvious problem with this paradigm is that we can't control how others view us. As a result, we feel uncertain, never knowing if we're really okay in their eyes. Further, our assumption that others and the external world could somehow give us real and lasting security is flawed. If we look deeply into how things truly are, we see instead that the world and everyone in it are always changing through a constant interplay of causes and conditions, most of which are outside of our control. Given these realities, it's no wonder we feel anxious. The real truth is, or so wise teachers say, the ultimate source of security and contentment must always come from within ourselves.

> Othering: the automatic mental movement of attention away from self to the other, based on the assumption that the other has more power, authority, or privilege.

The pattern of seeking approval and security from others while ignoring our own wisdom and knowledge is a deeply conditioned habit for many women in our culture. We unknowingly give our inner authority or agency away to the other person while ignoring, disconnecting from, or overriding our own authentic experience. I call this basic imbalance of attention "othering". Although the term "othering" has been used in a sociological context where one societal group classifies another group as inferior and less worthy of respect, I use this term differently.[1] I define "othering" as the automatic mental movement of attention away from self to the other, based on the assumption that the other has more power, authority, or privilege.

As a psychotherapist, I see this pattern operating repeatedly in the women who work with me, as well as in myself, friends, colleagues, and women of all ages who come to learn mindfulness. I see othering firmly embedded in our culture's messages about being female. I believe it's a root cause for the anxiety

> We give our inner authority or power away to the other person while ignoring, disconnecting from, or overriding our own authentic present-moment experience.

and depression that women suffer, and a barrier to creating vibrant, mutually empowering, and sustainable relationships. Many women, who on the surface appear successful and competent, feel deep down that something is wrong with them or they're damaged in some way. The effects of othering keep many trapped in self-doubt, afraid to fully and wholeheartedly take their seat at the table of life or to follow their dreams. This fear and entrapment deprive the world of the profound benefits of our feminine wisdom, intelligence, and compassion. Certainly, considering the current state of the world with its escalating bigotry, cruelty, and violence, the world needs us. We need to shed our internal limitations, encourage ourselves to live authentically, and bring our invaluable womanly ways to help our dear aching world.

This book explores the habits and patterns created in our minds that arise from our gender conditioning. As we journey from chapter to chapter, we will delve into how these habits become established and the different ways they play out, limit us, and cause us misery. We'll examine the Buddhist practice of mindfulness as the healing remedy and path to liberation from these patterns. We'll learn how mindfulness cultivates inner stability and security and rebuilds a deep trust in our own authority and ability to handle whatever arises in life. Because the teachings view attachment to self as the root cause of all suffering, we'll also investigate the question of self and what is meant by no-self. Along the way, we'll discover how mindfulness frees us to live our lives authentically and with unshakeable confidence.

It's true, of course, that men are also deeply conditioned in ways that create suffering for themselves and the world. It's my hope that they will do the crucial work of freeing themselves from the habits of their gender conditioning. We, however, must focus first on our own life as it's the one life we can actually save. Because everything is truly interdependent and nothing and no one exists completely independently, I hope you can view living from your own authority and cultivating your inner security as responsible, wise, and kind, rather than selfish. The more we can each take complete responsibility for our suffering and for our happiness, the more we naturally benefit those whose lives we touch daily. Those ripples will spread out to benefit every being.

Our Minds Are Powerful

The sages say that heaven and hell are created in our minds. I'm sure you've noticed that in one moment you can feel happy and successful, and in another moment you can feel awful, pathetic, or like the worst slug on the planet. It all depends on what you're thinking. "Okay, that was the best and most brilliant thing I've ever done!" Or, "That was the stupidest thing I've ever done! What was I thinking?" Because we each have the power to make ourselves stressed or happy, sick or well, it's crucial that we learn how to work with our all-powerful minds.

> Othering unmoors us from our inner base of stability and wisdom, and creates a chronic self-consciousness.

Through my work as a psychotherapist, I have the unique and sacred privilege of being allowed intimate access to many women's minds and hearts every day. Over and over, I see the power of the mind to make us feel happy or despairing, empowered or depleted. In particular, I see how the pattern of othering traps and exhausts us. We fixate on trying to figure out how to please others, tend to their needs, and make sure they are happy with us. No matter how much they reassure us that they think we're okay, deep down we fear they could change their minds at any moment. Othering unmoors us from our inner base of stability and wisdom, and creates a chronic self-consciousness. In our attempt to feel secure in the others' perceptions of us by pleasing and tending to them, we become paradoxically absorbed in our own insecurity. Further, the insecurity this pattern provokes, displayed through self-criticism, judgment, doubt, and second guessing, is at the root of our chronic anxiety, self-hatred, depression, eating disorders, and addictions of all kinds.

Seeing these patterns and the deep suffering they cause has led me on a journey to find a way to transform these habits so we can be free to live under the guidance of our own agency. In my own evolution, practicing meditation for thirty years, mindfulness and Buddhist philosophy have opened the door to a path of gradual self-acceptance and deep inner trust. In working with others, I have found this approach to be far more effective than insight-oriented psychotherapy, cognitive-behavioral therapy, hypnosis, and all the psychotherapy tools that I have used and experienced. As I've taught these practices, both individually and in classes, I've consistently witnessed women finding freedom from internalized oppression and strengthening their ability to trust and believe in themselves.

Naming the Problem

What's true for you? Have you noticed the tendency of your mind to dwell on others? By "dwelling," I don't mean thinking about how much you love, appreciate, or feel connected to someone. I'm talking about the "bad" kind of dwelling, where you fret about what's going on with them, whether they're happy, wondering how they feel about you, or worrying if they didn't like what you did or how you looked. This kind of dwelling on others often leads to feeling guilty, worrying you aren't doing enough

5

for them, or even wondering when they might finally confess and say, "You know what? You really aren't good enough for me." Or, perhaps you're more familiar with the kind of dwelling where you're constantly concerned about them. "Are they okay? Are they having trouble with their boss again? Are they going to be in trouble with their teacher? Are they drinking or gambling again? How can I get them to stop? It's really my fault they're so upset."

Fretful dwelling on others generates a basic uneasiness, an undercurrent of restlessness and tension, which is based on a deeply held fear that we aren't enough. This fear leads to relentless scanning and self-assessment. We habitually compare ourselves to others, which keeps us caught in worrying and striving to be better, more attractive, more considerate, or whatever we think is needed to please our all-important others. Yet, we never seem to reach the place where we feel we are okay enough, perfect enough. Consequently, we're never able to truly rest in ourselves, just as we are.

If you see yourself in some of these patterns, then welcome to the common pattern of women's conditioning in our western culture. Othering is a natural reaction and coping strategy to gender oppression. For thousands of years, the power structure of the world's prominent cultures has been patriarchal, making the male gender dominant and the female gender subordinate. A fundamental consequence of being subordinate is that one must learn to "other." Cultural conditioning teaches us the other is more valued and powerful than ourselves, and consequently we learn to disconnect from our authentic experience and center our attention instead on the more powerful other.

Simply because we were born female, we've been *unconsciously* trained to view ourselves as lesser and give our personal authority away to the other. We learned to place our frame of reference, or locus of control, in the external other, rather than within our own direct and actual experience. This all-powerful other can be anyone: our parents, partner, boss, colleagues and co-workers, children, siblings, friends, and even strangers on the street. We can give our power away to our children's teachers, the grocery store clerk, our neighbors, the car mechanic, or to any person, anywhere. In any moment, no matter where we are, we can be worrying about what someone else is thinking about us, unconsciously assuming their experience trumps ours. In waking up to this habit, more than one woman in my class has said, "I can't believe it! I realized that every time I'm in the checkout line at the grocery store I imagine the cashier is criticizing my purchases. I sense her judgments and I feel guilty and inadequate. But now I realize I'm making this all up!"

Until we recognize the mental habit of othering, we unknowingly continue to oppress ourselves. Moving attention away from ourselves to the other happens unconsciously. This is the nature of conditioned habits — we don't have conscious choice or control over them. When we're lost in othering, we're not aware of our authentic experience. Consequently, we become unknown to ourselves, often unclear about what we really want, feel, or think. We get cut off from our intuition, innate wisdom, and intelligence. Blind to ourselves as we actually are, we assume we reflect the distorted view we imagine through the eyes of the other. We react according to "shoulds," the mind's stories about how we think we're supposed to be. We may say "Yes" when we don't want to, pretend we're feeling things we aren't feeling, or want things we really don't want. We lose our center, the anchor to ourself, and become lost in the other. This often leaves us feeling like a fraud, or like we're

> Bondage to perfection keeps us stuck in a cycle of suffering.

skimming on the surface of ourselves, never fully alive, whole, or at home with ourselves. We may feel an ache or emptiness in missing ourselves. We come to believe that if we can just be perfect, then we will secure the other's approval and support permanently. Our striving for perfection is an ever-rising bar. We can never achieve it. This bondage to perfection profoundly limits our relationships and keeps us stuck in a cycle of suffering. As long as we remain attached to the illusion that perfection will save us, our sense of self and security will be submerged and swamped by feelings of inadequacy, shame, anxiety, and depression.

The Path of Mindfulness

Mindfulness is an ancient practice taught by the Buddha some 2,600 years ago to train the mind to be our friend rather than our enemy, and is a direct pathway out of the cycle of stress and suffering. It is aimed precisely at waking us up from the habits of our conditioning so we can see clearly how these habits actually create our misery. The method teaches us how to relate to our present moment reality in a stable, kind, and effective way, allowing us to live with more sustainable happiness and true freedom.

Over the past forty years, mindfulness has been steadily making its way into our mainstream society, due primarily to dedicated western teachers trained in the east by Buddhist scholars and the work of pioneering scientists studying its effects on the brain and body. Mindfulness is now taught in practically any venue you can imagine, from preschool classrooms to corporate boardrooms, factories, prisons, and public service agencies. Its value as a method for reducing stress is undeniable. Learning to be present with what is, versus getting swept away into the mind's scary, angry, or depressing stories is invaluable for our mental and physical health. Yet the practice offers much more than respite from stress so we can function more calmly as a worker or parent. Founded in a philosophy based on moral ethics, laws of nature, and a deep understanding of the psychology of our human hearts and minds, mindfulness has the power to free us from the root causes of suffering, cultivate the causes of true happiness, enable us to live with open and loving hearts for ourselves and all beings everywhere, and ultimately guide us to complete enlightenment.

Called a path of liberation and transformation, the practice asks us to first establish a steady and calm connection with our present-moment experience. By residing in that inner stability, we naturally see more clearly and deeply what is truly occurring — the exact thoughts and stories the mind is creating, the underlying assumed beliefs that create the story, and the accompanying feelings and sensations in the body. By learning to open to our thoughts with compassionate, kind, accepting awareness, the true nature of reality is revealed, and our experience shifts and changes on its own. Through clearly seeing how things really are, we find deeper understanding and insight. With practice, the mind gradually becomes deconditioned and we are able to live more authentically, ever freer from the habits of conditioning.

Practicing mindfulness is not a quick fix. It is a gradual process of waking up to the mind's habitual reactions and choosing wiser and more skillful responses to what is happening. In cultivating freedom from the habit of othering, we learn to stay on our own side, no matter what. We develop a balance in our awareness of what's happening with ourselves *and* with the other. We know what we are authentically experiencing in the moment *as* we are aware of and relate to the other. We can be truly who we are, vulnerable in our honesty, and able to maintain our own power because we trust and respect ourselves. We are released from needing the other's approval because we understand and accept ourselves. These qualities are fundamental to living with true freedom and unshakeable confidence.

> In cultivating freedom from the habit of othering, we develop a balance in our awareness of what's happening with ourselves and with the other.

Structure of This Book

This book is based on a class I've been teaching to women for over twenty years, and each time I begin a new class I'm urged to spread the word. Students repeatedly say, "This is amazing. No one ever talks about these patterns, and yet this is exactly what my mind does all the time. I'm always thinking about others, obsessing about them, and I feel totally trapped in this. It's such a relief to know I'm not the only one! It's so great to learn that there is a way to freedom and balance!"

The class was initially designed as a pilot study, part of my graduate research work. I wanted to study what impact mindfulness had on women's psychological health, particularly the habit of othering and building connection with authentic self. Because the results were overwhelmingly positive and statistically significant, I've been teaching the class ever since. I am so grateful for those first twenty-five women in the pilot class, and for all the women who have studied with me since, for having the courage to be vulnerable with themselves and each other as they learned the practice. This book is the ongoing result of what I've been learning from them and these ancient teachings. It's a work in progress and reflects my understanding of the practice and teachings so far.

I suggest you approach this book as if you were taking the class with me and view it as an exploration. In class, the lessons are weekly, but please work at your own pace. Don't hesitate to go back and reread sections and instructions. Most chapters end with suggestions for practice, which I call "Ownwork." You might want to read a chapter and then practice the suggested meditations and ownwork a while before moving on.

We begin by looking at the pattern of othering, first by exploring the notion of self, the conditioned mind, and what is meant by authentic self. We delve into just how we become trained to other, and describe the common characteristics of othering. Then we turn to mindfulness as the transformative remedy. We review the scientific support for the practice and explore the basic principles for its cultivation. We learn the practice of mindful breathing to establish our inner home base and begin the practice of spotting othering. Then we expand into mindfully connecting with the whole body, followed by learning how to relate mindfully to physical sensations, including pain. Next, we learn about the judging mind and how to work with thoughts in a way that frees us from their abduction and enables wise discernment.

After discussing the profound teaching called the Four Noble Truths, we explore how the wanting mind and clinging to desire create our difficult emotions. We learn about emotions and how to use mindfulness to change our relationship to those temporarily powerful and all-important feelings. We also explore the habit of over-responsibility, a deeply conditioned effect of othering, the habit of resisting what we don't want, and the alchemical power of acceptance.

Next, we turn to the ultimate painful effect of othering, self-hatred, and learn the potent antidote of the Loving Kindness (Metta) practice. We also engage in a process of investigative inquiry to transform and learn from our most difficult emotions, and then learn how to bring the healing power of compassion to ourselves. We return to the notions of self and no-self and how they relate to living authentically with unshakeable confidence. Finally, we review our journey and the benefits of freeing ourselves from the othering habits, and summarize suggestions for continuing on and deepening our understanding and practice.

If you're new to mindfulness, you'll understand its fundamentals by the time you reach the end of the book. Please experiment with the practices and see how they are for you. Although the method is essentially simple, practicing it is not easy due to the entrenched habits of the mind. Be patient and kind with yourself as you learn and practice. If you're already a mindfulness practitioner, I hope this book will provide a useful review of the method and offer new ways to apply mindfulness to expand your freedom and confidence.

My aspiration in offering this book is that you'll find mindfulness so intriguing and beneficial you'll be inspired to practice every day, because it's through daily practice that you'll witness your life changing for the better. Through relating mindfully to your present moment authentic experience, you'll come to trust your own knowledge and authority, and be able to respond to the challenges and delights of your world with greater wisdom, compassion, and ease. You'll discover how to create more reliable happiness for yourself and live your life with the confidence that you can handle whatever life dishes out. In that way, your life will be an even greater benefit to all those that you love, all you connect with every day, and to the entire planet.

By opening to these teachings and experimenting with these practices, my hope is you'll join the chorus of empowered women who repeatedly say by end of the class: "This practice has changed my life. This class has been life-saving! Mindfulness helps me stay steady with my true self. I feel like I'm getting to know myself again. It's so empowering to know I can choose how I want to respond. I now have the ability to say 'yes' and 'no' and really mean it. I'm learning to trust and respect myself in ways I never have before."

Guidelines for Experiencing This Book

Please read this book with an *experimental attitude and an open mind*. Consider being both the scientist and the subject of the experiment. Don't take my word for it that these practices are beneficial. Find out for yourself. Take these ideas and practices on to see what you can learn and discover about yourself. Notice what seems right to you and what works for you.

Whatever you are experiencing in the present moment is always valid and is exactly right. Remember that even though there are specific instructions for practicing mindfulness, there is no particular "what" you're supposed to experience. Instead, whatever you are experiencing in the present is always exactly right, simply because it is what you are experiencing. Trust and respect whatever is happening for you. Because you are experiencing it, it is valid. Period. There's nothing else you should be experiencing.

Approach your experience with curiosity. We are cultivating sincere interest in our experience, so please ask, "*What* am I actually experiencing right now?" and "Exactly *how* am I experiencing it?" Refrain from asking the familiar "*Why* am I experiencing it?" because "why" tends to propel us into our discursive problem-solving judging mind, taking us away from what is real and into ideas and concepts. Instead, we want to bring the energy of wonderment to our experience. Curiosity creates an internal openness, a roominess that brings us closer to what's here. Out of openness and enhanced intimacy with our own experience, new possibilities have room to emerge.

Be willing to change your relationship to yourself. A major effect of mindfulness is that it changes our relationship to everything we experience. As we wake up to our conditioning, we can *choose* how we want to respond instead of reacting automatically. Whereas conditioning breeds a judgmental, controlling, sometimes shockingly cruel relationship to ourselves, mindfulness trains us to relate to ourselves with acceptance, kindness, and trust. Through the practice, we develop respect for our experience, no matter what it is. We learn to let go of shaming self-assessments. We recognize them as conditioned reactions and not the truth. We are training our mind to be our friend instead of our inner bully.

Doing these practices does not require becoming Buddhist. This book is not about the religion of Buddhism. These ancient methods are intended to help our minds become so clear that we can experience reality accurately. The practice offers practical and effective ways to transform conditioned habits of the mind at the root of our suffering, regardless of our beliefs or religious background. It provides methods for learning how to create our own sustainable happiness. The principles and philosophy of Buddhism offer a contextual framework for life that is open to all and fully applies to the challenges of our times.

> *May you learn to accept yourself completely.*
> *May you learn that you are always enough.*
> *May you learn to be your own best friend.*
> *May you learn to reside and trust in your authentic experience.*
> *May you rest in unshakeable confidence.*
> *May all beings everywhere benefit from your efforts.*

2

Self: Conditioned and Authentic — Who Am I Really?

Our deepest fear is not that we are inadequate. Our deepest fear is that we are powerful beyond measure. It is our light, not darkness that most frightens us.... Your playing small does not serve the world.... There is nothing enlightened about shrinking so that other people will not feel insecure around you. We are all meant to shine....

Marianne Williamson

We all want to be happy, don't we? We all want lives that are fulfilling and joyful. We want to be loving, loved, and feel we belong. We want to be kind, generous, and patient. We want to conduct ourselves with integrity and self-respect. We want to be free from stress and suffering. Most essentially, we want to be ourselves as we honestly are. Yet for many of us, this deepest aspiration feels out of reach. We believe it's too risky to be our real selves because we're afraid if others *really* know us, we'd be rejected, abandoned, and alone. Why does lasting happiness evade us? Why is it so hard to be our real and true selves? What makes us so afraid of being authentic? Let's begin to explore these ideas of self as we look more closely at what it means to be authentic and what prevents us from living honestly as ourselves.

Conditioning: We Are All Wearing Sunglasses

As spirits living in human bodies, it is necessary and unavoidable that our minds become conditioned. Simply in the process of growing up, we develop habitual ways of experiencing and perceiving reality. Beginning in early infancy, when we first recognize we are separate from others because we exist in a body, we unconsciously begin to form perceptions and ideas about how we are supposed to be, not supposed to be, and what is supposed to happen to us. Over time these ideas become conditioned beliefs. It's like wearing a pair of sunglasses for so long, we forget they're in front of our eyes. This tinted view alters everything we experience and becomes our normal perception of reality. As our default programming, conditioned habits operate so automatically that we're living in a trance, a dream, or an altered state much of the time. Unless we wake up from the trance, we sleepwalk through our lives, reacting habitually without conscious awareness or choice.

Neuroscience tells us that habitual perceptions of reality create neural pathways in the brain. This concept is based on the simple truth that whatever we practice grows stronger. Consider the value of practice with piano lessons, learning a language, or any new skill. When we habitually make the same observations and hold the same beliefs, the neural connections in the brain become well-worn ruts and grooves. Every time you find yourself in certain conditions — you see a particular look on your parent's face, or walk into the dentist's office, or hear your child call, "Mom!" — your mind-body system reacts habitually. Those deep neural grooves truly run us.

The concept of self exists only through its relationship to something other than self. Practically speaking, we can define the notion of "self" as an awareness of our own being separate from other people and external objects. Referred to as self-identity, self-concept, or ego, self is created and shaped by the stories the mind habitually runs about ourselves, stories arising from the perceptions and beliefs embedded in our default programming. You have probably heard the advice, "Just be yourself," when you are preparing to interview for a job, give a talk, or meet a new important person and feel unsure of yourself. What's your reaction? Do you think, "Sure, no problem"? Or, are you more likely to think, "Yeah, right! Then they'll see who I *really* am, and that won't be good"? If we believe we aren't good enough the way we are, we try to appear the way we think the other wants us to be. On the inside, we feel phony because we know we're acting to win approval. This may leave us feeling deceptive or manipulative, which in the long run doesn't promote self-confidence.

Entire industries are built on the belief that being ourselves just as we are is not good enough. Look at the fashion and cosmetics industries, for example. My mother used to say that she couldn't go out into the world until she "put on her face," meaning she had to put on powder and lipstick. She was influenced by ads that told women they were more attractive and acceptable when they wore makeup. This may seem trivial, but when you witness a ritual like this as a child, you learn you have to look a certain way to be appropriate for the world. You need makeup to disguise yourself because how you are naturally isn't good enough.

Obviously, some of these conditioned habits are useful and help us function successfully in the world. In fact, when we first learned them, they were likely useful, and in many cases, essential. Useful conditioned habits include learning to look both ways before we crossed the street, brushing our teeth after eating, being "good" when Dad or Mom was on the rampage, learning how to be courteous, and practicing values of honesty and responsibility. To be successful in our lives, we need to learn moral, functional, and acceptable ways to behave. It's efficient for these acceptable views and behaviors to become automatic. In other words, learning these habits was intelligent and allowed us to survive our childhood as best as we could. However, to varying degrees, we also became conditioned to perceive reality in ways that cause misery. We developed the beliefs that we aren't good enough, that we aren't okay the way we are, that something is wrong with us, or that we have to be perfect to be loved. These are conditioned ideas about the self that *are not true* and create great suffering.

Sometimes the acceptable, conditioned ways of being serve us well at first, but cause suffering later. For example, when I was a girl, my dad taught me to smile instead of cry when I was upset. His teaching method was threatening to spank me if I didn't stop crying and give him a smile instead. He was surely operating out of his own conditioning in which he learned certain emotions were "bad," and he had no ability to understand or work with them. In turn, I learned to regard my hurt feelings as bad, to hide them out of sight, and act instead as if I were "fine." Learning this lesson created toughness and resiliency that gave me strength when I felt scared, lonely, or hurt as I was growing up. As an adult, I realized I was habitually cut off from my emotions and, consequently, I didn't know or trust myself. I maintained an emotional distance from others because it was too scary to let people know what I was really feeling, especially when I was upset.

Effects of Gender

Many factors shape our conditioning and the resulting beliefs we hold about ourselves, but the gender we are born into affects us at our root. It is the most basic and primary creator of our self-concept. Think of it: what was the very first statement made about you when you were born?

"It's a girl!" Gender's influence is so profound, so integral to our sense of self that it's hard to perceive it. I once heard Gloria Steinem say that we won't have real peace on the planet until we achieve true gender equality — that's how fundamental and powerful gender bias conditioning is for us as a species.

Because being female places us in a position of less power in our historically patriarchal world, we're conditioned to disconnect from our authentic direct experience and instead focus our interest, attention, and concern on others. We are trained to look to the other (i.e., parent, friend, teacher, lover, boss, children, or strangers) for validation that we are okay, worthy, lovable, and valued. We cut ourselves off from our core knowledge and wisdom through deeply ingrained habits of judging, criticizing, shaming, and trying to shape ourselves into being what we think the other wants us to be so we can win their esteem. This conditioning process happens unconsciously and insidiously, but the effect is that as we grow older, unless something happens to jolt us out of the habit of hiding our authentic selves, we are locked into these ideas. We form a self-identity that views our self as flawed — "I'm an anxious person. It's always my fault. I'm too heavy and not attractive. I'm not kind enough. I'm not okay." We strive to be perfect, hoping that when we are good enough, we will finally be okay and worthy of being accepted. Then we'll finally feel safe, secure, and protected. Paradoxically, bowing and scraping to the god of perfection keeps us trapped in our fears, anxious and insecure, blocked from the inner wisdom of our ultimate security — trusting and accepting our authentic selves just as we are.

> We are trained to look to the other for validation that we are okay, worthy, lovable, and valued.

Unfortunately, we have to learn these self-destructive habits to be successful as a woman in our culture. Dr. Jean Baker Miller, one of the early pioneers in establishing the field of women's psychology, said, "To be successful as a woman in our society, we must give up relationship with our self in order to be in relationship with the other."[2] In fact, our core training is to give ourselves away to the other. Research shows that by the time we reach puberty, our authentic self goes underground and the mental habit of referring our attention to the external is solidly in place.[3] Gender conditioning has high costs for ourselves and for any relationship we hope will be alive and satisfying. Often in my work as a psychotherapist, I hear women express their anguish over a relationship ending by saying, "I lost myself in the relationship, again."

> Othering cuts us off from knowing our actual thoughts and feelings.

Othering cuts us off from knowing our actual thoughts and feelings. It disconnects us from our innate wisdom, kindness, intuition, and trust in ourselves. We become confused about our boundaries, where our self begins and ends, and what we really want. We become afraid that what we're experiencing and feeling isn't okay because it isn't what we are supposed to be experiencing. Instead, we feel anxiety, shame, numbness, or depression. To the extent that we're bound to our conditioned identity, we live a fragmented rather than authentic life. On top of feeling fragmented, we're busy striving, trying to do things right, trying to be in control of what's happening, and worrying that it's all going to fall apart. We miss the only moment when we're actually alive and have the possibility of finding freedom: this present moment.

The Authentic Self

What does it mean to be authentic? What does it look, sound, and feel like? Consider the people you are naturally drawn to and are comfortable being yourself with, even though you may not know them well. Chances are, we'd call those people authentic.

Authentic people are open, transparent, and honest. They might not always be pleasant or pleasing. In fact, they can be difficult and challenging at times. Even so, we know what's going on with them, we know where we stand with them, and that's a relief. When we're around people we sense as authentic, we often are willing to be more real and honest ourselves, which is a relief.

Ezra Bayda, a wonderful mindfulness teacher, describes being authentic or genuine as "simply being aware of and connected with what we are actually experiencing in the present moment: the thoughts, emotions, sensations, and perceptions of the moment."[4] Being authentic is *whatever is true* for us right now, the facts of our actual experience. It's knowing and accepting, without judgment or rejection, the mind-body state we are experiencing in the present — anxiety, sadness, delight, boredom, anger, or tranquility.

For example, right now as I write this, my authentic experience is: I'm aware of a slight headache and feeling hungry. I'm smelling the odor of tuna fish because my spouse just brought me a tuna salad sandwich. I'm aware of feeling gratitude for her care. I hear the wind blowing outside. I'm feeling some satisfaction as I make progress on this manuscript, yet I notice a background thought of, "Gee, I hope I'm explaining this clearly," and a flicker of anxiety in my body connected to that thought. So the experience of being authentic is an ever-flowing and changing state, not solid, fixed, or permanent.

Authenticity requires radical self-acceptance and bravery.

Authenticity requires radical self-acceptance and radical bravery. It means having the courage to be open and vulnerable to our experience just as it is. It means staying connected with ourselves instead of abandoning or turning against ourselves when we don't like what we're experiencing. It means learning to love and accept ourselves exactly as we are: perfectly imperfect. That might seem scary, but the reward for doing so is freedom. By practicing knowing ourselves in a direct, honest, and accepting way, we can see through our conditioned assumptions and judgments and, over time, come to understand and relax with our true self. When we can accept ourselves completely, we don't need to defend or protect ourselves from others' opinions and judgments. We're not dependent on their approval. By being authentic, we stay steady in supporting ourselves with whatever we're feeling and thinking, even when what we're experiencing is different from others. We remain loyal and don't abandon ourselves in any way.

In author and researcher Brené Brown's groundbreaking work on examining shame and imperfection, she defines authenticity as "the practice of letting go of who we think we are supposed to be and embracing who we really are."[5] When we can be authentic — stand with ourselves in complete acceptance, trusting that we are enough, just as we are in this moment — we are empowered. We are centered and feel confidence and respect for ourselves, and we're aware of our whole experience: our thoughts, sensations, and emotions. We are transparent. We have nothing to hide. We aren't afraid of ourself in any way. We are anchored to our direct present moment experience. We can set boundaries and say "no" when we need to. We trust that we can handle whatever comes along, even if it's messy, scary, and hard.

Doesn't this sound great, to be so strong and brave and transparent? Wouldn't it be wonderful to be free to be yourself, just as you are, wherever you are, in every moment? Some of you might remember the Marlo Thomas award-winning album, "Free To Be You and Me," that encouraged boys and girls to be however and whoever they are, regardless of their gender. I fondly remember playing the album for my kids when they were little and enjoying its message of authenticity.

> When we can be authentic — stand with ourselves in complete acceptance, trusting that we are enough, just as we are in this moment — we are empowered.

Waking Up From Conditioning: Finding Our Authentic Self

To be free to be our real selves, we have to wake up from the trance of our conditioning and learn to see reality clearly and accurately. We have to take off our sunglasses. This requires dismantling the old conditioned assumptions and beliefs that tell us we are flawed. It requires letting go of the impossible belief that we have to be perfect to be accepted and loved. In short, becoming authentic requires healing our injured sense of self that grew from the false, conditioned view that we are lesser, and developing a sense of self that truly *knows*, without exception and regardless of gender, we are enough and equally worthy, valued, and precious.

As we know, simply choosing to believe in equality and attempting to rearrange our minds to think differently does not ensure change. If we could think our way out of our internalized oppression, we would have done so long ago. As I was beginning to wake up to the habits of my conditioning, such as giving my power away to my husband or my boss by feigning agreement with them when I disagreed, I'd feel furious with myself. I knew I was hiding what was true for me, but I couldn't stop because the habit to comply and please was so deeply ingrained. Even though I knew my opinion or idea was just as legitimate as theirs, my default programming was to give in to their view. Despite my intellectual understanding, my behavior remained caught in the conditioned pattern.

> Mindfulness has the power to transform our deeply conditioned habits.

This is where mindfulness can make a difference. Mindfulness has the power to transform our deeply conditioned habits. By waking up to our experience and seeing the ways we've learned to *habitually oppress ourselves*, mindfulness has the transformative power to gently free us from old patterns. It teaches us to relate to ourselves respectfully and kindly, no matter what. For example, let's say I'm aware of feeling angry with my friend because she didn't follow through with what she said she'd do.

I'm aware of the angry stories my mind is telling and the uncomfortable knot in my belly. I'm aware that I want my friend to shape up and be good on her word. My heart feels closed to her. The stories, sensations, and thoughts are my authentic experience. As I work with the reaction mindfully, holding it with acceptance and compassion, seeing into my genuine experience more deeply, my view expands as I recognize my judgments, expectations, beliefs, and deeper feelings of disappointment. I also realize my friend has a lot going on in her life right now.

Mindfulness heals our relationship with ourself.

Holding all of this in awareness, the anger and disappointment gradually dissipate, and a wise, kind response occurs to me: to forgive her and remember that disappointment (suffering) is a part of life. With this response, I find I can honestly open my heart to myself and to her.

Through mindfulness practice, we gradually become less hooked by our conditioned reactions. We take them less personally as we see they are only conditioned beliefs and not the truth of who we are. As we stop submitting to them, the deep neural grooves of the patterns gradually diminish. Eventually, the conditioned reactions lose the power to derail us altogether. In this way, mindfulness heals our relationship with ourself, and we can be who we authentically are in each moment.

Our true nature, which might also be called our higher self, spirit, or Buddha nature, is pure awareness. It is the unconditioned mind, our ultimate true consciousness, the universal consciousness that we possess. Our true nature is stable, luminous, spacious, kind, loving, generous, compassionate, and wise. It reflects a basic goodness and is always here, regardless of the habits of conditioning. Whereas western psychology tends to view the concept of self from the perspective of damage and illness, Buddhist psychology has us start with wholeness and perfection. A story about a famous statue of a Buddha in Thailand is a perfect metaphor for understanding the essence of our true nature and conditioned mind.

The Golden Buddha

For centuries a clay statue of a large Buddha sat in a temple in Thailand. Its origins were unknown, but it became a central aspect of the temple, the monks tending faithfully to the statue, fixing cracks in the clay as it dried out in the sun and heat over the years. One day when a monk was repairing an especially large crack, he peered into it to see how deep the crack ran, and to his surprise saw a golden reflection. Curious, he pulled off a piece of the dried clay and discovered more gold beneath the clay. And then more gold. When all the clay was removed, the now famous Golden Buddha was fully revealed.

We could say the Golden Buddha represents our true nature, our basic goodness that is always here, and the clay that covered the statue for so long symbolizes the grit and grime of our conditioned mind and incorrect views of ourself. I love this metaphor because it reminds us that no matter what happens, no matter how many negative habits our mind has, how much doubt or shame we have about ourselves, or how depressed we might feel or believe ourselves to be, underneath it all, undisturbed and unaffected by all this clay, our true nature, our basic goodness, our wisdom, is always here, shining, waiting to be accessed. When we mindfully accept our authentic experience and can explore it kindly and skillfully, we naturally access the wisdom, intelligence, and kindness of our true nature. We are finding our gold, our inner wealth.

What Is Selfless?

Ideally, to be our true genuine selves, we need to peel off the sunglasses of conditioning and connect with our authentic experience, which naturally allows access to the wisdom of our true nature. Many spiritual traditions call this being selfless or no-self. But, what does it mean to be selfless?

Some years into practicing mindfulness, I was listening to teachings at a nearby Buddhist temple when the teacher said, "The only route to happiness is to think of others before ourselves." This is a directive I had heard many times in my life, first as a kid in church, and later studying spiritual traditions, and reading Buddhist philosophy. My mother emphasized a version of this message when I was a teenager, warning, "If you think of yourself first, then you're selfish." Wanting to be good and never selfish, my mother's declaration propelled me into focusing my attention on others and to ignore my authentic experience. Looking back, I realize her statement was a direct instruction to other. I took it on hook, line, and sinker and became an expert in othering.

Upon hearing this message again in the temple, I resisted it. In fact, I felt angry and confused. By now, noticing what was true for me and for the women I'd been working with in psychotherapy, it was obvious that thinking about others first didn't seem to bring us happiness. Instead, it often created stress and suffering. It seemed to me that we women were in fact too selfless, too focused on attending to others at our own expense. Yet because many great teachers and traditions stress the spiritual message of selflessness, I assumed it must be a worthy goal. In fact, the Buddha taught that the root cause of all our suffering is the attachment to a sense of self, and the true nature of ultimate reality is no-self. How could this be, I wondered? Perhaps my understanding of what it means to be selfless was incorrect. Was selflessness really a goal for men, since in my experience, many men seemed so devoted to themselves? I wondered if women needed a different view to find sustainable happiness. Perhaps we could find a more balanced view where caring about others also meant caring about ourselves. Does accessing our true nature allow us to be selfless? Is this what no-self means? Is it simply being able to rest in the spaciousness of awareness? What would that be like?

I hope these questions intrigue you and pique your curiosity. For me, I can sense my understanding of both the meaning and actuality of dwelling in no-self is evolving. Realizing what it means to be selfless is at the heart of living with authenticity and unshakeable confidence. Let's keep our eyes on these questions as we delve more deeply into bringing mindfulness to the habits of othering and our conditioned sense of self.

Ownwork Suggestions

- Reflect on your relationship with yourself. Honestly observe whatever you notice with kindness, gentleness, compassion, and curiosity. How do you feel about yourself? How do you habitually treat yourself? Do you treat yourself kindly and respectfully or do you criticize, judge, harass, or demean yourself? What are some of your conditioned ideas and beliefs about yourself?

- Contemplate how you would ideally like to feel about yourself. How would you most like to regard yourself and treat yourself? Observe whatever arises with kindness, curiosity, gentleness, and compassion.

- Consider starting a mindfulness journal. Such a journal is a simple notebook filled with your thoughts and discoveries that you make along the way. Keeping a journal can be a helpful way to self-reflect and find your authentic self.

3

Othering 101:
How We Learn
to Other

What I am looking for
is not out there,
it is in me.

Helen Keller

Othering is a conditioned imbalance of our attention in which we focus almost exclusively on another person while ignoring our own experience. We're so intent on trying to meet the needs and ensure the happiness of others, we don't notice ourself. Because we overlook information about what is authentically true for us, we lose our sense of self. Instead, we define ourselves through the eyes of others and how we imagine they perceive us. Unconsciously, we're seeking their approval. We want them to validate we're okay, lovable, valued, and doing the right thing.

Effects of Othering

Besides the physical acts of caregiving most of us do on a daily basis for others, othering can be more than a full-time occupation mentally and emotionally. It creates an almost constant cascade of thoughts, imaginings, and feelings about the other. We dwell on them, wondering what they're thinking, feeling, wanting, and needing. We assume expertise about them. We know what's going on with them, what they need, and what will make them upset. We know what's wrong with them and exactly how they should change. We imagine how they will react to events and statements. We calculate and predict their reactions and feelings towards us, especially when we do something risky. Much of our world revolves around imagining and assuming their reactions and then modifying our own behavior accordingly.

Because it's so familiar and automatic, we're usually not aware we're othering. As one of my students said, "For me, othering is like the air I breathe. It's like water for fish. I don't realize it at all." We don't question our assumptions or imaginings. Disconnected from our actual mind-body-heart experience, we reside in our imagining mind, worrying or hoping about something that may happen, predicting how the other will react and how that will affect us. Or, we muck around in the past, remembering what happened with the other, wondering why it did, and often blaming ourselves for their unhappiness. Because we depend on their approval, and sometimes their financial resources, we try to behave in ways

29

that make others feel contented with us. Although we've been taught that loving and caring for others will make us happy, and while it does give satisfaction and delight at times, the fact that we don't feel as happy as we *should* is perplexing. We may conclude something is wrong with us, we're not doing something right, or we're failing due to a deep inner flaw.

The overall effect is we suffer. Besides having limited ability to control what the other thinks, feels, and does, othering leaves us feeling unmoored and unknown to ourselves. We may feel shaky and self-doubting, anxious or depressed, easily irritated by others, and at the mercy of their endless wants, needs, and feelings. When we do reflect on ourselves, it's often a negative critique. Over the years I've taught and counseled women, I've heard countless expressions of these effects of othering:

- *I don't know who I am, and I'm afraid to find out.*

- *I always lose myself in my relationships.*

- *I'm a chronic people pleaser.*

- *I feel like whatever is wrong is always my fault and responsibility.*

- *I constantly worry about what others are thinking about me.*

- *I feel selfish when I think about my own needs first.*

- *I don't trust myself, and second-guess myself all the time.*

- *I'm terrified of conflict and try to avoid it whenever I can.*

- *I feel responsible for everyone's happiness* and *their pain.*

- *I'm too controlling, but I can't stop myself.*

- *I feel scared and like I'm a loser when I'm not in a relationship.*

- *I feel like there's something deeply wrong with me.*

- *I don't know what I really want, and when I do it's really hard to be direct about it.*

- *I feel like a fraud a lot.*

Yet our hearts ache for real and honest connection with ourselves and with others. The desire to be authentic is a basic human need, a natural healthy longing. We know faking it doesn't feel good, like smiling when we don't feel like smiling, or outright lying in the hope of being seen the way we want to be seen. It harms us to pretend to be different from our genuine selves, even when it seems like the right thing to do. Pretending stifles and suppresses us, causing our inner light to dim. It hurts our relationship with ourselves and it maintains our limitations and distance with others. We yearn to find ourselves, but don't how.

Etiology of Othering: How It Begins

To understand the pattern of othering, let's think about how we grow up. When we are infants, toddlers, and children, our parents are completely responsible for us and have complete power and authority over us. We depend on them and need their care, help, love, and affection absolutely. They feed, dress, and bathe us, clean up after us, and strive to keep us warm and healthy. Because we are powerless, it's natural and intelligent to modify our behavior to please our parents. This requires referring and deferring to them, as well as watching, modeling, and learning from them.

What happens if we aren't raised in conditions where we learn our basic goodness: that we are intrinsically worthwhile and valued, precious and perfect just the way we are? What if we learn that simply being ourselves causes trouble and makes people upset with us? We're likely to unconsciously conclude: "There's something wrong with me. I'm not how I am supposed to be." Because we depend on our caregivers for our well-being, we aim to be good so they love, care for, and protect us. We learn life is easier when others, especially our parents, are happy with us. We're more likely to get what we want when we do things the "right" way. We begin *trying* to make ourselves better, good, and even perfect.

Disconnecting From Authentic Experience

To be good, we learn to judge and criticize ourselves to control and change ourselves for the better. We learn to blame ourselves when we aren't perfect, which makes us feel guilty and ashamed. If no one teaches us how to handle these painful feelings, we develop strategies so the feelings don't bother us. Strategies include suppressing or denying the feelings, projecting them onto others, or avoiding them by distracting ourselves. We learn to act as if we're okay. In short, we disconnect from our authentic experience of painful feelings and focus our attention elsewhere, hoping we can find relief and comfort from the distress. Over time, with repeated practice, the habit of disconnecting becomes our coping reaction, our default conditioned habit.

Recognizing the Power of Gender

As we grow older, we gradually step into our own authority and power, eventually assuming full responsibility for ourselves as adults. However, societal gender bias profoundly affects this development. Despite the second and third waves of the feminist movement towards gender equality, boys are still expected to be masculine, meaning strong, powerful, tough, independent, and authoritative. Girls, however, are expected to be both successful in the work realm and feminine, meaning soft, passive, sensitive, dependent, and nurturing. Debora Spar's book, *Wonder Women: Women, Sex, Power, and the Quest for Perfection*, is full of recent data about these trends, and shows not much has shifted during the last 40 years.[6] She sees the current generation of girls growing up deeply hooked on being princesses and forecasts a rude awakening when, as grown women, they'll be expected to be both pretty *and* brilliant. For the current generation of girls, trapped by the expectation of being a good mother and having a successful career, Spar predicts great stress and suffering. In addition, these cultural expectations of masculinity and femininity limit both genders, affecting our abilities as women and men to be our true selves and form relationships with the opposite gender that are mutually empowering and sustainable.

I remember attending a book reading by psychologist Lynne Brown, discussing the ground-breaking study she and Carol Gilligan conducted that documented, for the first time, how girls learn to disconnect from their authentic selves as they grow older.[7] As I listened, I felt grateful researchers were finally studying what happens to girls. Previously, psychological studies examined only boys and men, and then generalized the results (inaccurately) to girls and women. The Brown and Gilligan study was at last focusing on females. Despite the emphasis of their work, the first question from the all-female audience was, "But what happens to boys? Aren't they oppressed, too?" I was shocked by this question, though it perfectly reflected our conditioning. For the *first time*, a study showed what happens to *girls*, and the questioner couldn't reflect on her own conditioning for even a few minutes without shifting her attention to boys and men. We need to be brave enough to look deep within our own minds and hearts to discover the ways we oppress ourselves. If we are always paying attention to the other, we'll never find our own way.

Research shows we internalize gender oppression gradually during childhood, with a powerful shift happening around puberty. At this age, boys begin to blossom, assert their power, build confidence, and move away from the childhood habit of referring attention to others. Girls do the opposite. They shrink, become less confident, more concerned with tracking and pleasing others. The habit of othering becomes solidly entrenched. Unless an event or insight wakes us up to the causes and effects of othering, we are destined to be ruled by these habits for the rest of our lives. Nationwide mental health statistics reflect this conditioning. Women are two times more likely to experience depression than men.[8] Depression has been called the most significant mental health risk

> Oppression is fundamentally limiting and inherently depressing.

for women, especially younger women of childbearing age.[9] Approximately twice as many women as men suffer from a generalized anxiety disorder, panic disorder, or phobia.[10] These statistics are certainly not due to being weaker or inherently flawed. The cause is deeply rooted in our gender conditioning. Oppression is fundamentally limiting and inherently depressing.

Recognizing the Power of Power

We live in a world where, for thousands of years, the principal power structure has been based on domination rather than equality, mutuality, or partnership. Domination creates two fundamental groups: those on top, the dominants, and those below the top, the subordinates. The dominant group has power over the subordinate group.

> The dominant group has power over the subordinate group. Domination and othering go hand in hand.

Domination and othering go hand in hand, as members of each group inevitably identify with their own group and view members of the other group as different and separate. Historically, gender has been the basic determining factor for membership: men are dominant and women are the subordinate. Gender is the root separator, deeper than race, ethnicity, or class.

We know the resulting inequality and misogyny isn't right and harms all of us. Although women won the right to vote in the United States in 1920 (after African-American men were finally deemed worthy to vote), constitutionally we still don't have rights equal to men. The Equal Rights Amendment was never passed by enough states to amend the constitution. Women are still paid less than men for the same work, one in five women experience domestic violence and sexual assault, and choice over our bodies and reproduction rights continue to be challenged.

Dynamics of Domination

In our patriarchal capitalistic society, predominantly wealthy white men still call the shots. Their overriding job as the dominant group is to define and control reality for society. They determine *what* is valued and *who* is valuable, including who does and doesn't belong to the dominant group. They decide what resources are valuable and they control those resources. They make all the rules and laws governing everyone, distribute the privileges, rights, responsibilities, and roles various members of society may have, and create and define the institutions that implement the rules, functions, and resources. They create and control the government, including the economic, military, judicial, educational, medical, religious, and penal institutions. They define the dominant philosophy, morality, and social theory, as well as the acceptable science, psychology, religion, education, economics, health, and social programs. The dominant group defines what is normal and acceptable in society. The subordinate group must learn and accept the dominant group's view of reality and comply with its rules and restrictions.

Understanding the Master-Servant Relationship

The master-servant relationship is a vivid and classic model of the dominant-subordinate relationship. To sense how the dynamics of domination create othering, imagine what it might be like to live as a servant. Or, you might imagine being in a severely abusive relationship, as the same dynamics operate.

As a servant, the quality of your life depends on how skilled you are at pleasing the master who owns you and has absolute power over you. The little power you do have depends on the relationship you establish with him. If you have a family that depends on you, then how well you please the master also affects your family. You become expert at knowing your master, figuring out his needs and preferences, how to make sure he is happy and well served, and therefore pleased with you. This requires becoming sensitive to his moods and changing desires and accurately anticipating his wants. He is the primary object of your attention. Rather than yourself, *he* is your frame of reference. Everything else, including your family's activities and needs and your own feelings and needs, must remain in the background.

Consequently, your attention is habitually and constantly focused on the master. You're always thinking about him, wondering what he's feeling, what he needs and wants, and how he will react if you do or do not please him. You become so skilled at focusing on the master that you don't notice your own needs. You can't afford to notice anyway. Wanting something for yourself or something that doesn't involve the master is likely to create conflict, possibly danger, or at least confusion and unhappiness. Life functions more smoothly if you are not aware of yourself. As a servant, your mind naturally becomes conditioned to disconnect from your authentic experience as you focus on serving the master. Inevitably, the long-term effect of being seen and treated as lesser by the master, and having to treat yourself as less important, shifts your view of yourself. You come to believe, unconsciously, you are less valuable than the master. Shame and self-hatred become rooted in your sense of self.

Othering Is Required in Subordination

Observing the power dynamics between master and servant, we see the fundamental effect of being in the subordinate position is that we *must* externally reference to the other. In essence, this means giving up personal power, agency, and a sense of control over your life. Because our gender places us in the position of less power, we become conditioned in the same way as the servant, though to varying degrees. When we resist this programming by considering our own experience, needs, and wants, we are often accused of being selfish, self-centered, unkind, bitchy, or aggressive. To be normal and successful in our culture, we follow the rules of the dominant group and learn to other. In contrast, members of the dominant group internalize a sense of agency and locus of control within themselves. They presume they are in change of their lives. They assume privilege. Their habit of thinking, "What do *I* want, need, feel, think?" is conditioned and automatic.

> Relationships based on domination-subordination are not sustainable.

Psychology has also labeled othering as co-dependency. Emerging in the 1990s from the addictions field, co-dependency was defined as pathological. Treatment centers cropped up around the country to treat this "disease." They have since mostly disappeared. Not surprisingly, almost all of the patients were women, coded as "women who love too much." I remember chuckling with my friends and female colleagues, musing, "Well, come on, who isn't co-dependent to some extent anyway?"

Relationships based on domination-subordination are not sustainable in any kind of healthy, mutually empowering way. They only lead to feeling more disconnected, dependent, anxious, and depressed, and often head us toward addictive behaviors in our attempt to find relief. Further, because othering creates an unkind, hostile relationship with ourselves, the idea of being alone and single with our critical self can be severely painful. We may stay in unhealthy relationships longer than our wiser self advises because it's preferable to breaking free and being alone with our frightened, not-enough selves.

Othering Is Hardwired

Because women have been the base subordinate group for such a long time, othering patterns are hardwired in us. Passed down generation after generation, our mothers, grandmothers, aunts, and great-grandmothers have modeled othering seemingly forever. In their efforts to help us be happy and successful, they've taught us to other both directly and indirectly. I've heard countless women recall their mothers re-

37

minding them to be giving and never selfish, meaning, "Never think of yourself first." Institutions and influences in our culture continue to reinforce this message daily.

To understand and transform our conditioning so we can live authentically under our own authority, we must realize *othering patterns are not our fault*. Othering creates neural grooves that run deep, and we acquire them unconsciously, unintentionally, and innocently. The first step towards freedom is to recognize othering patterns in our lives. Please don't turn against yourself when the patterns arise. We need to see them clearly with understanding, compassion, and kindness instead of blame or shame.

Othering patterns are
not our fault.

Ownwork Suggestions

Sit with yourself quietly for a few minutes. Simply feel your body sitting there and notice whatever sensations you're aware of with curiosity and acceptance. Notice your body breathing.

- Now, contemplate the messages you received growing up as a girl in your family. What did your mother teach you about how you are supposed to be? What did your dad teach you? What did they model about relationships?

- What has been your experience in relationships? Have you lost yourself in relationships? Recall some experiences where you gave your power away or weren't true to yourself. How did you feel about yourself?

- Please notice all of this with plenty of curiosity, kindness, and *no blame*.

- Take a few moments to imagine yourself truly free of your internalized oppression. Sincerely practice noticing all that comes to you without judging yourself.

- If it's helpful, make notes of this practice in your mindfulness journal.

4

Trained to Please:
Characteristics
of Othering

The greatest hazard of all,
losing one's self, can occur very
quietly in the world,
as if it were nothing at all.
No other loss can occur so quietly....

Soren Kierkegaard

Characteristics of Othering

Because awareness is the first step to change, recognizing our conditioned thought and behavior patterns begins our journey on the path to freedom. Othering creates an uncomfortable chronic self-consciousness that manifests in many ways. As you read the following descriptions, notice how they may be true for you. When one feels familiar, please don't turn against yourself with a condemning judgment. The task is to notice with curiosity, taking note of the people and situations that tend to trigger reactions. Remember, *you* are not your conditioned patterns. They are not a reflection of your true self. These habits became established simply by growing up in our culture and operate automatically. So no blaming yourself. Practice kindness, curiosity, and acceptance instead.

Disconnecting From the Body

The body has its own needs and desires, which are always changing, and requires our wise attention to support its health and balance. However, when our main focus is on others, we may treat our own physical needs as inconveniences or distractions. Consequently, we learn to disconnect from the body and grow out of touch, often becoming numb to its language. In our mission to tend to others, we may regard our precious body as a source of pain, trouble, and fear, instead of a vehicle that allows us to interact with the world in amazing ways. Othering trains us to ignore, override, or deny the body's signals and therefore avoid conflicts that may occur if it wants something that interferes with taking care of others.

The first time I consciously spotted this habit, I was walking with a dear friend in a park. We were having an intense and wonderful conversation as we strolled with our arms wrapped around each other's waists. At a certain point, I noticed my arm was beginning to complain because I'd been holding it in the same position for quite a while. I didn't want to move my arm because I was afraid my friend would misinterpret the

Characteristics of Being
Disconnected From Authentic Self

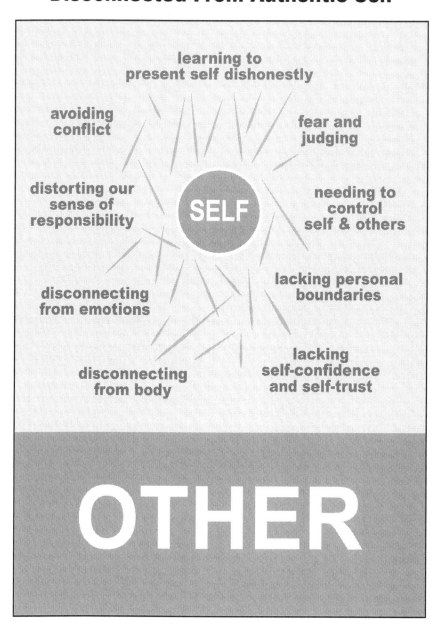

learning to
present self dishonestly

avoiding
conflict

fear and
judging

distorting our
sense of
responsibility

SELF

needing to
control
self & others

lacking personal
boundaries

disconnecting
from emotions

lacking
self-confidence
and self-trust

disconnecting
from body

OTHER

movement and think I was emotionally pulling away from her. I endured the pain until she made the first move to shift positions. Reflecting on this experience, I realized that enduring bodily discomfort out of fear of disturbing the other was a familiar pattern for me.

Our culture's incessantly skewed messages about how a woman's body is supposed to look also encourages disconnection. It's rare to find a woman who is truly content with her body. Most of us struggle with the one we have, wishing it were a different shape, weight, or height. We'd like our hair to be different, our breasts another shape or size, our complexion better, and so on. The beauty products we're supposed to buy continuously reinforce the idea our bodies need improvement. The dieting, fashion, cosmetic, and health industries flourish on our fear that we aren't attractive enough to please others. The high incidence of eating disorders and increasing reliance on plastic surgery are extreme reflections of these powerfully harmful conditioned beliefs.

Disconnecting From Emotions

Because emotions are felt in the body, disconnecting from our bodies goes hand in hand with disconnecting from emotions. Every emotion creates a sensation we feel in the body, which is why we call them feelings. When we're cut off from our bodies, we're also cut off from the sensations emotions create. Like bodily needs, emotions can arise inconveniently, getting in the way of devoting ourselves to others, so we learn to self-regulate. We try to allow only certain acceptable feelings — the good and ladylike ones — and suppress all others. Fear and sadness seem to be acceptable feelings for women, although too much crying is not okay. We're not supposed to be too upset, angry, or aggressive. From the dominant group's perspective, women are too emotional, and emotional is viewed as irrational, weak, and childlike. Historically women who were too emotional were labeled hysterical and crazy. They were disenfranchised, disempowered, drugged, locked away, or worse.

Conditioning teaches us to distrust and fear our emotions rather than respect them for what they are telling us. We attempt to control them through denial, suppression, shaming, distraction, and projection. When we're absorbed in a difficult emotion, we often turn against ourselves with the judgment, "I shouldn't feel this. If I were better, more perfect, more together, I wouldn't be upset." Consequently, we shut down, go numb and dead to ourselves. We feel the heavy grayness of anxiety and depression more than anything else.

> Conditioning teaches us to distrust and fear our emotions rather than respect them for what they are telling us.

Additionally, every month for approximately forty years of our lives, our bodies move through their hormonal cycles, affecting us physically, energetically, and emotionally. The hormonal cycles add another dimension to the task of keeping emotions under control. I know many women who describe themselves as feeling crazed premenstrually, making it even harder to meet the expectations of being emotionally "good."

Distorting Our Sense of Responsibility

One of the primary roles women serve in society is to care for the growth and development of others. We typically assume the responsibility of nurturing others. We feel responsible for the well-being of others and for the health of the relationships. Part of this responsibility is caused by our biology and genes. Another part is related to our conditioning in the subordinate position in society's power structure.

We are the ones, of course, who grow and birth babies. We are the primary caretakers of our children, although this responsibility is shifting in our culture as families become more equal and diverse. Even with more joint parenting of children, mothers take on the bottom-line, around-the-clock responsibility. We also take care of our spouse or partner and probably most of the household tasks. We respond to our friends and siblings when they are ill or in trouble. We help our sick and aging parents. We help our neighbors and colleagues. Taking care, responding, and helping are what we do as women now and what we've always done.

If balanced, our womanly instincts are the glue for families that build communities dedicated to helping, caring, supporting and healing. But often our sense of responsibility goes way overboard. We come to believe we are responsible not only for the happiness of others, but also for their misery, mistakes, problems, unhealthy habits, feelings, and failures. Essentially, we're trained to be overly responsible for others. When something goes wrong, when someone is upset or has a problem, it's our knee-jerk reaction to assume it's our job to fix it, or even assume it happened because we did something wrong or didn't do something adequately. We plunge in to try to make it right or obsess about what should have happened.

While being overly responsible for what's going on with others, we ignore our own needs. We become *under responsible* for ourselves. Trying to stay on top of everything and everyone can lead to feeling overwhelmed, burdened, and anxious. We may become frustrated, angry, or resentful of all we do for those we love. Panic attacks often surface under the weight of over responsibility. Eventually, exhaustion may force us to stop and seek relief by indulging in our favorite addiction, until the guilt inherent in over-responsibility prods us to get us up and going again. One woman I know, married with three teenagers and running her own business, realizes she's gone over her edge when she finds herself bristling and irritated by everyone and hiding in her bedroom binge-watching sit-coms on her smartphone.

Growing up in my family, my mother and I would recite a rhyme that reflects this pattern, usually while we were doing the dishes together. "Men may work from sun to sun, but women's work is never done." Sometimes we'd say it in the spirit of complaining and feeling burdened. Other times, we would feel pride and power, as in, "Because our work is never done, that means we're very important. We're really needed." Feeling responsible for practically everything can lead to feeling indispensable, which is a feeling of power. The power of martyrdom, however, is neither freeing or joyful.

Lacking Personal Boundaries

Closely related to our training to be overly responsible is our difficulty in setting boundaries. Having boundaries means realizing when your needs or perceptions are different from the other's, and then responding accordingly. You can say "no" to someone's request if what they want isn't right, wise, or respectful of what you want or are able to do. Because othering disconnects us from the data of our direct authentic experience, we lose track of ourselves, easily taking on the other's feelings, moods, desires, difficulties, and beliefs. We easily agree with the other's views or do things that aren't healthy or wise for us. When we do set a boundary, it's often scary to act on it because we fear the other's disapproval and rejection. Consequently, we tend to violate the few boundaries we do have.

When I was beginning to wake up to these patterns, I spotted my lack of boundaries during a cocktail party my husband and I were giving. As I moved from person to person, talking about the political affairs of the times, I agreed with the views each person expressed. Yet each person's view was somewhat different. I felt confused as I later mused about my experience. Was I flexible enough to understand each view? Or did I agree because I didn't know my own view? Was I too afraid to express my own view? I realized I didn't know what was honestly true for me and I was afraid to openly disagree. The feeling of not knowing myself was alarming. I felt phony, wishy-washy, and shallow.

Avoiding Conflict

Othering trains us to act as harmonizers and soothers rather than deal directly with disagreement. When you assume you have less power, conflict is threatening, so it's wise to avoid it whenever possible. Not rocking the boat is the surest way to keep relationships stable, safe, and seemingly under control. When we encounter differing ideas or desires, we suppress, ignore, or discount our own experience and defer to the other. Likewise, when someone hurts our feelings, it's too risky to be direct and honest about it, so we withdraw and may temporarily cut off communication with the person rather than risk a direct confrontation.

When I ask the women in my class what happens for them when they realize they have a want or need that may cause a conflict or highlights a difference with another, their first response is always anxiety and fear. They feel threatened by a possible confrontation. Many talk about finding ways to avoid the conflict or to present their idea in a way that will make it agreeable to the other. Some say they feel sad and depressed because they assume they won't be able to get what they want. Defeat is presumed.

Another common reaction to conflict is to assume responsibility for it by blaming ourselves, and then trying to change *our* reaction so everything will be harmonious again. Fear of the other's anger or disapproval can also keep us caught in pushing down our needs or feelings, giving us the appearance of being agreeable. However, suppression usually leads to resentment, which can build into a disturbing undercurrent that undermines the relationship. While our conditioned reaction to conflict is to give up, give in, or try to change ourselves to keep day-to-day life running smoothly, some part of us remembers the tally. This can create a storehouse of bitterness and irritation, and contribute to feeling victimized, powerless, hopeless, and depressed.

Learning to Be Dishonest

Because conditioning teaches us to believe something is wrong with us the way we are, we learn to hide our unacceptable parts and attempt to show only the likeable parts. Motivated by fear of disapproval and rejection (and for some of us, also by fear of violence and abandonment), our unconscious radar is continuously scanning, seeking information about how to manage the impression we are making on others so we can win their approval. Like the other patterns, deception can become so automatic it occurs without conscious intention and awareness. We are conditioned to habitually put on the "right" face, namely one that shows us to be as close to perfect as possible.

The habit of telling white lies is a common form of impression management. I caught myself in this pattern one morning when returning a phone call to a client. I heard myself saying, "Gosh, I'm sorry I couldn't call you back last night, but I was in a meeting until late." That was a lie. I hadn't called her back the night before because I was tired and didn't feel like calling. I realized behind my automatic lie I assumed my true reason for not calling wasn't legitimate. It wasn't "good enough." I was afraid if I had been honest she'd be angry or judge me as irresponsible. Although this was a little lie, it was still a lie and it hurt my integrity and self-respect. Habits of hiding and managing our impression can be as minimal as a fake "I'm fine" smile, or can be as extensive as living a double life. Regardless of the extent, the habit of dishonesty is an insidious self-betrayal that adds to a deeper disconnection and disturbance in our relationship with ourself.

> We are conditioned to habitually put on the "right" face.

Needing to Control

Being dependent on others' approval and feeling responsible for their happiness and pain means we also have an insatiable need for control. We expend enormous effort trying to make sure everyone is okay and happy, and everything is happening just the way it should. Consider the amount of time we spend planning, plotting, and rehearsing the right things to say and do so the other person will respond the way we hope they will, making everything okay, including us. This habit of fantasizing, rehearsing, and imagining conversations in detail is a prominent othering habit for most of us: You say this, and then I say this.... You respond with this, and I then say.... Eventually in our imaginary conversation, everything works out just right. Not only are we trying to control the other person, including their thoughts, feelings, and actions, but to achieve the desired outcome, we also have to exert control over ourselves. We have to make sure we appear the right way, and we say and do the right things to prompt the other person to respond the way they are supposed to, all according to our fantasy.

This habit of trying to control propels us repeatedly into an imagined future, where we cling to our hopes and fears, and meanwhile miss what's *actually* going on in the present, where life truly happens. I remember a poignant moment near the end of a nine-day meditation retreat when a participant said she realized she spends her entire life in fantasy, lost in daydreams about her life. She now wondered what it would be like to live in the present moment where life is real. I understood her insight, because othering keeps us living in fantasy.

The anxiety bred by the need for control leads us farther away from what's authentic and creates more misery. Because we'd all like people and events to be how we want them to be, the desire for control is natural to human nature. Still, we hate it when someone accuses us of being controlling. We aren't supposed to be controlling. It's not attractive; it's not perfect. No one likes someone who is controlling, and no one likes to be controlled. These judgments lead to more self-condemnation, anxiety, and depression, creating a painful self-defeating cycle.

Being Caught in Fear and Judging

Fear is the root emotion underlying the entire pattern and all the various ways othering manifests in us. We're afraid of not being good enough. We're afraid we aren't smart, kind, funny, attractive, or anything enough.

We're afraid we aren't acceptable the way we are. We're afraid we aren't doing, saying, feeling, or even thinking the right thing. We're afraid something is wrong with us. We're afraid we are damaged goods. We're afraid we don't matter, don't belong, or aren't lovable. We're afraid of being rejected, abandoned, and alone. We may not always be conscious of these fears, but if we sincerely explore our anxieties, we'll likely find them, along with the shame they provoke at the core of our conditioned sense of self.

We're afraid
of not being
good enough.

Messages from the dominant culture expect women to be perfect. We're supposed to be in control and responsible, giving and caring for others. We're supposed to be attractive and appealing, as well as a perfect mother, partner, daughter, friend, and worker. We're supposed to do it all competently without complaint. We feel tremendous pressure to meet these superwoman expectations and fear we cannot. The conditioned mind generates strong internal voices that continuously judge, compare, and monitor our experiences, all aimed at controlling our feelings and actions. The neural grooves of self-judgement and comparison keep us caught in rigid thinking and often brutal bouts of self-criticism. Fueled by our need to control, we judge and criticize others, and then turn around and judge ourselves harshly for judging them. It's a very painful trap.

One of my dearest friends is a woman who experiences chronic anxiety and episodic depression. She is an amazing, thoughtful, creative person, dedicated to integrity and healing. She told me of a major insight that came to her in a recent meditation. She realized that with *everything* she thinks, feels, says, and does, her mind reacts with an immediate self-critical judgment. The harsh, instantaneous message is always, "That isn't right! That wasn't good enough! You aren't enough! There's something really wrong with you!" Despite her previous efforts, it wasn't until a moment of deep clarity in meditation that she realized how her mind habitually torments her with a false conditioned view. With great under-standing and compassion, she could now see the root of her suffering.

Lacking Self-Confidence and Trust

The cumulative effect of being disconnected from our authentic ex-perience is pervasive self-doubt. We don't trust, love, and respect our-selves. We don't believe in ourselves. We don't trust our perceptions, feelings, or intuition as valid. Instead, with our center anchored in the other, we wait for someone else to validate our perceptions. Nearly every woman I've worked with in psychotherapy, every woman I've taught mindfulness to, suffers from self-doubt and varying degrees of self-hatred and low self-esteem. We resist acknowledging these con-ditions because they are painful to realize and accept. If we are honest and can find the courage to look deeply, we're likely to discover a pain-ful core of self-loathing, hatred, and shame.

We suffer from self-hatred not because we aren't adequate, but because the habit of looking outside ourselves for approval inevitably creates self-loathing. The inescapable effects of being in the subordi-nate position and continuously bombarded with the culture's sexist messages coerce us to succumb to those views. Without being aware of it, we hold a deeply embedded belief that we aren't as worthy as others and we don't matter as much. In particular, we don't matter as much as men. We've internalized the patriarchy's view and posi-tion, and unintentionally maintain its oppression through the habits of othering.

Othering Limits Relationships

The fundamental inequality of power is at the root of most relationship dysfunction. When both genders are trained to conduct relationships in the dominant-subordinate paradigm, it limits our ability to have authen-tic and intimate connection with each other. Even if your parents were feminists, the cultural messages of domination rather than mutuality are so deeply embedded in our culture that, wanted or not, they creep into our psyches and styles of relating.

This imbalance naturally forces relationships to center around issues of control and power rather than honest, authentic, and intimate connection. As author and scholar bell hooks teaches in *All About Love*, love is about connecting and joining, whereas domination promotes separation. Domination opposes love.[11] Instead of connecting with exactly what's happening right now as we interact, our habit is to wonder what's behind that look or gesture, or to make up a story about what they just said *really* means, or to second-guess what we just said to them. Being habitually caught in the mind's stories about the other and doubting our own authentic experience, we cannot be fully present and intimate with another. When we're not aware of our own experience, we're not present with our self, and we can't be authentic with the other either.

In the subordinate position, we must exert control over ourself and the other to make sure they're happy and we're behaving "correctly." The person in the dominant position must exert control over the subordinate to make sure she's in her place so that his independence is not threatened, while his need for the relationship is still secured. In other words, both participants seek to control the other by various strategies: becoming defensive, manipulating, projecting, lying, hiding, and withdrawing. Rather than express the honest truth of our experience, we say what we think will be effective to create what we want. Our cultural conditioning has trained us to substitute control for authentic connection, and relationships based on control are inevitably limiting and oppressive for all.

There Is Hope

If you recognize yourself in these mental and behavior patterns, you may be feeling disheartened. That's how it feels when I present these descriptions in class. Students often cringe and say, "Oh no! This is me!"

Please take heart because mindfulness offers true relief and healing from these oppressive habits. Practicing mindfulness shifts our imbalanced attention back into balance.

With attention balanced between self and other, we discover the vital data of exactly what's happening for us in the mind, heart, and body — our authentic experience. We know what's true for us and take full responsibility for it. When we bring the information of our authentic experience to our interactions, it profoundly changes how we relate to ourselves, others, and the world.

> Practicing mindfulness shifts our imbalanced attention back into balance.

Through mindfulness we can connect with our body and respond to its needs and signals appropriately. We no longer judge and turn against ourselves when an uncomfortable emotion arises. We know how to stay steady with ourselves and respond skillfully. We realize the old belief that we aren't enough is a lie. We lose our fear that others are judging and disapproving of us because we're no longer judging and disapproving of ourselves. Instead, we trust we're acceptable as we are, and come to respect and love ourselves. We learn to take appropriate care of others and ourselves. Conflict isn't scary because we understand our views and experiences are as valid as anyone else's. We're willing to be transparent, knowing the power of vulnerability that accompanies undisputable honesty. The need for control diminishes because we trust we can be present and handle whatever happens. We're aware of our boundaries and can say "no" without fear.

As we come to know and accept ourselves through mindfulness, we gradually relax, lose our painful conditioned self-consciousness, and build trust and confidence in ourselves. Over time we open our heart to everyone and everything. We realize we have nothing to fear from others because the stability and power of approval and acceptance lies within ourselves, within our own agency. By knowing, trusting, and accepting our direct authentic experience, staying steady with ourselves no matter what, we naturally respond to all that happens in our life with more ease, kindness, wisdom, and skill. This is the central hope and gift of practicing mindfulness, and it is deeply and sustainably liberating.

We have nothing to fear
from others because approval and
acceptance lie within ourselves.

Ownwork
Suggestions

As you consider the characteristics of othering, let it stimulate your curiosity. I invite you to begin noticing othering habits as they come up in your mind, and in your reactions to what's going on with the people and activities in your life.

• Reflect on the characteristics of othering that resonate in you: in your sense of your body, emotions, responsibility, and boundaries, and in your reaction to conflict, showing yourself honestly, habits of judgment and self-criticism, attempts to control yourself and others, and the tendency for self-doubt.

• Notice whatever seems true without judging yourself. Strive for absolute honesty without blame. Remember that othering habits are "normal," even though they create so much suffering.

• Imagine what it might be like to be free of these habits, simply accepting and connecting with your own authentic experience as you pay attention to the other person.

• Record what you notice in your journal, if you find it helpful.

5

The Remedy Is Mindfulness

The secret of health for both mind and body is not to mourn for the past, worry about the future, or anticipate troubles, but to live in the present moment wisely and earnestly.

The Buddha

Because we've been trained to anchor our attention in the other, leaving us disconnected from our authenticity, the remedy lies in hauling up that anchor and dropping it within ourselves. We must learn to connect with our own experience, rather than giving our attention and power away to others. In this way, we affix authority for ourselves to ourselves. We need to understand that no matter what, our direct experience is always valid, simply because it is our own. By knowing whatever is true for us, we can bring discernment to our experience. We can discover whether we are reacting out of conditioned habits or seeing reality clearly. After recognizing our reaction, we can choose to make skillful adjustments.

> Our direct experience is always valid, simply because it is our own.

Mindfulness is a perfect tool for responding and adjusting because it guides us to recognize what we're experiencing in the moment and to open to that experience with curiosity and compassionate acceptance, instead of judgment or rejection. Mindfulness creates a safe container for self-reflection. As we practice it over time, we build a genuine connection with our bodies. Our emotions become less scary as we accept and learn from them. We realize what we can be responsible for, set real boundaries, and be more honest in how we present ourselves to others. Conflict becomes workable. As we grow more accepting and compassionate of ourselves, we become more genuinely accepting and compassionate with others. Our attention becomes balanced: we are aware of ourselves as we are aware of the other, our need for control diminishes, and self-confidence grows. We spend less time "in our head" worrying, fretting, planning, and wondering about things over which we have no control. We can respond with integrity to the needs and moods of others, as well as our own. Being fully present radically improves the quality of the current moment and allows natural access to our innate wisdom, kindness, intelligence, compassion, and joy.

Purpose of Mindfulness

More than 2,600 years old, mindfulness is the primary method the Buddha taught for freeing the mind from its conditioning so we can perceive reality clearly, access our true nature, and ultimately become free from suffering. Mindfulness trains our mind to be our friend instead of our enemy, or inner bully, and provides a skill set we can use regardless of religious beliefs. To be clear, mindfulness is not a religion, so practicing it does not make you a Buddhist.

Through mindful awareness, we can see reality clearly. We see the habits of the mind that cause suffering — our painful and habitual thoughts, beliefs, assumptions, and distorted perceptions. We also realize what creates our happiness — inner stability, peacefulness, love, generosity, and joyfulness. We experience the innate basic goodness of our true nature, the blue sky mind inherent in all of us.

> Mindfulness trains our mind to be our friend and provides a skill set we can use regardless of religious beliefs.

However, our conditioned or ordinary mind blocks access to our true nature. Often likened to a tree full of monkeys, our ordinary mind tends to be chaotic, distractible, and restless. Does your mind ever feel like that? This "monkey mind," as it's sometimes called, is unstable, easily affected by the slightest distraction, continuously zooming back into the past and forward into the future. It's busy, busy, busy, flitting from one thought to another, rarely focusing or staying in the present moment, where we are actually alive, for more than a second. Our minds can exhaust us and make us crazy.

In contrast, mindfulness gently slows mental activity and leads us to remain steady with ourselves, stable in the present moment with whatever is happening. The quality of equanimity, or inner stability, creates inner security. Over time, stability begins to foster the confidence and trust that we can handle the various challenges in life.

Pema Chödrön, an American Tibetan Buddhist nun and one of the country's most beloved Buddhist teachers, says that our ordinary mind is like a heavy cloud cover that keeps us from accessing our blue sky true nature and natural intelligence.[12] I love this view — that our true nature, who we naturally are — is open, wise, compassionate, and always here. Each moment of mindfulness, such as, "Oh, here's feeling sad (angry, scared, or confused, for example). How am I experiencing this?" pokes a hole in that cloud cover so that little by little, over time, more of our blue sky mind shines through. With practice, we gradually have more access to our natural wisdom, compassion, patience, and intuition and can start to become a true friend to ourselves, and then to others.

When we know how to relate to ourselves mindfully, we develop access to our true nature. Mindfulness is not, however, a self-improvement course. We're not trying to make ourselves better; rather, we're clearing away the obstacles blocking access to our true self, our natural loveliness, wisdom, and radiance, that is always here.

Definition of Mindfulness

We can define mindfulness as the moment-to-moment nonjudgmental investigation of the mind-body-heart experience through calm, kind, accepting attention. A more user-friendly, practical definition that I especially love comes from the author and teacher Sylvia Boorstein.[13] She suggests mindfulness involves asking ourselves three basic questions:

1. What's happening right now? What am I actually experiencing (thinking, feeling, sensing, seeing, hearing, tasting, and smelling) in this very moment?

2. What's my reaction to that? In other words, how am I relating to what is happening? Am I judging it, trying to change or control it, trying to get away from it? Am I open to it? Accepting it? Am I letting it be?

3. Given what I'm experiencing, what's the wisest and kindest response I can make to myself right now?

With each question, we open to our direct experience, without judgment or criticism. The goal is to observe our actual experience, whatever it is. We are simply intending to see what's real and true in this moment. We're saying "yes" to whatever is here: to a headache, to feeling anxiety rising, to the traffic light turning red, or to the deliciousness of an ice cream cone. By turning towards what's happening and relating to it without bias, we're connecting directly with what is — reality — right now.

While mindfulness connects us to our direct experience, it also changes our relationship to it. We shift from being enmeshed with the experience, carried away by it, or resisting and fighting with it, to simply observing what we're experiencing. When we feel difficult emotions, we can step back and *watch* the storm of the disturbing emotion, instead of being swept up in it and *being* the storm. As we know all too well, when we become the storm, we're caught, whipped around and frequently hurt by its intensity.

When we are snared in the habit of othering, we are vulnerable to whatever we *imagine* the other sees or feels because we don't realize we are making it all up. We automatically believe whatever our mind is creating. We take it to be THE truth. In contrast, with mindful awareness of what's happening, our experience is different and better. For example, I have a deeply conditioned pattern of shyness. Before learning mindfulness, attending a social event where I didn't know anyone was very stressful. Anxious and unable to think of anything to say, I'd hardly talk to anyone and count the minutes until I could leave. I'd obsess over how self-conscious, awkward, and shy I felt, convinced others were noticing how tongue-tied I was, which only created more anxiety. Later, I'd feel ashamed for being so ridiculously shy. It was always painful.

With mindfulness, and applying Sylvia Boorstein's questions, I can now bring my attention to what I'm experiencing when shyness arises:

♦ I first acknowledge it and ask myself: *What am I experiencing right now?* Oh. Here's anxiety, shyness. My belly feels tight. I feel more tension in my body, especially in my jaw and shoulders. I'm imagining people turning away from me and thinking, "That was a really dumb thing she said! Who is she, anyway? I don't like her!" I feel a strong sense of contracting, of pulling in and shutting down.

+ Next, I ask: *What's my reaction? How am I relating to this?* I don't like it. I hate being like this. Wow, these feelings are very unpleasant. Those thoughts are really negative. No wonder I feel anxious. Here it is again, the old shy reaction.

+ Lastly, I ask: *What's the wisest and kindest way to respond to myself right now?* After a moment or two, what likely comes to me is: Yes, this is the old feeling of shyness, and it's okay that I'm feeling it. Just give it space and let it be. Stay with the feeling, relax around the sensations, and remember that I'm okay just as I am.

When I can relate to the experience of shyness this way, I have greater ease with it. The experience passes through me more quickly than when I resist and judge my reaction. When the feeling subsides, it's over. I'm simply in the next moment, free and present. I don't have any backlash against myself. Because I'm more relaxed as I accept the uncomfortable experience, I often feel comfortable enough to talk to other people. By observing my experience closely and accurately, I learn more about my mind's habits and how to stay steady rather than getting hijacked by them.

Furthermore, each time I have the chance to practice these three steps, I become less afraid of the unpleasant feeling of shyness and build tolerance for the discomfort. I become more familiar with all the judgments and stories I imagine others are thinking about me, and I build confidence in my ability to handle the feelings of shyness. As Pema Chödrön might say, I've poked some more holes in the cloud cover of my conditioned mind.

Science Validates Many Benefits

An enormous amount of research has been conducted investigating the effects of practicing mindfulness. Scientifically, we know that it's beneficial for us on every dimension: physically, emotionally, mentally, and spiritually. Jon Kabat-Zinn, beginning in 1980 at the University of Massachusetts Medical Center, was the first researcher to systematically study the effects of mindfulness.[14] He first taught the practice to a range of medical patients whose doctors had run out of treatment options for them. These patients had complicated chronic illnesses and diseases, often involving acute and chronic pain that affected their ability to function in their lives, as well as anxiety, depression, and chronic stress. Jon developed the Mindfulness-Based Stress Reduction Program (MBSR), an eight-session class applying mindfulness to handling stress. Because his research showed such effectiveness, he went on to mainstream this practice, training other professionals (including myself) in the program. Now MBSR is taught in 250 major medical institutions around the country as an effective method for reducing pain, stress, and improving quality of life for patients dealing with conditions ranging from depression to cancer.

Today mindfulness is taught in practically any venue you can imagine, including prisons, law offices, businesses, clergy offices, police and fire departments, government agencies, day care centers, and nonprofit organizations. It's offered as a self-care tool for workers in the healthcare professions, such as nurses, social workers, and counselors, where burn-out and compassion fatigue are risks. Increasingly, mindfulness is taught to teachers and students in schools as research shows it improves the quality of teaching and learning. It is now accepted as an effective modality in psychotherapy, in the field of chemical addictions and recovery, as well as with eating disorders, obsessive-compulsive disorders, and post-traumatic stress disorders. Further, it's highly effective for childbirth and handling the whole gamut of difficult medical procedures. Many Fortune 500 companies and other large businesses and organizations are offering mindfulness to their employees because they are discovering that it improves overall well-being, making workers happier, healthier, and more productive.

Richard Davidson, a pioneering neuroscientist at the University of Wisconsin and founder of the Center for Healthy Minds, has developed a state-of-the-art, high-tech lab where, through the use of functional

Scientists have discovered that mindfulness meditation improves overall well-being and benefits the body in multiple ways:

- *Lowers heart rate, respiration, and blood pressure*
- *Boosts the immune system*
- *Decreases suffering with acute and chronic pain*
- *Reduces insomnia*
- *Decreases the negative effects of stress and builds resilience to stress*
- *Increases the brain's neuroplasticity*

Mental and psychological benefits of mindfulness include the following:

- *Lowers anxiety and reduces depression*
- *Increases self-confidence and self-esteem*
- *Stabilizes mood and decreases emotional reactivity*
- *Improves concentration and attention span*
- *Builds compassion and kindness*

magnetic resonance imaging, it is now possible to measure and detect changes in the brain when people are meditating. Davidson and colleagues have discovered that when a difficult emotion arises, breathing mindfully coupled with even a moment of mindful awareness, such as, "Ah, here's fear," makes a remarkable difference. It slows the firing of neurons in the amygdala, the emotional center of the brain that's activated when difficult emotions arise, allowing the mindfulness practitioner to *choose* how to respond to the feeling, instead of reacting automatically. It's as though mindfulness functions as a dam that calms the waters of a raging river, and the slower flow naturally enables a wiser, more skillful response.

Other scientists from around the world are contributing to the rapidly growing body of knowledge of mindfulness, and much is being learned about how it changes patterns in the brain. In *Buddha's Brain*, Rick Hanson documents how mindful meditation strengthens positive neurochemical systems that contribute to well-being. A daily meditation practice reduces activity in the default mode network, the part of the brain that gets stuck in rumination, a major mental habit in othering. Neuroscientists have also learned that, even though habits of conditioning create well-worn neural grooves in the brain, the brain is changeable and adaptive. Our brains are shaped by our experiences, so intentional practice changes the brain's patterns. Old neural grooves can grow weaker and even diminish, and new neural pathways can be established. Further, studies have shown that after eight weeks of a daily 20–30 minute meditation, the density of the brain's gray matter (areas having to do with memory, attention, problem solving, empathy, and emotion regulation) increases and grows thicker, and the size of the amygdala (the area having to do with stress, fear, and anger) decreases.[15]

Mindfulness changes
the brain,
which in turn
changes the mind.

From this research, we now know that when a conditioned pattern is activated and we're automatically pulled into it, mindfulness has the power to interrupt the momentum of the reaction and pop us out of its neural groove. Once freed, we can connect with what is real and true in the moment. With practice over time, the neural grooves formed from conditioning diminish and gradually lose their power to trap us and then sweep us away. What's going on in our mind — what we perceive, think, imagine, and feel — affects our brain, and we can use our mind, via mindfulness, to change our brain for the better. In other words, mindfulness changes the brain, which in turn changes the mind.

Mindfulness Takes Practice

Mindfulness is a set of skills and attitudes, a practical tool set, that we develop most directly through meditation practice. Formal meditation practice is like going to the gym. It's the workout period for building mindfulness "muscles," requiring intentional effort and concentration. Mindfulness is also practiced informally, "off the cushion," so to speak. Informal practice is the bridge for bringing this skill set into our lives, where it matters the most.

The specific practice I teach is called Vipassana, or Shamatha Vipassana, meditation. Its roots come primarily from Theravaden Buddhism. In the western world, the practice is commonly called Insight Meditation. Loosely translated, *shamatha* means calm abiding, and *vipassana* means insight, seeing into clearly. The formal practice includes two basic aspects. First, it calms the mind-body-heart system, which helps slow the system so we can be more stable with whatever we're experiencing in the moment. In a calmer state, it's easier to see our experience more precisely, which allows clearer insight and understanding to arise naturally.

The most fundamental guideline for practicing mindfulness is simple: *we bring attention to whatever is most predominant in the present moment.* What am I actually experiencing in this moment? Next, we notice how we are relating to the experience. Are we open and accepting of it, or resisting and fighting with it? This is the point at which simple may become difficult. When we're experiencing something uncomfortable — such as anxiety, sadness, anger, doubt, or shame — our instinct and habit is to turn away from it. We don't want to pay attention to it. We want to get away from it as quickly as we can using any of our well-practiced exit strategies: distracting, denying, numbing out, repressing, or projecting. We often invoke one of our favorite addictions such as eating, drinking, shopping, or texting to escape what we don't want to experience. *Anything* but opening to the experience just as it is. Now mindfulness becomes radical because despite our desire and our culture's encouragement to escape from what's unpleasant, mindfulness asks us to do the opposite and open directly to it.

Instead of turning away, we turn towards what's upsetting or uncomfortable, *but* with the skill set and attitudes that are inherent to mindfulness. This makes it possible to identify what's happening in our mind to create our suffering. We recognize the habits and triggers for judging and criticizing. We see how the mind is easily agitated by grasping and clinging to our desires, assumptions, and beliefs. With practice, we become more discerning and can see exactly what causes our suffering, as well as what creates more peacefulness, calmness, and happiness. An old Zen proverb describes it this way: *The obstacle is the path.* In other words, the way out is through. It takes courage and skill to face what is difficult and unwanted. Who enjoys feeling uncomfortable and in pain? Yet bringing mindful attention to what's upsetting moves us through our upset much more quickly than our habitual reactions, and we emerge wiser, stronger, and more compassionate towards ourselves. The practice is, therefore, more than a tool to create inner calm; in fact, it's a truly healing, revolutionary practice. Therefore, it's often referred to as the path of liberation.

Coming Back to Our True Selves

Mindfulness is a direct pathway back to our true selves. In a simple and immediate way, we connect with what we are authentically experiencing in this moment. We notice whatever it is without judgment, but instead with kindness, curiosity, and acceptance. In this way, mindfulness wakes us up to what's real, alive, and true. It pops us out of the bubble of dwelling on the other so that we find ourselves, even for a brief moment. Waking out of the trance of habitual thinking and returning to the present over and over cultivates access to our true nature. Little by little, or sometimes suddenly in a lightbulb moment of epiphany, the clouds of conditioning part and a new awareness or insight comes to us. This is exactly how we develop freedom from the habit of othering and learn we can trust ourselves.

Practice

Beginning Meditation: Moment of Mindfulness

I invite you now to experiment with a mindfulness practice, as it's one thing to talk about being mindful, and quite another to experience it. The transformation is all about the experiencing. *Please read through the instructions first and then experiment with the practice.*

• Close your eyes and bring all of your attention into this present moment, turning attention towards yourself. Arrange your body in a way that feels comfortable, really noticing how the posture feels. Feel your back, your head and neck, your shoulders and arms, your chest and belly, your hips and bottom, your legs and your feet. Be aware of all of you sitting here, your whole being. You're saying "hello" to your body, just as it is. Stay with your body for a few moments as you are.

• Now shift your attention to listening to the sounds you are aware of right now – the sounds within you and the sounds outside of you, including the sound of silence. Listen for a few moments.

• Move your attention back to your body and feel the physical sensations of breathing. Notice what the sensations feel like with as much curiosity as you can muster. Stay with these sensations for a few moments.

• Shift your attention directly to your mind, noticing your thoughts, perhaps some judgments, visiting a to-do list, remembering a conversation, wondering if you're doing this practice correctly, and so on. Notice your thoughts for a few more minutes. Notice it all without judging but, instead, simply be curious about your experience and accept whatever you notice. Open your eyes and notice the effect of this simple practice.

What was that practice like for you? How did it affect you? Was it easy? Hard? Do you feel more awake and connected to yourself right now? Please notice whatever is true for you, and accept whatever you notice as valid, because it is. You successfully completed the first meditation practice.

Ownwork Suggestions

Practice the short "Moment of Mindfulness Meditation" several times throughout the day.

Afterwards, notice how it affected you. Be very sensitive to all you notice.

• Periodically and frequently throughout the day, intentionally pause, turn your awareness in towards yourself, feel your body breathing several breaths, and then ask the three core questions:

1. What am I experiencing right now? Thinking? Imagining? Feeling? Sensing? Hearing? What's happening in my body? Notice with lots of curiosity.

2. What's my reaction to that experience? How am I relating to it? Am I accepting or resisting?

3. Given what's going on, what's a wise and kind way to respond to myself right now? Be open to whatever occurs to you and follow your advice.

• If it's helpful to you, record your observations in your journal.

6

Basic Principles:
The Nuts and Bolts
of Mindfulness

You only have moments to live.

Jon Kabat-Zinn

Long before I attended my first meditation retreat, I became intrigued with mindfulness after hearing about the experiences of a friend's brother. For a good part of his early adult life, Nick saved money so he could travel in Asia for long periods of time. When he returned to the United States, he'd transition back into our western world by completing a three-month silent meditation retreat at the Insight Meditation Society (IMS) in Barre, Massachusetts. Afterwards, he'd find a new job and save until he had enough money to return to Asia, followed by another three-month retreat. I was curious about what happened in his mind when all he was doing was meditating, in silence, day in and day out for those months, so I asked him about it when he came for a visit. He said in the silence and continuous practice, his mind became so slowed down and quiet that he could sense when a thought was beginning to form. He'd watch it slowly coming, sense it gradually getting closer, see the thought clearly when it fully arrived, and then watch it pass and fade away. He'd remain present in silence and spaciousness, resting, and open. At some moment, he would sense another thought beginning to arise.

I was fascinated by his account and longed for a similar experience. At that point in my life, my mind felt like a jungle full of monkeys. I felt no spaciousness in my mind. In fact, I felt mentally exhausted, as though I was a giant head perched on top of a tiny body, constantly thinking, analyzing, and planning seemingly *all the time*. Nick's experience started me down the path of mindfulness.

Mindfulness: What It Is and Is Not

Today after thirty years of practicing mindfulness, my mind is more spacious and feels proportional to my body. The speed of thoughts arising is remarkably slower. However, being thought-free, or achieving a blank mind, is not the primary purpose of mindfulness meditation; it is simply a by-product of intensive practice and very deep concentration.

Mindfulness is not about entering an altered state. Rather, it's just the opposite. It is about waking up from the trance of our conditioning so we can know ourselves more deeply and wisely. It is a practice in being just as we are, rather than trying to be something or somebody else. Mindfulness teaches us radical acceptance: we accept our experience just as it is, no matter what. We learn to connect with whatever our true experience is right now, even if we're not comfortable with it, instead of trying to change it to be more to our liking. This is not selfish or indulgent navel gazing, but rather an act of self-responsibility. It enables us to fully embody our lives and take complete responsibility for exactly what we're experiencing and how we respond to that.

Here's how it works. Typically, we try to change things we don't want to experience: there's a pain in my knee, I'm feeling sad, someone disappoints me, the kids are driving me crazy. We tend to react to these situations, even minor discomforts, by struggling against them and trying to make them go away. If we can't, we squirm and suffer until they do somehow finally change. In contrast, with mindfulness we let it all be, we let ourselves be, with life as it is in the moment. It's often said that mindfulness develops a "fair witness," or an observing part of yourself. We open to it all with curiosity and acceptance. We let go of struggling to make the experience different.

> Mindfulness develops a "fair witness," or an observing part of yourself.

For example, when you're suddenly upset, you mindfully note your reaction and open to it in detail. You become interested in exactly how you are experiencing the feeling rather than running off in the mind's stories: "I just felt a wave of discomfort moving through my belly. What was I just thinking? Oh, wow! I just imagined that my neighbor thinks my kids are too noisy and I'm the worst mother in the world. No wonder I felt upset." Accepting your actual experience doesn't mean that you agree with the content of your mind's story, but you see how it arises and how you are truly experiencing it. When you accept your actual experience, your perspective shifts from being the target of the disturbance, from taking it personally and getting swept up in it, to observing it and watching it go by.

Furthermore, because nature is impermanent, everything is always changing. Any uncomfortable experience we have will change without our having to fight with it and strive to make it different. As we accept our experiences, we're gradually changing our relationship to ourselves. We're developing a new and deeper intimacy with ourselves. Remarkably, as we stay with our experience, we discover it's workable as it is, and we are likely to learn something useful about reality and ourselves that could be freeing.

Meditation is not necessarily relaxing. It can be, but relaxation is not the purpose of mindfulness. However, a core aspect of the practice is cultivating a deep inner calmness, the ability to calmly abide with what's here. With time and practice, you develop a deeper inner stability that's available even in the midst of chaos, agitation, and disturbance.

Six Basic Principles

Practicing and developing mindfulness involves six key principles. As you enter into a practice, I want to make it clear that mindfulness is not a quick fix. Although many people do notice benefits right away, the more profound effects come through gradual change. Freeing ourselves from our deeply conditioned mental patterns and shifting our understanding of reality is an organic process that can be working away in our psyches for the rest of our lives. It's a gradual awakening. Take a long view and be patient and kind with yourself all along the way.

1. Present Moment

Mindfulness brings our attention to the here and now. The present moment is the power moment. If you think about it, the present moment, this moment right now, is the only moment when we are actually alive. Thus, it's the only moment we can take action.

Our ordinary mind is wild and untamed. It is used to going off in whatever direction it wants, whenever it wants, continuously swinging between remembering the past, wishing an event or feeling was still happening or wishing the past had been different, and then zooming into the future, fantasizing about what we hope will happen or are afraid will happen. As you've discovered by watching your own mind, the conditioned mind rarely stays in the present moment for more than a second or two. This zooming back and forth, attention captured in thoughts and emotions about the past and future, directly affects our present moment experience, and makes us miss what is happening in the here and now. We miss the beautiful sound of the robin's song, or the eager look in our child's face as she's telling us about something exciting, or the gentle feel of the soft breeze on our face as we walk because we're lost in thought, carried away into the mind's current version of the past or future.

> The present moment is the only moment when we are actually alive.

Much of what occupies our attention is made up in the mind, either memories of the past or fantasies of the future. The past is over and done with; it's dead and can never be alive again. It can only be brought into the present moment through memory, and with it the distortion of memory's recall. Likewise, the future never arrives. It is always ahead of us, something we can only imagine. We are only alive in this very moment. We can live only one moment at a time.

Through mindfulness and understanding the mind's habit of wandering, we bring our attention back to the present moment over and over. More than anything, mindfulness is the willingness to be aware of where our attention is, pop out of the bubble of being elsewhere, and escort our attention back to the present. By repeatedly returning to the present, we train our minds to become more familiar and skilled with connecting to the reality of the moment. We're establishing new brain pathways; the neural grooves to be here now.

We have umpteen habits that take us away from the present and off into the mind's dramas, stories, and preoccupations, so it's a big deal to wake up and see the present moment clearly. A woman who has taken several of my classes reported a major insight during a one-day silent retreat. She said that as she was meditating, she became aware of an overwhelming urge to flee. "Suddenly I felt like I had to get out of the meditation hall. My mind was screaming 'Let me out!'. I wanted to run out as fast as I could. As I saw this so clearly, I suddenly realized that I'm always moving hurriedly to do something else, the next thing, any next thing, versus being fully here in the present moment. I realized I'm always trying to escape the present moment." She was encouraged and excited by her insight, hopeful that in seeing it clearly, she may now have more choice and ability to stay in the present moment.

2. Direct Experience

With our attention here in the present, we focus on what is called our direct experience. This is whatever we are experiencing with our senses right now. We connect with our six "sense doors," as they are called in meditative jargon: what we are seeing, hearing, smelling, tasting, and sensing in the body, and what's happening in the mind. The sense door of the mind includes our perceptions, thoughts, and emotions. In any moment of mindfulness, you might be aware of thoughts, a familiar body ache, a hot flicker of anxiety, a sweet smell, a feeling of calm, a painful judgment, the sound of traffic, and an itch between your fingers. The direct experience might be pleasant, unpleasant, or neutral. It might be what you want and like; it might be what you definitely don't want and don't like. It doesn't matter. The point of practice is to realize what's actually here, just the way it is, right now. In mindfulness, whatever you are experiencing is always exactly right. It's your direct experience. It's valid. It's what's true for you right now. *It is your authentic experience.*

Our habit, though, is to *add on* to our direct experience with reactive stories. These stories can take us far away from our present moment actual experience into judgments, imaginings, memories, worries, and fears, which arise primarily from our conditioning. The add-ons pull us away from present reality and often create suffering. For example, when I first began meditating, I realized that in trying to concentrate on the sensations of breathing, I'd start wondering about the next breath before the present breath was completed. Anxiously I'd think, "Where's my next breath. What will it be like? Is it comingnow? Oh, wait. I'm still breathing this one." Seeing this reaction, I'd think, "Wow, I'm so anxious. I'm not good at meditation, I can't even stay with this one breath. I am so uptight. What's wrong with me anyway?" Then I'd go off in my various judgements, getting even farther away from my present moment direct experience. At some point, I'd release myself from the inner drama and come back to the sensations of breathing, but usually not before I'd whip myself around. With mindfulness, we learn to see these add-on reactions, choose to let them go, and return attention to the present moment reality.

> Whatever you are experiencing is your direct experience. It's valid because it is your authentic experience.

3. Unconditional Friendliness

Another key principle is to pay attention to our direct experience with an attitude of unconditional friendliness. We train in simply noticing what's here with gentleness, kindness, and respect. We bring the energy of loving kindness to our experience. This means not abandoning or turning against ourselves when our experience is uncomfortable, when we realize we're intensely othering, when we make a mistake, or when we're mad, afraid, jealous, or ashamed. We are developing the ability to be a real friend to ourselves by relating to our experience with loving kindness, no matter what we are experiencing.

Because othering breeds a hostile judgmental relationship with ourselves, when I first began to meditate, it felt awkward and strange to treat myself in a kind and loving manner. If this is true for you, here are some suggestions for how you might encourage yourself to relate with more kindness and gentleness:

• *Modify your tone of voice (out loud and in your mind) so that it's softer and slower.*
• *Talk to yourself as if you were a young child, innocent and open, and you are the child's loving mother.*
• *Treat yourself like you treat a being that you never or rarely lose your patience with, such as your favorite pet. Use that same feeling and voice towards yourself.*
• *Hold the view that you are always doing the best you can in any given moment, and forgive and accept yourself when you think you could have or should have done better.*
• *Bring as much lightness and humor as you can to yourself and what you notice.*

Learning how to relate to ourselves gently, kindly, and lovingly is one of the most enduring benefits of the practice. We come to accept ourselves and heal the harsh and painful critical relationship we've unintentionally created through conditioning. Through unconditional friendliness, we create a reliable loyalty towards ourselves, no matter what. You're the one person in your life who will always be here for you, no matter what, so learning how to accept yourself is liberating and necessary. Mustering even a tiny amount of friendliness begins the healing and feels better than the old familiar critical way.

> Mindfulness develops the ability to be a real friend to ourselves.

4. Acceptance

As we connect with our direct experience in the present, relating to it with unlimited friendliness and kindness, we also refrain from judging the experience. Instead, we accept it just the way it is, regardless of whether we find it comfortable or pleasing. Acceptance is a radical act, because it's the opposite of our conditioning. If our experience is pleasant and we like it, acceptance is a piece of cake, no problem. If it's unpleasant, uncomfortable, or painful, acceptance is hard. We don't like the experience and want it to change right away.

As humans, we seem to have a limited tolerance for the unpleasant. Sometimes changing things for the better is easy. If you're hungry, you can usually find something to eat. If you're cold, you can put on more clothes. If you feel a hard pain in your body that won't go away, or you're feeling sad because your dear friend moved or a loved one died, these experiences can't be changed as easily. If we look more closely, we'll see we can't change many experiences in the ways we'd prefer. Because so many conditions are out of our immediate control, we practice accepting whatever is here, just as it is right now. When that experience is uncomfortable, we practice holding it in our awareness with spaciousness, giving it lots of room. We learn to relax around the unpleasant experience. Allowing more room makes it easier to accept the experience and stay with it with less suffering.

When I first heard the instructions to accept all experiences as they are, I felt tremendous relief. In my previous attempts to meditate, I'd judge my experiences relentlessly. I would criticize my wandering mind, my posture, my breath, and on and on. I felt like a failure at almost every sitting practice. These judgements were self-inflicted spankings. Instead of becoming more patient with myself through meditation, I was becoming more irritated and impatient. The instruction to explicitly and intentionally refrain from judging my experience, no matter what, was powerfully transformative news. It shined the light of awareness on my deeply ingrained habit of perfectionism. I realized I was always trying to do things exactly right, and judged myself severely when I didn't measure up to my standard. By practicing both acceptance and unconditional friendliness, especially when I realized that I was judging myself, I could more easily see the patterns and the pain they caused.

5. Curiosity

While bringing kindness and acceptance to the present moment, we also bring curiosity to it. We approach each moment as if we've never experienced it before, which in reality is true. Every moment is a brand new moment. Curiosity asks us to relate to whatever is here with freshness and sincere interest. This is not analytical curiosity, but an eager inquiry. It's the kind of natural curiosity we all had as kids. Instead of asking, "Why am I experiencing this?" we ask, "Exactly *what* am I experiencing? *How* am I experiencing this?" Those "Why?" questions engage our discursive mind, where we easily zoom off into stories and theories about ourself, taking us far away from our direct experience, and often into familiar painful territories. "Why am I like this? Why aren't I different? What's the matter with me anyway? When am I going to change?"

With curiosity we're cultivating what is often called "beginner's mind," or "don't know mind." In truth, we don't know what the next moment of our life will be like. By embracing that innocence, we bring a more childlike curiosity to our experience, a kind of wonderment. We investigate the moment with openness and precision. The goal is to discover exactly what an experience is like in this moment, even if, or especially if, we've experienced it many times before. When something is familiar, we assume we know what it will be like again, so it's hard to stay present, fresh, and open to it. Instead we get lost in our assumptions and miss what it is truly like right now. Our mind closes and we lose interest. As the highly respected Zen Master Suzuki Roshi said, "In the expert's mind there are few possibilities. In the beginner's mind there are many, many possibilities."[16]

To practice the curiosity of beginner's mind, ask questions such as, "Exactly how am I experiencing this ache, fear, excitement, or boredom? What's it actually like in this moment? Exactly what am I imagining, remembering, concluding, or projecting? Does it feel pleasant, neutral, or unpleasant? How am I relating to it? Am I trying to change it, fix it, or ignore it? Or am I letting it be here, accepting it?" A curious inquiry deepens and amplifies what we're experiencing by bringing us closer to it, making the experience more interesting. It expands our knowledge and understanding about what's really going on. It also helps us stay present with what's difficult, and allows us to see what happens as we do so.

Here's an example of how curiosity works. Not long ago when my daughter and grandkids were coming over for dinner, I noticed a feeling of anxiety starting to rise when I looked at the clock and realized they were over an hour late. I turned towards the anxious feeling with curiosity and friendliness, and I asked, "Okay, exactly what am I experiencing? How am I experiencing this feeling of anxiety?" I realized that my belly was tight, my heart was beating faster, and my palms were sweaty. I asked myself, "What am I actually thinking?" I discovered I was imagining a horrific story where they had been killed in a terrible car accident. I imagined a police officer calling me to tell me the tragic news. Then I imagined I was devastated beyond belief, and dropped into a deep depression and never recovered. Thankfully, seeing all of the thoughts mindfully, I took several full deep breaths and reminded myself these very scary stories were all fantasy, and I chose to deliberately let them go. A few minutes later, the doorbell rang and they arrived, safe and sound. I was so thankful for mindfulness. The disaster story was only a dream.

Curiosity is a beneficial attitude to cultivate because it automatically creates more space or room with the event, helping us accept it more easily in the moment. Inner spaciousness also helps us take the whole experience less personally.

6. Disidentifying

The sixth basic principle is to disidentify—to be aware of what we're experiencing without identifying with it or taking it personally. Taking what we experience personally is a big habit of the conditioned mind. The mind makes an egocentric interpretation by spinning a story about what the experience signifies, or what will happen to us because of it. We assign meaning to it about ourselves. It's fascinating to see how pervasive the I-me-mine habit is. As you pay attention to the stories your mind creates, you're likely to see that most of your mind's stories are about what did or could happen to *you*. Even in the last example where I imagined a tragic car accident, the final imagined pain was about how *I* would be affected. This automatic attachment to our personal self, our identity, destines us to suffering.

Instead, the view in mindfulness is that experiences, based on conditions, are continuously arising and passing away, changing moment by moment, and as human beings we are all subject to these experiences. They are not unique to us individually, but are universal to being human. In certain conditions, we experience anger, fear, or sadness. In other conditions, we feel joy, delight, or peace. By learning to disidentify with our direct experience, we can be aware of it with less attachment and more friendliness, acceptance, and curiosity. When we understand that an experience is not about "me" personally, but rather arises from the current conditions, it's safe to become intimate with the experience. We create more room around it. We can then understand the conditions that caused the event or reaction to arise, and we can choose to let it go and pass on by without making it into a bigger deal by adding on an interpretation of what it means about me.

After a meditation I led in which the instruction was to focus on opening to the sensations in our bodies with kindness, acceptance, curiosity, and without identifying, a student said that it had been a difficult meditation. All she had noticed was the pain in her neck. Although she tried to work with it mindfully, she kept feeling so much aversion to the pain because, as she said, "It showed me how rigid and uptight I am. I'm always closed and resisting things. I'm so judgmental and critical. I've always been like this and I'm afraid I always will be." Although her direct experience was neck pain (clearly unpleasant), she added the painful interpretation that the pain meant *she* was rigid, judgmental, and critical. By identifying with her experience, she added misery to her physical pain.

Mindfulness Builds Mental Muscles

As we practice, especially through formal sitting meditation, we develop four important mental skills, or muscles, that build internal strength and power to free us from our painful conditioned patterns. These are concentration, awareness, intention, and letting go. Every

```
┌─────────────────────────────────────────────────┐
│                                                   │
│     Mindfulness Builds Four Mental Skills:        │
│                                                   │
│         • Concentration                           │
│                                                   │
│         • Awareness                               │
│                                                   │
│         • Intention                               │
│                                                   │
│         • Letting go                              │
│                                                   │
└─────────────────────────────────────────────────┘
```

time we meditate, we are exercising and developing these indispensable mental capacities.

Concentration is the ability to focus attention deliberately. When we concentrate, we gather our mental energy and aim it onto a chosen object and then sustain it there. Concentration strengthens our ability to stay connected, focused, and present for longer periods of time. It promotes calmness, as well as a deeper experience of whatever we're paying attention to. This focused attention contrasts with the more familiar monkey-mind state, where we're distracted, restless, agitated, and only superficially connecting with our experiences.

When attention is concentrated, neural and hormonal activity shifts in helpful directions. Research shows that concentrating on one object, such as our breath, activates the prefrontal cortex of the brain. This is the region of executive function that guides thought, action, and emotion. It is sometimes called the Wise Owl of the mind because it's where we have natural access to our wisdom and common sense. Concentration also stimulates the parasympathetic nervous system, releasing hormones including dopamine and oxytocin, which help the body relax and slow down.[17]

Awareness is the ability to know what we are actually experiencing right now. When we are aware, we are cognizant, realizing what we're sensing, feeling, seeing, hearing, perceiving, and thinking in the present moment. Awareness is being awake, alert, and sensitive to the changing flow of events and experience. It's recognizing when attention shifts from the chosen object of concentration to something else. Awareness brings a sense of aliveness to our experience. The opposite of awareness is spacing out, not knowing what's happening for us, feeling sleepy, sluggish, or dull. Unaware, we don't realize we've been carried off and become lost or preoccupied in the dream of our thoughts and fantasies.

Intention, the third mental muscle developed through mindfulness, is the ability to decide where we want to aim and focus our attention. Intention informs and guides action. Like setting our compass in the direction we want to go, intention points attention toward the chosen object, purpose, or goal. It keeps us aligned with what we want to cultivate. When we feel undirected, scattered, without purpose or a goal, lost in wherever our undirected attention takes us, it's helpful to remember and renew our intention.

> Letting go is deciding to release attention from where we're caught, which gives us the freedom to move attention to where we want it to be.

Letting go is the ability to release attention from what we've become involved with, or absorbed into, that we no longer want to focus on. It's the ability to relax and release our grip when we want to, at will. Letting go is deciding to release attention from where we've been caught, which affords us the freedom to move attention to where we want it to be. The opposite of letting go is holding on, clinging to something and not being able to put it down or get free from it. If you've ever been caught in obsessing about something, ruminating, unable to stop thinking about it, you know the suffering of not being able to let go. We do a lot of ruminating when we're caught in othering.

Meditation Practice Is the Gym

Formal meditation practice is the daily intensive mental workout period for training the mind. Each time we sit down to meditate, we're exercising and developing the four mental skills or muscles of concentration, awareness, intention, and letting go. Understanding that the basic intention of the practice is to be awake and compassionately aware, we begin by *concentrating* on a chosen object, usually the sensations of breathing. Concentration helps the mind and body come fully into the present moment, and invites our whole system to slow and calm down. When we become *aware* that attention has left the breath and we're now thinking about something or being carried away by a sensation in the body, we remember our *intention* to be awake and concentrate on the breath. We then choose to move attention back to concentrating on the sensations of breathing, *letting go* of wherever we were. Over and over, we practice *concentrating* on the breath, being *aware* of attention wandering off, recognizing where it's gone, *intentionally* concentrating on the breath again, and *letting go* of where our drifting or restless mind took us.

Each time we practice meditating formally, we are strengthening these mental muscles. Then when a challenge arises in life, off the cushion, we can use our mindfulness muscles to respond with greater stability, wisdom, and ease. Over time when feelings of discomfort arise, we'll increasingly be able to recognize what's happening, realize the disturbing reaction the mind has created, remember our intention to be awake and connect with what's real in the moment, and then let go of what's causing our suffering.

Practice:

The Raisin Meditation

The raisin meditation is a useful first meditation practice because it provides practice in the mindfulness principles, especially concentration and curiosity. I encourage you to challenge yourself with this practice to learn how much you can discover with beginner's mind, and see what it's like for you.

Read through the following instructions, and then observe what you notice and experience during the practice. You may be surprised. If you're not fond of raisins, pick something else, such as a dried cherry, fresh grape, or strawberry. Even a small piece of chocolate will work. The food needs to be small so you can hold it in the palm of your hand.

• Hold the raisin lightly in the palm of your hand. You've never known this raisin before, so exactly what is it like? The goal is to be aware of what you are actually experiencing right now, with lots of curiosity and interest. Watch for the ever prominent habits of judging and assuming — they are pervasive.

• Begin with the sense door of seeing. As you cradle the raisin in your palm, what do you see? What's its shape or shapes? Colors? Does it cast shadows? Is it opaque? Translucent? Is it smooth or rippled? Turn the raisin over and examine it completely, noticing all you can *literally* see.

• Now experience the raisin with sense door of smell. What odor or fragrance do you detect? Be open and curious.

• Next, close your eyes and feel the raisin with your fingers. What can you learn about it through touching? Is it rough, smooth, cool, dry, sticky, hard, soft, heavy, or light?

• Put the raisin next to your ear and listen, the sense door of hearing. You never know, you might hear something.

• Place the raisin between your lips and roll it around, noticing what you can experience just with your lips. When you're ready, let the raisin fall into your mouth and move it around, not biting into it yet. What does it feel like in your mouth? Can you sense any flavor? Notice when you start to salivate.

 • Intentionally take your first bite into the raisin. Stay with this first bite for a few moments, really experiencing what it's like. Now continue to slowly chew it, staying present with all you notice. Notice how the raisin changes as you chew it. Stay present with the experience of chewing and eating the raisin until it's completely gone. After it's all chewed and swallowed, notice if you can still taste the flavor of the raisin.

Take a moment to pause and notice the effect of the meditation. What are you like after concentrating on the raisin? Do you feel calmer, stimulated, more here, or the same as you did before? Notice whatever is true for you. Remember whatever you are experiencing is exactly right. There's no particular way you should feel. The point is to collect your own data from the experience and notice with curiosity. Did you enjoy the practice? Did you discover new things about the raisin? Can you imagine what it would be like to eat a whole meal mindfully?

Mindfulness is anti-multitasking.

Formal meditation practice trains the mind to be more awake in our everyday life and activities. Mindfulness changes the quality of our experience, making it more interesting, fresh, alive, and engaging. Imagine what it would be like to do ordinary activities with mindfulness: mindfully shower, wash the dishes, fold the laundry, drive, or chop vegetables. I can guarantee that eating mindfully is transformative and greatly beneficial for the body. Kissing your sweetie or your child mindfully is heavenly. Mindfulness is anti-multitasking. It brings all of our attention here, focused on the one thing we're doing right now, rather than getting lost in thought, and mindlessly doing the task. This gives our busy monkey mind a chance to rest, and an opportunity for the wisdom of our authentic true nature, our blue sky mind, to shine through.

Ownwork Suggestions

To get familiar with these principles — present moment, direct experience, unconditional friendliness, curiosity, acceptance, and disidentifying — as well as the notion of building the muscles of concentration, awareness, intention, and letting go, here are some simple and powerful ways you can *practice informally*. Please be sure to always notice your experience with acceptance and kindness instead of criticism. Othering has trained us to be critical towards ourselves, and this habit hurts us far more than helps us. Be gentle and curious towards yourself, and see what you can learn about your mind's conditioned habits.

• Where am I? Throughout the day, notice where your attention is by frequently pausing and asking "Where am I right now? Is my attention here in the present moment, or is it in the past or the future?" Remember — no judging, just be curious. Notice exactly what you're focusing on, such as remembering a conversation, worrying about someone, or watering the house plants.

• Eat mindfully. Take the raisin meditation further and experiment with eating a meal mindfully. See how much you can actually experience and notice all the habits of eating without awareness. When you realize you've drifted away, bring your attention back to eating, kindly and gently.

• Connecting with all of your senses. Because we're caught up in thoughts much of the time, it's helpful to intentionally connect with our physical senses. Besides helping to balance our experience and energy, connecting with each of our senses can add wonderful experiences to the day. Every now and then, pause and connect with one of your other senses. Ask yourself, "What can I smell right now?" Or, "What can I actually hear right now?" Or, "What sensations are happening in my body right now?" Make a point of looking at the amazing blue sky or clouds above you at least once in the day.

7

The First Formal Meditation: Don't Just Do Something, Sit There and Breathe

To undertake a period of meditation is to offer a gift to yourself. It is an act of caring for your own well-being and consciously nurturing inner connection. It is a time for exploring the most intimate relationship in your life — the relationship with yourself.

Christina Feldman

Mindfulness of Breathing

Now that you've practiced being aware of where your attention is, coming back to the present moment, noticing your direct experience, and experimenting with eating mindfully, it's time to learn the first and most basic part of the formal sitting practice: mindfulness of breathing. Mindful breathing is home base for the entire practice of mindfulness. It is the anchor we return to when other experiences arise and draw us away. Concentrating on the sensations of breathing is our tether to the present moment. Learning to breathe mindfully can be liberating and transformational. I've heard teachers say that we can reach complete freedom from the habits of conditioning — enlightenment — simply by practicing mindful breathing. Don't underestimate the benefit and power of learning to concentrate on the sensations of the breath.

Mindful breathing is home base for the entire practice of mindfulness.

The breath is home base for a number of reasons. Because breathing happens in the body, bringing awareness to the sensations of breathing automatically brings attention into the body and out of our thoughts. The breath is completely portable. Wherever we go and as long as we are alive, we're breathing, so the breath is always available to us. Breathing also happens only in the present moment. When we're concentrating on the breath, our mind and body are aligned and we are grounded in the here and now. The breath also provides a neutral focus. Finally, although we can intentionally control breathing to some extent, the body knows how to breathe on its own so breathing doesn't require our direct control. We can trust the body's ability to breathe, which allows us to relax and rest with the sensations of breathing.

Mindful breathing has a calming effect, which invites the mind and body to slow down and become more collected and condensed. Concentrating on the breath shifts neural activity into the prefrontal cortex of

Checking in

• What was it like to intentionally notice where your attention was every now and then throughout the day? Were you surprised at what you observed? How much of the time were you ahead of yourself imagining into the future? In the past? Actually here in the present moment? Was it useful to track your attention?

• What was it like to eat a meal mindfully? Did you enjoy your food more? Did you eat less than you usually do?

• Did you remember to connect with your various senses? What was it like to intentionally focus on smelling? Listening? Feeling sensations in your body? Seeing what you were looking at? Did you notice more?

• If you intended to do these practices but forgot, welcome to the world of living on autopilot. It's hard to remember to wake up and be mindful. So do be understanding and kind to yourself. Although these practices are simple, they are not easy because our minds are so deeply entrenched in their habits.

the brain and activates the parasympathetic nervous system. This encourages the release of relaxing hormones, further helping us to drop into a more stable state. Remember that as we are concentrating on the sensations of the breath, we are exercising and developing important mental muscles of concentration, awareness, intention, and letting go.

Choosing a Place to Sit

Find a place to meditate where you will be undisturbed by others, such as a spot in your bedroom, office, or porch. Use the same place every day if you can. If you live with other people, ask them not to disturb you while you're meditating. Consider meditation your sacred time and make a deal with yourself and your family or housemates to honor your commitment. Everyone will benefit. If you live alone, make the same agreement with yourself. This is your designated time to be free from paying attention to anyone and anything else. It's a respite, an othering-free zone. Turn off your cell phone and computer; you may even want to put them in another room.

Choosing a Time to Sit

Most people find it works best to practice around the same time every day. This helps to establish the discipline of the practice. Some women find it's easiest to practice first thing in the morning, before everyone else gets up. Others find lunchtime is more workable, while some prefer the end of the day right before bed. You'll have to experiment with what works best for you. You might want to write "meditate" in your schedule.

The most benefit comes from meditating every day, even for a short amount of time. You are learning a new skill set, so practice is essential. What's most important is to establish the habit. Bring a watch, timer, or alarm clock with you, and before you sit, decide how long you'll practice. Start with an amount of time that feels doable. I suggest starting with

5 or 10 minutes. No matter what, sit for that amount of time. (You can download free phone apps for timing your meditation.)

A daily sitting practice requires time, and like any new and healthy habit, we must make room for it in our lives, somewhere. Not surprisingly, the mind tends to resist meditating. After all, it's blatantly against our conditioning because we're paying attention to ourselves only. Neither are we getting anything done on our "to-do" list unless we include meditating on the list. In addition, we're going against the grain and asking the mind to do something unfamiliar and out of the norm. For most of us, finding time to meditate means choosing to let go of another habit we've become accustomed to. Consider what you may need to change to make room in your day for meditation. Will you set your alarm earlier and get a little less sleep, or go to bed earlier to get the sleep you need? Will you change your routine at the end of the day so you have time to practice? Will you say "no" to hanging out with your family for a few minutes in the evening so you can meditate? Do you need to ask your partner or spouse to cover for you while you practice? These are important practical considerations. It is difficult to establish a practice if we try to squeeze in meditation somewhere between all that we are now doing. Something has to give — at least a little.

Meditation Posture

Formal meditation can be practiced in any posture: sitting, standing, or lying down. Traditionally, it's practiced sitting on a zafu, a round meditation cushion, or a meditation bench, which is why meditation is called a sitting practice. You can also sit in a straight-backed chair or lie down if that's the only posture comfortable for you. The goal is to arrange your body so you feel as stable and comfortable as possible, and your body feels balanced and aligned. Ideally, you want to arrange your body so you can sit in stillness, without moving for increasingly long periods of time. Because the body and mind are connected, the more the body moves, the more the mind moves.

To arrange your body on a zafu or dense cushion, sit on the very edge of it so that as you cross your legs, your knees are below the top of your pelvis. Meditation benches are an alternative if you aren't comfortable in the cross-legged posture. You can also sit in a chair. However, rather than leaning against the back of the chair, scooch yourself forward so you're sitting on the edge of the seat and your feet are resting on the floor, legs uncrossed.

Whether sitting on a cushion, bench, or chair, the position of your back is most important in meditation. The idea is to sit erect, in a dignified posture. We want to hold ourselves upright, not rigidly, but in an aligned, self-respecting way. Maintaining a straight spine helps you stay more alert and breathe more naturally.

Sitting comfortably, let your arms and hands rest gently on your thighs or lap, and invite your spine to become aligned and lengthened. Sometimes it's helpful to imagine a helium balloon floating above you, attached by a string to a tuft of hair on the crown of your head. Let your sense of the balloon subtly lift your head and spine. Your head and neck can rest in a neutral position, your head neither dropping forward nor backward.

If you have a back injury and need to lie down, make the same intention to arrange yourself comfortably and with all parts of your body aligned. Uncross your legs and feet. Sleepiness is always a challenge in meditating, and meditating lying down increases the challenge. Be sure to guard against sleepiness. In fact, the only way you can perform the practice incorrectly is to fall asleep while you're meditating. Then you're simply sleeping instead of meditating.

Your eyes can be open or closed, whatever is most comfortable to you. If you prefer to leave your eyes open, set your gaze in front of you at about a 45-degree angle and let your eyes unfocus so you are not concentrating on what you're seeing, but rather merely resting your eyes softly on that spot.

Finally, invite everything to relax and soften. Invite all the muscles of your face to relax, especially around your jaw and mouth. Let your tongue rest behind your front upper teeth. Invite your shoulders, arms, and hands to relax, as well as your chest and belly. Simply open to the direct experience of sitting here just as you are, in this precious body, noticing what it is like with lots of curiosity and kindness.

Instructions for Breathing Mindfully

As you tune into the sensations of breathing, notice where you feel them most easily in your body. Some people feel the sensations mostly at the nostrils where the air enters and leaves the body. For others, the sensations are more obvious in the upper chest, and still others find them most pronounced in the belly. When you find the most obvious location, plant your attention there.

Focusing on your breath in the belly is ideal because the belly is closest to the body's actual center (just below the navel) and farthest from the head (where we tend to dwell in thinking). Don't force anything. This practice is inherently noncoercive and nonviolent. Please find the location that's the easiest and most comfortable for you. Over time you'll discover there's a consistent location for stationing your home base.

Once you've discovered where you can feel these breathing sensations most easily and set your attention there, bring beginner's mind to what you notice. Invite yourself to get really curious and interested in exactly what the sensations of this breath are actually like, just as they are happening right now. Concentrate on the sensations from the very beginning of the inhale all the way through to the completion of the exhale. Then open to the next breath as it happens. You want to ride the wave of the breath precisely as it is happening in your body.

We're connecting with the sensations of the ordinary and miraculous breath just as it is. We aren't trying to breathe in any special way. It doesn't matter if it's fast or slow, shallow or deep, irregular or stable. We accept the breath exactly as it is, with unconditional friendliness and tons of curiosity. In initially learning how to do breathe mindfully, you might ask a few questions: What are the sensations actually like? How much does the chest or belly expand and fall back with each inhalation and exhalation? Is the breath warm or cool? Can you sense the gap at the end of the inhale before the exhale begins or the next inhale happens? Remembering each breath is brand new and unique can help our curiosity. We also let go of identifying with the sensations, understanding that this precious body is simply breathing, or perhaps more accurately, simply being breathed. We practice not taking the breath personally, not making the breath a reflection of me and how I'm doing.

It's helpful to concentrate on the sensations of breathing with lightness and spaciousness, like a butterfly landing on a flower. We use our awareness to touch it lightly and sensitively, not crowding the sensations with our attention or watching too closely. We want to allow enough internal room in the field of our awareness so the breath can change however it may. As we concentrate, we hold the breath in the foreground of our field of awareness and allow all other phenomena to recede to the background: sounds, smells, other sensations, thoughts, and feelings. We will be somewhat aware of these other factors, but they are not prominent.

Sooner or later, we'll lose our connection with the breath and attention will wander away to a story in the mind, a sound, some other sensation in the body, or an emotion. This is normal. Wandering is what the ordinary mind does, so when the mind wanders, you haven't messed up. Recognizing when attention has left our chosen object — here it's the breath — and then gently and kindly returning it to what we want to attend to is a fundamental aspect of meditation practice. When we realize attention has gone somewhere else, we gently return to the breath and reconnect with its sensations. Sharon Salzberg, author and one of the country's leading Buddhist teachers, has played a crucial role in bringing meditation to the West. Salzberg suggests that coming back to the breath is similar to recognizing a friend in a crowd of people. You keep your eye on your friend as you gently and steadily make your way towards them. You don't aggressively push people out of the way to get to your friend.[18] We come back to the breath gently and kindly. We practice returning over and over and over.

Practice:

Meditation:
Mindful Breathing, First Practice

Find a timer or use your cell phone or watch to time the meditation for five minutes. Get a solid cushion, bench or chair to sit on, and pick a spot to practice. Please read over these instructions and then guide yourself through this first sitting practice.

• Sit comfortably with your spine aligned and lifted. Invite the mind, body, and heart to relax. Notice what it's like to be sitting here in this moment, receiving yourself just as you are. Remember that whatever you are experiencing is exactly right. Notice what you're aware of right now: sounds, thoughts, sensations, or smells. Notice without judging, but with curiosity and interest....

• Now notice your amazing body breathing. Let the breath be just as it is. Begin to get curious about where in your body is the easiest place to feel the sensations of breathing.... Position your attention right at this location. With your attention stationed here, receive the sensations of breathing as they come to you here.... Encourage yourself to get really curious about the actual sensations of this breath, staying with these sensations from the very beginning of the inhale all the way through the completion of the exhale. Open to the sensations of the next breath as it arrives.... Bringing the sensations of breathing into the foreground, while thoughts, sounds, and sensations fade to the background.... Whenever you realize attention has left the breath, pulled into some other experience, gently and kindly return attention to the sensations of this breath.... Each breath you breathe is unique, so be curious about the actual sensations of this one.... Relax around the sensations, giving the breath plenty of room to be however it is.... Rest in the aliveness of the present moment as the body you live in is breathing.

Reflecting on the First Practice

Take a few moments to notice how you were affected by these 5 minutes of practice. How do you feel in your body now? Your heart? What's your mind like? What did you notice in the practice? Did you find it easy or hard? Where was the easiest place to feel the breath? Did the meditation create more calmness or anxiety? Was it hard to stay focused on the breath? Did you have a lot of thoughts or other sensations?

In reflecting on this first meditative experience, whatever you experienced, even if it was difficult, hard, boring, or frustrating, was exactly right because it was your experience. The whole point of practice is to be aware of what we are experiencing and learn to relate to it wisely and skillfully. It's not about having, or trying to have, a sublime, relaxing, blissful experience. On the other hand, if you had a sublime experience, then by all means enjoy it. Just don't get attached to it, or think that's what you're supposed to experience.

Many women find the first meditation relaxing and refreshing. Others find following the breath actually creates anxiety because it's hard to let the breath be and simply relax with it. If this was your experience, don't be discouraged — you will get better at meditation. It can be hard to companion the breath when in the rest of our lives we are used to thinking we have to control everything that's happening, including our own experience. Mindfulness of breathing, in fact all of mindfulness, is a receptive practice. Through being conditioned to other, many of us are inexperienced at letting go of control and being receptive. Please remember not to judge yourself, but rather be curious and open to your experience, whatever it is. Fundamentally, mindfulness is the willingness to come back to the present moment and begin again.

> Mindfulness is the willingness to come back to the present moment and begin again.

Did you discover sensations in your body you didn't know were there? Mindfulness is an embodied practice. It's common with the first practice to find aches, stiffness, or pains we weren't aware of before. This may be a reflection of how distant we are from our bodies, due to being in our heads and habitually focused on the external. It's great news, though, that with just a few minutes of practice we can reconnect and discover what's going on with the body. In addition to being precious vehicles for living our lives, our bodies contain valuable information for us, so it is wise to learn to connect with their sensations and messages.

Did you find your attention wandering away from the breath, thinking about other things completely? Mental wandering is completely normal. It's what the ordinary mind does. It's used to thinking about whatever it wants to, not concentrating on one object and staying focused with that. When you noticed your attention wandered away, that was great. You were being mindful. You were being aware and awake. Sometimes when I meditate, I become so absorbed in a fantasy, planning or remembering something, that a large chunk of time will pass before I wake up and realize I'm off in my bubble and forgot I was supposedly meditating. This is what the conditioned mind is used to doing: going off on its own whenever it wants to. The intention of mindfulness is to be aware of the wandering and bring attention back to the present, over and over and over.

Maybe you noticed judging. Perhaps you caught a glimpse of thinking you weren't breathing correctly, that your breath should be slower, deeper, or more regular. Or maybe you judged yourself when your attention wandered away from the breath. Or you thought you weren't sitting properly. These kinds of judgments are common. Whatever the content, it's helpful to spot judging and recognize it as a powerfully ingrained habit of our conditioning. This is a key. We are working toward being able to see the mind's habits, without judgment, so we can have more choice with our thoughts.

Puppy Stay

When we realize attention has wandered from the breath, exactly *how* we bring ourselves back to the present is critical to our training, healing, and freedom. Remember, whatever we practice grows stronger. If we react with frustration and impatience, then we'll be strengthening the habits of turning against ourselves through frustration and judgment. Instead, understanding the mind is wild, and wandering is what it's used to doing, we bring our attention back to the breath gently and kindly. This way we both teach the mind to be here where we want it to be, and we cultivate acceptance, patience, and kindness with ourselves.

An apt metaphor I learned from Jack Kornfield, another renowned mindfulness teacher and co-founder of the Insight Meditation Society, is that of house-training a puppy. You spread newspaper on the kitchen floor so your puppy learns to pee or poo on the newspaper instead of anywhere else in your home. You put your cute, innocent puppy on the newspaper and you say to her, "Stay, stay." What does she do? She has no idea what you mean by "Stay," so she runs off to play. If you get mad at her and yell and tell her she's stupid and bad, what do you think she'll learn? Most likely to be scared of you, or the paper, or the word stay. If you continue this hostile, judgmental method, she may eventually learn to stay on the paper, but she'll most likely be neurotic and unsure of herself.

Instead, as the wise puppy owner, when she runs off the paper, you pick her up and put her back on the paper saying again, gently and kindly, "Stay, stay." She runs off again, you bring her back, gently and kindly saying, "Stay, stay." Eventually your puppy learns what "stay" means, and as she grows older she is well trained because you consistently responded to her gently and kindly every time she wandered away.

We want to train ourselves to stay in the present moment with the breath in the same wise and skillful way. Whenever we realize attention has gone somewhere else and we're no longer aware of the breath, we simply notice where we've wandered to—a memory, imagining, sound, sensation—and then *gently and kindly* escort attention back to the breath. We return our attention over and over and over again. It really doesn't matter how many times attention wanders away in a given sitting. Each time we're aware of it and bring our attention back, it's a moment of training the mind, "Not over there dwelling on that right now, back here, please." When you've lost focus on the breath, you haven't done anything wrong, you simply begin again by coming back to the breath and reconnecting with the present. In this way, by gently and kindly returning and beginning again, the practice is inherently forgiving.

Softly Noting

Another useful method to aid concentration and stay present is called "softly noting." This mindfulness tool sharpens the precision of attention. You make a mental notation or label of whatever is most predominant in the moment, and you say it to yourself with a soft, light, neutral tone in your inner voice. With mindful breathing, here's how it works: at the beginning of the inhale you neutrally and gently say in your mind, "breathing in," or only the word "in." At the beginning of the exhale, you softly note "breathing out," or only the word "out." Briefly marking these two points in the breath cycle helps maintain contact with the breath. It's like using a bright highlighter pen to mark your experience more clearly.

We use this method to build concentration and hone awareness for other experiences as well. We can softly note worrying, judging, aching, hearing, sadness, and so on. This helps create an inner sphere of awareness, a calm interior space to observe our experience without reacting. It's also a way to directly square up to and fully face what's most prominent in the moment. Softly noting aids concentration both in the beginning stages of learning the practice, and at other times when the mind is foggy or dull and concentration is difficult.

Not About "Me"

A core principle of mindfulness is to disidentify with experience, to not attach personal meaning about ourselves to what's happening. Taking things personally is a deeply conditioned habit that binds us to suffering and distorts our understanding of reality. Notice that we softly note what's happening without adding the "me "pronoun. We say, "breathing in," and not "*I'm* breathing in." At the exhale, we say, "breathing out," not "*I'm* breathing out." Deleting the personal pronoun automatically takes the "me" out of concentrating on the breath and makes the experience feel less personal and more universal. We step back and observe the breathing in and breathing out. Without the personal pronoun, we're decreasing the sense of self.

I encourage you to experiment with this approach and see what gives you the most freedom. As you practice being mindful of the sensations of breathing, notice the difference between softly noting with and without the "I'm" pronoun. Discovering what's true for you, what's most beneficial, based on your own direct experience, is what mindfulness is all about.

Practice

Meditation:
Mindful Breathing, Second Practice

Let's practice again, adding "softly noting" to mark the beginning of the inhale and the exhale, and bringing yourself *gently and kindly* back to the breath when your attention wanders away. I suggest you practice for 10 minutes this time, so please set your timer accordingly.

Before you practice, consider the advice of an ancient Zen master about breathing mindfully: "Learn how to enjoy keeping the mind with the breath. When you spend time with the breath, you become sensitive not only to the breath, but also to what the mind is doing in the present moment and to how it causes unnecessary suffering for itself. The mind is like an animal: if it hasn't been trained, it's difficult to live with. Once we train the mind, it stops creating suffering for itself. We begin by staying in one place with something simple: the breath."

• Sit comfortably with your spine aligned, inviting the mind, body, and heart to soften, relax, and open.... Notice what you're aware of as you sit here right now receiving yourself. If you notice areas of tension in the body, gently invite relaxing and letting go....

• Bring your awareness to the experience of breathing. Move your attention to the place where it's easiest to feel the sensations of breathing (belly, chest, or nostrils) and anchor your attention there.... Now become really interested in the actual sensations of this inhale and exhale, concentrating on these sensations from the very beginning of the inhale through the completion of the exhale.... Open to the next breath as it arrives...staying very receptive, accepting, kind, and gentle with each breath. Commit to being fully present with this breath....

• Softly note the beginning of the inhale with the words "in" or "breathing in," and at the beginning of the exhale with "out" or "breathing out" to help you concentrate on the sensations of breathing. Remember each breath you breathe is fresh and new, so practice opening to it with curiosity and beginner's mind.... Whenever you realize attention has wandered away from the breath and something else is predominant — planning, remembering, hearing, feeling — simply notice it without judgment then gently and kindly escort your attention back to the sensations of this breath, reconnecting with the sensations of breathing again.... Invite yourself to be very sensitive and receptive, curious and open to each inhale and exhale, following the rhythm of the breath just the way it is, letting it change however it does. You are cultivating calmness and spaciousness...allowing the busy thinking mind to rest, even for a moment, in the awareness of the sensations of breathing....

Reflecting on the Second Practice

Take a moment now to notice the effects of the second practice, collecting data about your experience. What are you like now? What do you notice in your body, your mind, and your heart? Was it helpful to softly note the sensations of breathing? Did your attention wander? Could you escort yourself back to the breath gently and kindly? What was it like to treat yourself kindly? How did your body do as you sat in stillness?

In the beginning, many people find it difficult to sit without moving. We are used to adjusting our posture at the slightest twinge of discomfort, often without awareness. When we sit still, intending not to move, sooner or later we experience discomfort: maybe you felt knee pain, back pain, an itch, or restlessness and the desire to move. The basic approach when starting to practice is to notice all of the discomfort with curiosity, friendliness, and acceptance, and to do your best to let it be just as it is.

But please, meditation is not boot camp! If your foot has fallen asleep and the prickles and numbness become uncomfortably unbearable, please go ahead and move so you can find comfort, however, move *mindfully* so that you include the experience in the meditation. In other words, instead of automatically moving your foot because it's asleep and hurting, first bring awareness to the actual sensations of tingling and numbness, being curious about it and letting it be as it is. When you conclude that your numb foot is really too uncomfortable to bear, choose to intentionally move it, bringing all of your awareness to the experience of moving it, staying with the changing sensations as the numbness and tingling recede. When the sensations are no longer predominant, return your focus to the sensations of breathing again.

Another common experience in learning to meditate is worrying about time. Time often seems warped in meditation. Sometimes it seems excruciatingly slow, sometimes it seems fast, and other times it seems timeless. A thought might arise such as, "I wonder how much more time I have to go? The ten minutes must surely be almost up." If that thought becomes compelling and you want to check the time, go ahead and *mindfully choose* to open your eyes and check. "Oh. Wow. There's seven more minutes to go." Return to practicing until the time is up. No problem. You've checked the time mindfully.

Resistance can also arise as your mind starts to whine, trying to convince you to stop: "This is boring. This really doesn't matter. No one will know if I stop now." While no meditation police will ticket you for quitting early, you will know that you did. That matters. Meditation practice is about staying with ourselves no matter what, and especially when the going gets rough. In the moment your mind is trying to convince you it doesn't matter if you quit early, see

> The goal is to develop a kind discipline to stay with ourselves no matter what.

that as resistance, let the thought go, remember your intention, and return to concentrating on the breath until your practice time is up.

The goal is to develop a kind discipline to stay with ourselves no matter what, even if we are in pain, feeling anxiety, tiring boredom, or whatever the unpleasant experience might be. Staying through to the end of the sit builds confidence in our ability to handle whatever comes along. Staying with ourselves cultivates inner strength and security. Please continue to practice until your timer rings and your sitting time is completed.

Informal Practice: Dropping In

Of equal importance to formal sitting meditation is informal practice, simple methods for bringing mindfulness into our lives as we're living them. "Dropping In" is a powerful core informal practice, a simple and direct way of connecting with ourselves, discovering what's going on, and then making skillful responses and adjustments. Dropping In cultivates self-acceptance as we get to know ourselves.

Here's how it's practiced: periodically throughout the day, pause in whatever you're doing, shift attention to your internal experience, and mindfully breathe several breaths. Use your breath to fully connect to yourself in the present moment. Then, ask yourself the following three basic mindfulness questions:

1. What am I experiencing in this moment? What's happening for me? You want to know where your attention is and what's going on with you. What are you thinking and feeling in your body? Are you affected by an emotion? What's your energy like? You are finding your authentic experience just as it is in this moment.

2. How am I relating to the experience? Are you open, curious, and accepting of what's happening? Can you let it be here, even if it's not pleasant or what you want? Or are you resisting it in some way, judging it, wanting it to be different, trying to control and change it?

3. What's the wisest and kindest way to respond to myself right now? Given what's happening and how I'm relating to what's here, what do I really need? With the last question, you are opening to the blue sky of your mind. You're considering that there could be a wise and kind way to respond to yourself. Ask and hold the question gently, opening to whatever occurs to you.

Each time you remember to Drop In, you turn off autopilot and connect to your direct experience and authentic self. You're practicing relating to yourself in a respectful way, and building connection to your true self. Each time you have the possibility of learning about yourself. You may see the unkind and unwise habits of your conditioned mind, habits of othering, judging, and turning against yourself. You may also see the beauty of your true self, your kindness, compassion, love, and tenderness.

I can't overemphasize how helpful informal practice is. One woman who wanted to learn mindfulness to change her relationship to her body relied solely on informal practice for the first two years, because the formal sitting practice was too difficult and painful for her. She said Dropping In led to remarkable changes in her body and in her relationship with herself. She lost a lot of weight, her sleeping patterns improved, and her anxiety and depression decreased. At the beginning of her third year of classes, she felt ready for formal sitting practice and was curious about where that would take her.

Please experiment with the Dropping In practice. You can do it wherever you are, with your eyes open, and no one but you knows you are doing it. I practice it whenever I'm waiting, such as waiting for the elevator, waiting in line at the grocery store, waiting for a red light, a train, or a client to show up for an appointment. It's a much better use of my time than fretting and getting lost in stories. It's also wise to practice it before any important meeting, phone call, or appointment — any situation where it would be beneficial to have your wits about you.

Ownwork Suggestions

Formal Practice:
Mindfulness of Breathing

Practice formally every day for the next week. Sit for 5–15 minutes each time, or an amount of time you can manage, and then stick it out, no matter what. Remember practice is your sacred time with yourself and you are building connections to your authenticity. After you sit, reflect on what the practice was like and its effects. It's often helpful to write in a journal about the experience.

Informal Practice: Dropping In

Throughout the day, practice intentionally Dropping In to the present moment and focus on the sensations of breathing. Mindfully breathe at least three full breaths. Pause and connect more deeply by asking the three basic questions:

    1. What am I actually experiencing right now? Thoughts, feelings, sensations – what am I aware of?

    2. How am I relating to that? Am I judging, resisting, or trying to control or change it? Or am I accepting it, letting it be?

    3. Given that, what's the wisest and kindest way to respond to myself right now?

You might experiment with Dropping In before an important meeting or conversation, before you walk into your work or home, when your kids yell for you (or they just yell), or whenever you feel upset or out of balance. Each time you do these practices, pause for a moment to notice their effects. Collect your own data on whether the practice is useful.

8

Awareness
Is the First Step
Towards Freedom:
Spotting Othering

At the center of your being
you have the answer;
you know who you are and you
know what you want.

Lao Tzu

Losing connection with our authentic self through othering has serious consequences. We disconnect from our bodies and our emotions, our sense of responsibility gets distorted, and we fear and avoid conflict. We try to appear how we think we're supposed to be, instead of being authentic. We have a tremendous need for control and find it hard to set boundaries. Because the underlying emotion of othering is fear, we believe we aren't enough as we are, so we're highly judgmental and critical, not only of ourselves, but of others, too. These judgments and criticisms are attempts to dominate and control conditions so that everything turns out right for everybody, and then consequently, for ourselves. The cumulative effect of these habits is a chronic and painful self-consciousness We don't trust ourselves, our self-confidence is shaky, and at a deep, core level we feel shame and even hatred towards ourselves.

> The cumulative effect of othering habits is a chronic and painful self-consciousness.

Please remember, simply because women are in the subordinate position, we are destined to feel inferior. This is deeply buried in our psyches, making it nearly impossible to relax with ourselves. Constantly assessing and judging, vigilantly on guard to protect and defend ourselves, we tend to take things personally. Ironically, this preoccupation makes us self-centered, and being self-centered is not how we are supposed to be. Yet we repeatedly obsess about how we're doing. "Did *I* say the right thing? Is he upset with *me* now? Maybe *I* should have…." The sense of self, although negative and painful, looms large at times. The habit of taking things personally serves to keep us stuck in feeling inferior and insecure. Further, when we act out of these internal reactions, we create more suffering. Is this cycle familiar to you?

All of these thoughts and habits are normal—sadly, terribly normal. How extensively these patterns operate varies, of course, depending on the degree of inequality in the significant relationships in our lives. If we were raised in families with more than the normal amount

Checking in

• How are you doing with finding some time to meditate each day? A hearty "Hooray" to you if you've been able to mediate. However, most women find it hard at first to carve out even five minutes to formally meditate. If this is true for you, please be kind and keep encouraging yourself. Some find the only place they can meditate is while sitting in the car waiting to pick up their kids. No interruptions then. Great — that's a fine place to start. Changing our own habits, and the habits of others who depend on us, can be very hard. If you keep working on it, at some point when you realize it's truly beneficial and important enough to sit every day, you will find the time.

• How about the informal Dropping In practice? Have you remembered to do it now and then during the day? Was it helpful? Did it allow you to connect in the moment and slow down a bit? Were you surprised at what you noticed about your direct experience? Many women find this practice amazing and very useful. Besides being simple and something you can practice anywhere, you might discover habits you've never noticed before, such as tension in your body, observing how your mind is caught up in worrying and fretting, or realizing how wild and crazy those thoughts are sometimes.

of dysfunction—abuse, neglect, alcoholism, incest, or other forms of violence, trauma, and loss—then the effect of othering is magnified. It's also likely to be greater if we're not heterosexual or from a race, nationality, or religion different from the dominant group.

Beginning to Wake Up

We may abhor misogyny, believe in gender equality, and know in our heart of hearts that as women we are just as valuable and worthwhile as men. We don't want to give our power away or feel shame about being female. Still, regardless of our intellectual understandings and intentions, the patterns of oppression are deeply embedded in our psyches. Because these patterns are hard-wired, it takes a lot of intention, diligence, and the right set of tools to uproot them.

In the early phase of waking up to my internalized oppression, I thought because I was now aware of the many ways I disempowered myself, I could simply choose to change my reactions and behavior. I clung to that belief for a long time, trying again and again to force myself to change, to liberate and empower myself, but my progress was painfully slow. In reality, I was caught in the patterns. As I became more aware of the habitual face I showed others (always smiling), I realized that face was a mask I hid behind. I was trapped under my perfect wife, mother, woman, and professional dictums, trying to be a superwoman. A gap separated my inner life from how I was engaging with the external world, and maintaining that gap was painful. I also became more aware of the underlying anxiety of self-doubt and insecurity. When I'd find myself repeating the old oppressive messages, I'd feel angry and impatient for doing it to myself, once again. Although I recognized the patterns, I also saw how I was caught and unable to change them. That awareness increased my suffering.

> Patterns of oppression are deeply embedded in our psyches.

The pain was not entirely bad, because it became my teacher. From the perspective of mindfulness and Buddhist philosophy, suffering isn't "bad." Suffering is a part of our human condition, and when it claims our attention, that's potentially beneficial because it can wake us up. In my case, awareness of the painfulness of the patterns motivated me to keep searching for liberation.

Eventually I realized I had been trying to *think* my way out of these patterns. It's a common myth that if we think about something long and hard enough, it will change. I bought into the myth. I'd logically counsel myself when I gave my power away. "There's no reason for me to have said that. He isn't any smarter than I am. He doesn't even have as much experience as I do. There's no reason for me to be shrinky here. Next time I'll hold my own." I'd judge, criticize, and correct myself, over and over. However, there's a limit to how much thinking is useful. I came to see I needed another route.

While awareness and insight are essential for true healing and change, they alone are not enough. Clearly, if we could think our way out of our challenges, we'd all be free by now. Mindfulness was the *transformative* power I needed. Remember the core purpose of this ancient practice is to decondition the mind, freeing it from the habits of conditioning so we can see reality clearly and access our true nature. Through regular practice, both formal and informal, we transmute and change those deep neural othering grooves, build connection with our authentic experience, shift the balance of power back to ourselves, and cultivate unshakeable confidence.

Mindful Awareness
Is the First Step

Awareness is the first essential step in becoming free from othering. We cannot respond differently to a habit until we realize it's happening in this very moment. As long as we remain unaware of the habit, we are its victim, and we'll repeatedly be caught in acting out of it.

Remember the principle of practice: whatever we practice or repeat grows stronger in the brain and mind. Becoming aware of othering patterns as they happen in the moment is the key to changing the habits. Indeed, it is only in the present moment that we have the chance to respond differently.

Exactly *how* we spot our conditioning and *how* we relate to it, are crucial. If we relate to othering in our habitual way with irritation, impatience, and disdain, we aren't helping ourselves. We're doing the same old thing we've always done: blaming ourselves for something we have no control over because it operates unconsciously. This is the way of all conditioned patterns. They are the brain and mind's automatic, default reactions. If we get mad at ourselves when we recognize othering, we dig ourselves deeper into the pattern and feel worse. It's far more useful and wise to respond with appreciation and sincere interest whenever you spot othering. In fact, practice feeling glad and even encouraged whenever you spot it. When you spot the habit, you're aware and awakening to your direct experience.

> Whatever we practice or repeat grows stronger in the brain and mind.

Responding with curiosity and acceptance creates internal psychic room. Reacting with judgment and aversion closes the mind, contracts the body, and keeps us bound in struggle. We fixate on what we hate. In contrast, acceptance and curiosity instantly create inner spaciousness around the pattern. With repetition, inner roominess enables an organic, natural letting go and promotes the internal conditions where we can exercise choice about either staying caught in the pattern or stepping out of it. Please invite yourself to become really interested in discovering all the ways othering happens for you. The more you can become aware of othering and how it affects you, the more you'll be motivated to transform it.

Common Sightings of Othering

We have to catch ourselves othering before we can do anything about it. Here are a few common ways it can show up. See if any of these scenarios ring a bell for you.

+ You walk into the yoga studio or gym, glance around at the other women, and think, "Geez, they're all in way better shape than I am." Your attention lands on the most gorgeous woman in the studio and you go off into a long fantasy about how perfect her life must be. As you're doing a head-down-dog pose, you sneak a look at her excellent form, lose your balance, and think, "I hate my stupid body!" You spend the rest of the workout thinking you pale in comparison.

+ You've finished making an important presentation at work on a topic you feel passionate about and worked hard on. Your boss makes a terse but polite nod towards you and says, "Thank you." He looks around the room at your colleagues and says, "And what other ideas do people have?" You feel discounted. Hot tears instantly well up, and it's all you can do to keep your composure. The rest of the day you are sure everyone thinks you're stupid and second rate, you get no work done and go home ruminating over your fears of incompetence.

+ After getting everybody in your house off to school and work, getting yourself to work and doing your job, and then making supper, supervising homework, helping your daughter through a meltdown about a test, and making treats for your son's class the next day, your spouse or partner has a crisis over their job. Once again they're feeling down, despairing, and hopeless. You do everything in your power to make her or him feel better, but nothing you say makes any difference. You go to bed feeling exhausted, depleted, hopeless, worried, and responsible for everybody.

+ Your friend asked you a few weeks ago to help her with a move across town and you said "Yes" because you always say "Yes." It's the right thing to do. Today, moving day, you feel worn down and need a day of rest. Like always, you override your feelings, pull yourself out of bed, and get over to her house. You help, just like you said you would, but you're grumpy the whole time, feeling resentful, though you try to hide your feelings and be pleasant. You fall into bed at the end of the day, irritated and more tired.

⁎ You're excited because you've begun a new relationship, and this one might be a keeper. Last night, as you were telling each other stories about your selves and your lives—the usual getting-to-know-you stories—you said something and your new friend reacted unexpectedly. Now you can't stop thinking about that moment. You keep going over it in your mind—remembering what you said, how they reacted. You second-guess yourself and worry you've now ruined things. You're driving yourself nuts, but you can't stop thinking about it.

⁎ It makes you squirm every time somebody gives you a compliment. Anxiety arises instantly, and you want to hurry up and turn the compliment back onto them. "Anyway, they don't really know me," you always think, "because if they did, they wouldn't really be saying that."

As these examples show, the other can be anyone or anything outside of ourselves. The most important others are our spouse, partner, children, parents, friends, boss, colleagues, teachers, and spiritual or religious guides. As you're likely to discover others can be complete strangers on the street, clerks in the store, people you pass in your car, and the ubiquitous "them or they" that are so often present in our imagining mind. One woman, beginning to track her othering habit, said, "I couldn't believe it! I realized as I was waiting in line at the grocery store, my mind went off in a long fantasy about what the checkout woman was thinking about me from the groceries in my cart. I imagined she had some mighty big judgments and I felt lots of shame."

Another category of other that disconnects us from our own experience is the realm of work, activities, doing, and performing. We can become so absorbed in our work, whatever its form, that we lose ourselves in it, letting how well we do the work become the measure of our worth. Because we're taught to believe in our culture that *we are what we do*, we identify with it and take our work, our activities, our "doings" personally. How well we do our "work," or how much we get done, links directly to the people that we are aiming to please by what we do. A fifty-year-old woman who is working hard to wake up from the effects of being the eldest daughter among ten siblings and an oppressive relationship with her husband recently discovered these insights and questions: "Unless I do for others, I have no sense of worth. Who am I if I'm not performing? Am I worth taking care of myself, just as I am? Up until now I haven't thought so."

Other Common Expressions of Othering

- *Rehearsing what I'll say in my mind over and over so the other will take it the "right" way.*
- *Imagining that my neighbor/clerk/ boss/stranger is judging me.*
- *Dwelling on all the things that are wonderful about the other.*
- *Dwelling on all the things that are wrong with the other.*
- *Caught up in trying to do my work, or any activity, perfectly.*
- *Knowing more about what the other feels, wants, and needs than I know about myself.*
- *Worrying that they think I'm not _____ enough (clever, attractive, thin, smart, kind, generous, loving, capable, or spiritual).*
- *If something is wrong or someone is upset, assuming it's my responsibility to fix it.*
- *Feeling I should always say "Yes" when somebody wants my attention, help, or anything else. It's scary to say "No" to someone's request.*
- *Protecting the other's feelings by not saying what's on my mind.*
- *Believing it's really up to me to make sure everyone is happy.*
- *Assuming I don't matter as much as the other person does.*
- *Putting my needs last, after I make sure everybody else is okay.*

As you begin to see these patterns, don't be surprised if you discover how pervasive othering is. As we become aware of othering, many report it seems othering is all their mind is doing. One woman said, "I don't know what I'd pay attention to if I didn't other! I wonder what I'd be like or who I'd be?" Another woman, mother, wife, and head of a local nonprofit agency, said that she was shocked to discover that when she recently had a much longed for day by herself, free of her responsibilities, all she thought about were others. She tried to be happy about being aware of this preoccupation, as I had suggested, but in truth she was bummed out by how extensive her othering habit was. Only when she brought her attention to her breath could she find a few moments respite from dwelling on others. Another woman, a business owner, who is taking the class for the second time, said that now, because she's been meditating daily for three months, the extent and frequency of her othering has significantly decreased. Her mind is much calmer and she's is much less anxious.

Core Practice

To move towards freedom, our intention is to be mindfully aware of when we are othering. Please remember that instead of feeling frustrated when you recognize othering, congratulate yourself for seeing it. Spotting it means you're waking up. Each time you spot your mind othering, drop into the following seven-step mindfulness practice:

1. *Softly note*, "Oh, here's othering." Do not judge yourself. Instead, observe yourself othering with curiosity, kindness, acceptance, and appreciation. Cultivate an attitude that says, "Good, I'm seeing the pattern in myself. This is really helpful." Please note "othering" without the pronoun "I'm" , as you're learning to observe your experience with less identification. Simply see the conditioned pattern, which is not who you are.

2. *Mindfully breathe.* Move your attention to the sensations of your breath, and mindfully breathe. Bringing awareness to the sensations of breathing automatically connects you to what's real and to what's actually happening in this present moment. Each

time you mindfully breathe, you find yourself. You connect with your authentic and true experience.

3. *Connect with your direct authentic experience.* Expand and deepen the sense of your authentic self by connecting with the direct experience of all of your senses. Ask: "What am I actually *experiencing* right now?" Observe your thoughts, feelings, and sensations, what you're hearing, seeing, smelling, or tasting in this moment.

4. *How am I relating to this?* Ask: "How am I *reacting or responding* to my experience? Am I judging and criticizing my experience, wanting it to be different from how it is? Am I open to it, accepting and curious about it and letting it be?

5. *What is a wise and kind response?* Ask: "Given what's happening and how I'm relating to it, what's the *wisest and kindest way to respond to myself* right now? In other words, "What do I really need?" Please listen receptively to yourself. This question opens the door to your deeper, wiser true self. It reminds you of your wisdom and gives access to your blue sky mind, your unconditioned true nature.

6. *Follow and apply your advice.* You are not searching for a strategy to fix your experience or find a clever response to give to the other person. You are creating the internal conditions in which you access your own inner knowing about what would help you remain stable, open, and honest in this moment. For me, the answers are often basic reminders such as, "Remember I am enough." Or, "This difficult sensation or feeling is impermanent. It will pass." Or, "Remember this reaction is not who I am." Or, "May I be kind and gentle to myself with this."

7. *Observe the effect.* Lastly, pause for a few more moments and observe what you're like now. How did this affect you? Accept whatever you notice with curiosity.

Every time you practice these steps truly matters. As you shift your attention from the other to yourself, you connect with your direct authentic experience and move your frame of reference from being in the other to being within yourself. You balance your awareness. By observing how you're relating to your experience and inviting your wisest and kindest response, you build connections with your deeper natural wisdom and knowledge. You disconnect from the conditioned pattern and create a new neural groove of connection in your brain. You are cultivating an internal frame of reference, a home base within yourself that is kind, accepting, and stable. From your own home base, your power base, you can then respond to what's happening in the external world with greater self-knowledge. With awareness of your own data — what you're thinking, feeling, and wanting — you can respond wisely and skillfully to the other.

This is the basic core shift in attention that enables deep transformation. Every time you wake up from the trance of conditioning and respond mindfully with the seven-step practice, you are literally building new neural pathways, new synapses, in your brain. You are clearing out the obstacles blocking access to your true nature. You are changing your brain and developing the freedom to be who you really are. As you learn to relate mindfully to whatever is here in the moment, your trust in yourself and your ability to handle whatever arises will steadily deepen, and consequently, your habitual need for approval and validation from others will steadily diminish. You are planting and watering the seeds of authenticity and unshakeable confidence.

You are cultivating

a home base

within yourself that

is kind, accepting, and stable.

Ownwork Suggestions

Formal Meditation Practice: Mindful Breathing

Set your timer for how long you'll practice, and then no matter what, practice until the time is up.

Sit comfortably with your spine aligned, inviting mind, body, and heart to soften, relax, and open.... If you notice areas of tension in your body, gently invite relaxing.... Now notice the body you live in is breathing.... Move your attention to where it's the easiest to feel your breath (belly, chest, or nostrils) and anchor your attention here.... Now bring lots of curiosity to the actual sensations of this inhale and exhale, from the very beginning of the inhale through the completion of the exhale...Open to the next breath as it arrives.... Stay very receptive, accepting, kind, and gentle with each breath.... Softly note the beginning of the inhale with "In," or "Breathing in," and at the beginning of the exhale with "Out," or "Breathing out.... Remember each breath is new, so open to it with curiosity.... Whenever you become aware that attention has wandered away from the breath and some other experience is predominant — fantasizing, planning, remembering, or feeling a sensation or an emotion — simply notice this without judgment, and *gently and kindly* escort your attention to the sensations of this breath, intentionally reconnecting with the breath again....

In this way you are cultivating calmness and spaciousness, dwelling in the present moment, allowing the busy thinking mind to rest in the simple, amazing sensations of breathing....

At the end of your practice, pause for a few moments and reflect on what it was like and its effect. What are you like now?

Informal Practice

• Drop In as often as you possibly can throughout the day. Be sure to notice the effect each time. Collecting this data increases your self-knowledge.

• Intend to *spot othering* throughout your day. Recognizing this habit is the first step to changing it. This is very important. Practice the seven-step core practice each time. Please note the effect.

• Make a record of all that you notice about othering and mindfulness in your journal. Practice noticing with curiosity, acceptance, and appreciation.

9

Oh, My Body!
Connecting With
This Precious Body

Attention to this human body
brings healing and regeneration....
Through awareness of the body
we remember who we really are.

Jack Kornfield

We Live in Our Bodies

Mindfulness is a fully embodied practice. In fact, the Buddha taught that it's possible to become fully liberated through practicing mindfulness of the body. How we relate to all that goes on in the body reflects both the ways that we can create suffering for ourselves, as well as how we can create peace and happiness. Thus, along with mindful breathing, mindfulness of the body itself is essential. In my early reading about Buddhism, I remember learning that some monks, who begin the practice as young boys, can become so sensitive to their bodies they can sense an illness or infection beginning within their body long before symptoms start to emerge. That really impressed me.

We are living this life thanks to our body. Yet, because the body is temporary, when it dies, the life we're living will suddenly end. In other words, we depend on our body for our very life. It allows us to do so much. We have our five sense doors — seeing, hearing, smelling, tasting, and touching — and a brain (the sixth sense door) that enables our minds to work through our body and its senses. These amazing senses give us our world on this earthly plane. Think of it for a minute: our skeleton and muscles, nerves, organs, hormones, intricate cell life and body chemistry are so complex and interconnected, operating continuously and automatically, moment to moment to moment to moment.

We can feel a soft subtle warm breeze and the frigid blast of an icy northerly wind. We can undulate delicately in our favorite dance or run powerfully fast, blasting all out at full speed. Aromas can excite, disturb, and calm us. Every day we see, taste, and smell the food we must eat to fuel this body so it grows, stays alive, and remains in balance. We can see the beauty of nature in the panorama of our world, and we can look tenderly into the eyes of a person we deeply love. We can hear the sweet song of bird outside our window, as well as the expanding restful sound of silence. Through our bodies, we experience amazing physical pleasure and excruciating pain. We love, work, connect, create, destroy, give, and receive with our bodies. We also fall ill, may develop serious or chronic

Checking in

• What's it been like to intentionally spot othering and then apply the seven-step core practice? Have you been surprised at how often othering occupies your mind? Has it been helpful to pop out and mindfully breathe and find yourself again?

• Do you feel you're gaining more skill at attending to the sensations of breathing in your formal practice? Please remember to bring yourself back to the breath and the present gently and kindly. Always return gently and kindly.

• What are you noticing as you practice Dropping In throughout the day? Are you finding you're more present, more here, than you used to be? If it's hard to even remember to drop in, you might try a prompt. Find some sticky colored dots (at the office supply store) and put them up where you know it would be smart to be present. Stick them on your phone or computer screen, in your car or the mirror in your bathroom. Each time you see a dot, Drop In and find yourself.

illnesses, have accidents and injuries, and will inevitably experience the death of the body.

Because our consciousness, our mind, extends beyond the body, it's accurate to view our bodies as being inside of us. Our body is the house, or vehicle for our consciousness, but its regions are not limited to the physical form of the body. Consciousness goes well beyond the body. We all have energy, which the ancients call energy fields, that emanate from the body. Although most of us cannot see energy fields, we are familiar with the experience of feeling someone's energy. Perhaps our training in othering even teaches us to be extra sensitive to "reading" energy in others.

Because mind, body, heart, and spirit are interconnected, our bodies give us essential information about what's going on with us and what we need. Besides letting us know when we need to eat, drink, sleep, pee, exercise, and rest, the body lets us know when we're stressed and when we experience emotions. Every emotion has a sensation or feeling within the body. We access our intuition through the body as "gut" feelings. If we're paying mindful attention, the body tells us when we say "yes" to something, as well as alert us to our boundaries — when we need to say, "That's enough," "Stop," or "No." Because we depend on our body for our life, it seems wise and responsible to be good caretakers of it. I once heard Ram Dass, a highly renowned spiritual teacher, refer to the body as a space suit that our spirit rents for a lifetime. He encouraged us to be good stewards and take good care of it.

Othering Harms Our Relationship to Our Bodies

Taking wise care of our bodies is easier said than done. Because our bodies have been objectified, abused, mistreated, and controlled by the dominant group for a long time, othering distorts and damages our relationship to it. We're trained to be relentlessly concerned with how we look. Deep down, we're often afraid we're not attractive enough. How do you honestly feel about your body? Do you like your body the way it is? Do you have a kind, accepting, appreciative, and respectful relationship with it? Or do you wish parts of your body were different?

In my experience, it's rare to find a woman who respects, accepts, and loves her body as it is. How could we, given our conditioning? I'm certainly not completely accepting of my body, although I'm moving in the right direction. I can still hear the "judge" at times complaining that my breasts are too small, my ears aren't right, my hair is too limp, I'm too scrawny, or I need more muscles in my butt and thighs. What's your litany of complaints?

The intensity of our criticism and rejection varies. Sometimes we outright hate our bodies for being the way they are. Sometimes the aversion becomes so violent, we turn on ourselves and do mean, destructive things, such as starving ourselves, overeating, binging and purging, or undergoing plastic surgery. Our constant struggling and fretting about our body's appearance can bring stress on our relationships, as well as fuel our painful self-consciousness in social situations.

After my son broke up with his girl friend of many years, he described a dynamic between them that became chronically frustrating and divisive. Although naturally beautiful and elegant, Lucy needed frequent reassurance from Dave about her looks. In the early years of being together when they'd dress up to go out for an event, she'd ask for his opinion about how she looked. When he'd say, "You look great!" she would press him to tell her how she could look even better. Wanting to be honest and helpful, he'd search for some suggestion, but then when he'd express it, she'd fall apart. She'd sink into feeling criticized and deeply hurt, and they'd be caught in a painful tangle of "But you're beautiful just the way you are!" "No, I'm not, and you don't really think I am either!" Around in circles they'd go, Dave trying to reassure her and retract his suggestion, and Lucy caught in her conditioned fear that she truly wasn't attractive enough. Sadly, Dave eventually learned to avoid the struggle by shutting down when she'd ask, "How do I look?" Because he did honestly appreciate her beauty, but felt sad she was so painfully absorbed in her self-doubt, over time, this became one of many places where they could not connect from their open and loving hearts. It was a painful obstacle between them.

Not surprisingly, men hardly ever ask us, "How do I look?" Have you noticed that? I have it on good authority — discussing this issue with a lot of men — that they aren't very concerned with their appearance. This makes complete sense, given their position in the patriarchy. My hunch is their conditioning teaches them to assume they are generally okay, and winning approval through attractiveness is not a core issue for most.

I'm Too Fat

Weight, body size, and shape are issues for most women in our culture. Even though the pendulum for the perfect woman's body is shifting away from unsustainable thinness that began with the super model Twiggy fad in the 1960s, we still receive many messages about being thin in order to be attractive. Practically every woman goes through periods of dieting in attempts to control her body, which deeply distorts our relationship to food and eating. Eating disorders remain alarmingly common among teenage girls, following some of them into their adult life, and becoming a life-long, painful, and dangerous pattern.

Teaching mindfulness to a 15-year-old girl who was struggling to heal from her eating disorder, I learned it's a social ritual for girls to complain about their bodies. Sandra would tell me that when she'd get together with her friends, they would obsessively criticize their bodies: "My thighs are too big. My butt is huge. My hips are too wide. I've got to lose at least five pounds." Clearly, these self-loathing messages don't necessarily stop as we get older. My mother was always complaining about her weight, and although she was never fat, she was never content with the size of her body. I had my own time-limited binging and purging disorder in college, and then went on to diet and obsessively measure calories in my twenties, always tracking my weight through a daily and usually depressing visit to the scales. It wasn't until my husband had the wisdom to hide the scale that I began to regulate my eating based on authentic feelings of hunger and satiation in my body.

For many of us, the litany of self-loathing rants goes on subliminally much of the time. A subconscious running commentary constantly evaluates our body, and the remarks are cruel. This self-induced suffering is based on a culturally created view that we all agree to believe. To counteract this conditioning, Harriet Brown, an author and editor with a teenage daughter struggling with anorexia, woke up to these deeply embedded patterns and created the "I-Love-My-Body Pledge" with which women and girls promise to not talk negatively about their bodies. Through her books and website (www.harrietbrown.com), Brown spreads her efforts to uproot these painful habits.

I Love My Body Pledge

I, _____,

pledge to speak kindly about my body.

I promise not to talk about how fat my thighs or stomach or butt are, or about how I really have to lose 5 or 15 or 50 pounds. I promise not to call myself a fat pig, gross, or any other self-loathing, trash-talking phrase. I vow to be kind to myself and my body. I will learn to be grateful for its strength and attractiveness, and be compassionate towards its failings. I will remind myself that bodies come in all shapes and sizes, and that no matter what size and shape my body is, it's worthy of kindness, compassion, and love.

We've been receiving persistent and pervasive messages about how our bodies are supposed to look since we were very young. Because our sense of self is attached to our body's appearance, our self-esteem often is determined by our relationship with our body. I heard my seven-year-old granddaughter vehemently vow the other day that she would never be fat. Thin-is-beautiful is a pervasive message if it's reaching even seven-year-old girls.

Besides being attractive, sexy, and alluring, our culture also expects us to be giving and nurturing all the time. We're expected to be both saintly and seductive. As objects of passion, we're here to give pleasure. We're also supposed to have babies, run the household, take care of the family, and be happy and giving, all while looking and acting desirable. We receive these messages blatantly and insidiously throughout our entire life. Because they are deeply rooted in our psyches and brains, we're stuck in believing our bodies aren't wonderful and amazing just the way they are. The heartache and suffering is tremendous.

Of course, what we're aiming for in our body-hating rants is perfection. We believe we are supposed to be perfect and therefore our bodies are supposed to be perfect. What is perfection, anyway? I'm sure we each have a unique variant on the definition. A *New York Times* article reported on a group of girls who were seniors in an elite public high school outside of Boston.[19] These girls were successful in every aspect of their lives. They were smart, high achievers, leaders, star athletes, attractive, popular, and creative. All were planning to attend prestigious colleges. Despite their successes, they sadly also explained that it was more important to be hot than smart. "Effortlessly hot," one of the girls said. My hunch is their concern reflects much more than the raging hormones of adolescence. It reflects the deep beliefs about female physical perfection in our culture. Even though we all know real beauty is much more than skin deep, we're still co-opted by the superficial allure of physical attractiveness.

I am certainly still biased by our culture's gender conditioning about appearance and attractiveness. When I see a video of a woman leader, my mind habitually evaluates her appearance. I zoom in with a comment on her hair, her clothes, or her weight. I clearly don't have the same reaction when I see a video of a male leader. I hold women to a different standard. Does your mind react this way, too?

Because we're attached to the belief that our body has to be perfect and it's not, we feel angry at our body and ourselves. We slam ourselves with judgments, develop schemes and plans to change, only to be upset and disappointed when the change we want doesn't happen. We've developed an adversarial relationship to our body. We struggle and fight with it. We may even be afraid of our body. We try to control it, even though our control is limited. Over and over, I've heard women express hatred and shame about themselves because their body isn't how they want it to be. They try to change themselves by using force — harsh and degrading criticism — and they get locked into a battle that just gets worse with repeated struggle.

Listening to and Respecting Our Bodies

Beyond its physical appearance, we don't give the body much reverence or appreciation. We take it for granted and become impatient when it doesn't do what we want. Our lives are often so busy, taking care of everything and tending to others, it's difficult to carve out much time to attend to the body. Of course, we'd rather not have sickness and disease, allergies, menstrual cramps, headaches, stomach problems, sleep issues, and so on. We want our bodies to be forever healthy, strong, comfortable, and steady.

> Othering makes us self-conscious, disconnected, and hypercritical of our bodies.

Because othering makes us self-conscious, disconnected, and hypercritical of our bodies, we learn to ignore, deny, or override the body's messages and complaints. We also tend to obsess about what we think is wrong when something does goes haywire. As we get caught up in critically judging, denying, and disconnecting or fretting and worrying, we distort our relationship with our bodies. Biased

129

against them, we can't connect with our bodies just as they are. We don't know how to listen to the body's needs and amazing wisdom.

Karen, a mother of two, promised herself after her second child began school that she would take good care of herself again. She knew she had significantly lost track of herself in mothering, and needed to rebuild her relationship with herself. Shortly after she resumed a daily practice of yoga, resting, meditating, and journaling, she discovered she was pregnant again. Although unplanned, she welcomed a third baby, knowing it was the last child she would have. When the third child began preschool, she developed a severe pain in her belly. The pain appeared off and on over a period of several weeks, and was sometimes so strong she doubled over in agony. One night it was so severe she sought emergency care. The many tests she endured couldn't clarify what was wrong. Finally, in the midst of a painful episode, she decided to meditate and ask her body what was going on. As she listened deeply, her body told her very clearly she had forgotten her decision to take care of herself. Upon hearing this and remembering her promise, the pain dissolved. Heeding this wise reminder, Karen resumed daily self-care practices and became pain free. Whenever she would forget and lose herself in the lives of her kids and husband, the pain would return. This pain became her wise reminder to take good care of herself, always.

> Learn to listen to your body deeply and to trust its inherent wisdom and healing powers.

The great thing about living in our bodies is that *bodies never lie.* Our minds can be clever and tricky. We can rationalize, deny, and distort. We can convincingly fool ourselves, at least for a while. If we pay attention to the body and notice it with mindfulness — if we bring our conscious and open awareness to it — we will discover the body responds to everything we think, perceive, judge, fear, and feel.

We need our body to live this life; it is a vital source of information. Our lives depend on cultivating a relationship to our body that is sensitive, accepting, kind, loving, respectful, and wise. We can learn to listen to it deeply and to trust its inherent wisdom and healing powers. We need to rebuild a connection with our body just the way it is — including its so-called imperfections. We also need to remember its impermanence and be wisely present as the body ages, falls ill or becomes injured, experiences diseases, and at some point can no longer hold us and dies.

It should be obvious by now, with everything your body has experienced in your life so far, that it is a miraculous vehicle. You've likely fallen sick and recovered countless times. Maybe you've had accidents and injuries that needed casts or required stitches. Maybe you've healed after surgery. Perhaps you've given birth or had a miscarriage or an abortion. Maybe you endured sexual abuse or a physical assault. Maybe you survived incest or rape. Your body now has scars and scar tissue, and you have memories of those events with your body. Energy medicine and many body workers teach that the body has its own memories, that each cell has a kind of consciousness, intelligence, and memory. The bodily events of your history and the memories, both conscious and cellular, contribute to how you relate to your body now. If the events were traumatic, those memories may be disturbing to recall. You may find it hard to be present in the parts of your body that were hurt. If that's so, please be very gentle and kind with yourself. Practice being tender and appreciative of your precious body and all that it's experienced, just as it is.

I've had experiences with my body that revealed its amazing ability to heal and return to balance. In addition to the miraculous experience of pregnancy and childbirth twice, I completely healed from a torn ligament in a sports injury doctors said I'd never fully recover from. I also healed from a severely broken femur from a skiing accident, and I am an 18-year cancer survivor. I remember after surgery to remove the tumor, the first time I got up from the hospital bed to use the bathroom, still foggy from the anesthetic and painkillers. As I sat on the toilet, my body, on its own, remembered how to pee. I was amazed and said right out loud, "Thank you, body." I felt so grateful for its knowing how to perform basic functions, and I had a very clear sense that my body was a vehicle that was once again working as designed, but my body wasn't actually me.

The view that our bodies are not who we are, but are physical vehicles for this life, is a helpful perspective. If you believe that when our bodies die, our spirit, soul, or life force doesn't, but moves on to somewhere or something else, then it makes sense that we are not our bodies. This view helps us not take our bodies personally. When we do identify with them, thinking we are our bodies, we're more likely to struggle and suffer when our bodies fail us, or when they don't function or appear how we want them to be.

Body Sweep

Due to these harmful and pervasive cultural messages about the "perfect woman's body," along with our habit of identifying, we need a strong method for righting our relationship with our body. We need to become friends with our body. It's our ally, not our enemy. The mindfulness practice of the body sweep is a simple and powerful method for helping us cultivate a receptive, friendly and respectful relationship with our body.

To do the body sweep, we systematically and slowly move our attention through the body, observing and sensing whatever we notice with as much sensitivity as we can muster. We practice relating to what we notice with kindness, curiosity, acceptance, and appreciation, rather than with judgment, criticism, or aversion. As we practice observing with sensitivity and acceptance, our habits of judging and condemning often become more obvious. This is good. Awareness is the first step to change. We want to spot judging habits. When you realize you've judged part of your body the way you always do, simply notice that judgment with curiosity and appreciation for realizing it, and then choose to let it go. You may find that because you're connecting with the body from the inside rather than the outside, many of the habitual judgments fall away naturally. The body sweep is a lovely practice of greeting, appreciating, and thanking your precious, amazing, resilient, and smart body.

Practice

Meditation: The Body Sweep

Practice the body sweep in a comfortable posture. Feel free to lie down if that's the most comfortable posture for you.

• Arrange your body comfortably, and then simply open to yourself just as you are. Be aware of whatever you notice: sounds, sensations, thoughts, and feelings. Notice it all with curiosity, acceptance, and kindness.

• Practice breathing mindfully for a few minutes. Be alert to when attention shifts away from the breath to thoughts, sounds, or other sensations, and gently and kindly escort your attention to the sensations of breathing again.

• Now let go of focusing on the breath and bring your attention to the area of your head and face. Let your attention be like an atmosphere that can completely infuse and surround the area of your head and face. Bring lots of curiosity and sensitivity to all you're aware of here: perhaps the feeling of hair, the hardness of the skull, perhaps a sense of your brain, ears, eyes, sinus cavities, and any sensations, odors, and smells. You might feel muscles in the forehead, jaw, or tongue. You might feel the teeth or moistness or dryness in the mouth. Practice being aware of whatever you notice with interest and amazement. Take some moments to really appreciate this part of your body, and thank all that goes on here continuously in service of your body and your life: these amazing organs that allow you to see, smell, hear, taste, chew, think, smell, taste, and express yourself.

• Move your attention to the area of the neck, throat, and the top of the back and shoulders. Here you may become aware of the vertebrae of the neck, the muscles of the neck and of the back and shoulders. You may sense the esophagus, the trachea, the larynx. You may feel sensations of tightness or tension, or you may feel relaxation and ease. Practice saying "Hello, and thanks so much" to this amazing part of your body.

• Move your awareness into the shoulder joints, both right and left, and down into the upper arms, elbows, forearms, wrists, hands, fingers, and thumbs. Open to all you notice here: sensations of muscles, joints, ligaments, and bones, the flow of blood and energy, tension and relaxation, warmth or coolness. Being curious and open, sensitive to all that's here. Appreciate and thank all that these shoulders, arms, hands, and fingers make possible for your life.

• Move your attention to the area of the back: upper back, middle back, and lower back. Here you may sense the spine with all its vertebrae stacked on top of each other, forming protective housing for the spinal cord and all the nerves that flow out from it into the body, innervating movement, sensation, and operating energy for the body's vital organs. You may feel the muscles of the back, layered and powerful. You may feel areas that are relaxed and comfortable, and areas that are tense and uncomfortable. Notice them all with acceptance and steadiness. Take some time to thank this amazing back for all it allows you to do in your body.

• Move awareness to the area of the upper chest and the front of the body. Here you may connect with the muscles of the upper chest. Sense and appreciate your breasts. You may feel the movements of the ribs and the diaphragm, and more internally, the rhythm of the lungs as they fill up and empty out of air. You may also feel the heart, continuously beating, opening and closing as it pumps blood throughout the body. Pause here and really appreciate all that goes on, every moment, in this part of the body.

• Shift your attention to the belly. Notice the muscles around the abdomen that support and hold this area. Now let your attention move deeper to connect with the stomach, liver, spleen, pancreas, and gall bladder. Be open to any sensations here. Notice the kidneys towards the back of this area. Thank all these organs for what they continuously do for this amazing body you live in.

• Shift into the lower belly. Sense the small intestine and the colon. Connect with the bladder. Feel into the ovaries, uterus, cervix, and genitals. Notice the boney bowl of the pelvis itself. Take a few moments to fully thank and appreciate all that happens in the lower abdomen for your body and your life.

• Move your attention into the hip joints and buttocks, and notice whatever sensations are here. Drop into both upper legs, down into the knees, into the lower legs, down into the ankles, feet, and toes. Notice the long bones of the femur, the strong muscles of the upper legs, the amazing and complicated knee joints, the bones and muscles of the lower legs, and sense the intricate bones and tiny muscles of the feet and toes. Really appreciate and thank these amazing legs, knees, ankles, feet, and toes and all that they make possible for this body and your life.

• Now expand the field of your awareness to include your entire body lying or sitting here, covered by the largest organ of all, the skin. That amazing and thin protective envelope helps the body receive what it needs and release what it doesn't need. Feel your whole body covered by this protective layer, and sense all parts connected, interdependent, working together continuously and automatically. Take a few moments to really appreciate the miracle of this body.

• Notice once again the sensations of breathing as they are happening now. Stay here with the sensations of breath a little while longer until it feels like just the right moment to bring yourself gently out of this practice.

• Now notice the effect of practicing the body sweep. How do you feel about your body right now?

Many women find the body sweep relaxing, while others find it makes them feel more alert. When I was teaching the body sweep to a group of parents and kids, the youngest child in the class, a four-year-old girl, announced after the body sweep, "Now my body feels organized!" Some women find this practice makes them feel so relaxed they feel sleepy. The body sweep can be a wonderful practice to do in bed to help the mind settle before falling asleep, or to employ if you wake up in the middle of the night and find the mind caught up in worries. Be especially kind and patient if you wake with worries.

If you find your mind wanders as you do the body sweep, please be patient and kind. Because we often have so much aversion towards our bodies, it can be difficult to stay present. You might try concentrating on breathing mindfully for a few breaths and then scoot back to wherever you remember leaving off. Always be very kind and gentle.

Some find the body sweep disturbing because it connects us with parts of the body we've learned to ignore, distrust, or fear, especially if they were wounded or abused. When this has happened to us, it's not uncommon to skip over parts or major swaths of the body. If this is true for you, please be especially gentle with yourself. Judy, a woman in her mid-thirties, said the following after she practiced the body sweep at home: "In class I was fine doing it. But when I did the body sweep at home, guiding myself, it felt so intimate I couldn't bear it. It was so, so painful! I was really surprised by my reaction. But as I looked deeper into my experience with curiosity, I realized I actually had so much hatred towards my body and myself! I deeply love my horses and my dogs and their bodies. But I was stunned, horrified actually, to realize how much I hated my own body." Regardless of your response to this practice, respect your experience and be kind and tender with yourself. We aren't used to paying appreciative attention to our bodies. It is a radical practice.

As we continue on in learning the meditation practice, you will learn to work with all the various aspects of your experience mindfully, but it's useful to periodically practice the body sweep as a method for deepening connection with the body and developing a friendly, kind, and trusting relationship with your life's amazing vehicle.

Ownwork Suggestions

Formal Meditation Practice:
The Body Sweep

Practice the body sweep every day for at least a week and notice the effect. Allow for around 15–20 minutes. Either start at your head and proceed downward, ending with your feet and finally your skin, or start at your feet and proceed upward, ending with the skin. When you lose track of where you are because attention wandered away, just come back to where you left off. Go slowly through your body, and pause to genuinely appreciate each area of the body. Always notice what you're like after completing the practice.

Informal Practice

• Throughout the day, keep redirecting your attention back to the body whenever you can. Notice what you experience each time with curiosity, kindness, and appreciation instead of the familiar judgments and criticisms.

• Continue the Dropping In practice as much as you can, and especially pay attention to what you're noticing in your body.

• Keep tracking the habit of othering. Practice the seven-step core practice. Notice the circumstances, your exact thoughts, feelings, and sensations, all with lots of curiosity. Remember to be glad that you noticed.

• Take the I-Love-My-Body pledge and practice refraining from the habit of trash talking about your body. Instead, speak very kindly to it.

• Be on the lookout for your mind's habitual judgments, criticisms, and comparing your body to others, the effects of othering on your relationship to your body. Be happy when you recognize the habits and shift to the sensations of breathing.

10

We Are Sensational, But Do I Have to Feel That? Our Amazing Sensations

Meditation practice is a powerful tool for revealing our conditioned reactions to unpleasant experiences...we learn to go to the heart of each moment's experience even if it's painful, because there – unclouded by conditioning –we discover our lives.

Sharon Salzberg

Our bodies are full of sensations. I'm sure you realized this directly in practicing the body sweep. We like the sensations that feel good. We don't like the ones that make us feel uncomfortable. Some we hardly notice at all. Of course, we much prefer the lovely and comfortable sensations, but we have limited control over which ones arise. Because our bodies are vulnerable to illness and injury, are always growing older, and will die, it's certain that sooner or later we will experience sensations that are painful and difficult to bear. Othering trains us to disconnect from our bodies, developing habits of ignoring, denying, and sometimes dissociating from the sensations we feel. We have many conditioned reactions that can create misery.

It's possible to experience pain without suffering.

Mindfulness teaches a way to relate to sensations so we can thoroughly enjoy the pleasurable ones without getting carried away, connect with the neutral ones, and be stable and present with the difficult and painful ones. Because experiencing the whole gamut, including the painful ones, is part of living in the body, it's wise to learn this approach. The great news is, through mindfulness, it's possible to experience pain without suffering.

Feeling Tone of Experience

To learn to relate mindfully to sensations, consider that every experience we have, moment by moment, creates a sensory flavor, texture, or feeling tone. This sensory perception (called Vedana) is either unpleasant, neutral, or pleasant. When we feel a sensation in the body, it is unpleasant, pleasant, or neutral. Every thought, emotion, sight, sound, taste, and smell creates an experience that we perceive as unpleasant, pleasant, or neutral. When a sense organ, an object, and consciousness connect, our very first perception of this experience is as a feeling tone. For example, when my eyes (sense organ), see a dog running (object), and I become aware of seeing the dog (consciousness), I perceive that as pleasant (feeling tone). Our

Checking in

- How are you finding the body sweep? Some women really enjoy it and find it relaxing. Some find it hard to do or can't stay awake through it. Whatever you are experiencing is exactly right for you. Trust your experience and keep noticing the effects of the practice.

- How is it going spotting othering? Are you discovering how pervasive the pattern is? Many women report, as they become more aware of their thoughts and feelings, that a shocking amount of mental time is spent dwelling on others at the expense of being aware of themselves. Often their thoughts about themselves are full of judgments and self-doubt. Second guessing creates anxiety and discomfort. Try to see the patterns of othering without blame and with lots of curiosity, kindness, and compassion.

- Remember to come back to your breath and body each time you spot an othering pattern. Dropping In to your breath and direct experience changes the pattern. Remember to ask, "What's the wisest and kindest way to respond to myself right now?" Learning to ask this question and then opening to your inner wisdom is one of the most immediate beneficial effects of mindfulness.

- Please establish times and places where it would be beneficial to train yourself to Drop In. For example, before you open the door to your workplace, or right before your kids pile into the car when you pick them up at school.

perceptions of the experience are subjective, based on past experience and conditioning. If you had a scary experience with a dog, your first impression at seeing one might be unpleasant.

Our perception of the feeling tone happens instantaneously and unconsciously. Yet it prompts a cascade of reactions. For example, imagine you feel a painful twinge in your knee. You may think, "Ouch! This hurts! What did I do to my knee? What if it gets worse? What if it gets so bad I can't stand it? What if there's something really wrong and I have to have surgery? I won't be able to run and I'll get fat and won't fit into my clothes. I'll look awful." Within a few seconds, the mind creates a dramatic and depressing story predicting your future, all in reaction to an unpleasant sensation in your knee. Now you're anxious and depressed on top of feeling the twinge in your knee.

Is this experience

- Pleasant?

- Neutral?

- Unpleasant?

Learning to bring mindfulness to the feeling tone of the experience can interrupt these reactions, freeing us from being trapped in suffering with even the most painful sensation. Beyond recognizing the feeling tone, learning how to relate to physical sensations mindfully builds skills for companioning painful emotions with less suffering. This skill set is fundamentally life-enhancing.

Pleasant Sensations

Let's explore what typically happens when we experience a sensation with a pleasant feeling tone. Perhaps someone is giving you a great back rub, or you're lying on a beautiful beach or a park bench, soaking up the warm sun. Without being aware of it, the first reaction to the pleasant feeling tone is to *judge* it as good: "Yes! This is great!" On a preverbal level, the mind makes the judgment that this experience is good and right.

We like it just the way it is. We agree with it. Depending on how much we like it, how much we are enjoying it, or how hungry we are for this lovely experience, we form an *attachment* to the experience. We want it to continue. We never want the massage to end or the cloud to block the sun from warming us.

However, any pleasant experience is inevitably interrupted because conditions are always changing. The massage ends; the weather changes. Impermanence is unavoidable. Everything is in the process of change, continuously. This is a basic law of nature. When the ending inevitably arrives, depending on how attached we are to wanting the experience to continue, we suffer loss. We feel varying degrees of disappointment, sadness, or impatience. If we believe experiencing pleasure is what life is about, or how it's supposed to always be, then seeking pleasure can be a prison.

Unpleasant Sensations

When we experience a sensation with an unpleasant feeling tone — perhaps a headache, hunger pang, discomfort, or other pain in the body — the mind makes the *judgment* that the sensation is negative and our whole system reacts with a "no." We don't like the sensation. We think it's bad or not right. Something is definitely wrong. We don't want to keep experiencing the unpleasant sensation. We form a negative attachment to it: we resist it and feel aversion towards it.

Because we don't like the unpleasant sensation, we react by trying to change it, fix it, or make it go away. Often we will do whatever we can to get away from it, distract ourselves from it, or numb out to it. We shop, go online, check our phone, turn on the TV, rummage through the fridge, pour ourselves a drink, or shift our attention to othering and think about someone else. Othering can serve as a strong distraction from unpleasant sensations. In fact, all our various addictions are rooted in attempts to keep our experiences pleasant and avoid or numb out to the unpleasant.

141

Fortunately, the law of impermanence applies to unpleasant sensations, too. Sooner or later conditions change and the intensity of the unpleasantness diminishes or vanishes entirely. Still, unpleasant experiences leave a mark. We may become afraid of feeling the sensation again, thinking it will be unbearable or overwhelming. This fear can lead to further suffering. We may make decisions to play it safe in our life. We may choose to avoid situations that could cause pain, and in that way, our life may become limited and our world smaller.

Impermanence is a basic law of nature.

Avoiding the dentist's office is a prime example for me. Visiting the dentist scares me. I had enough painful experiences with dental work as a child to assume whenever I go in for a dental exam or tooth repair, I will experience pain. Sitting in a strange reclining chair with the dentist's hand in my mouth, poking around with her pointy little tools, is not my idea of fun. I lie in wait, dreading the next horrible, surprising pain. Even when having my teeth cleaned, I'm perpetually tense, moving as far away as possible from the hygienist's hands.

Recently, I practiced mindfulness while having a crown repaired. To interrupt my mind's habit of anticipating pain, I decided I would practice noting the feeling tone of my experience moment to moment as the dentist worked on my tooth. Doing so helped me stay present with exactly what was true. At one point as I was concentrating and softly noting the feeling tone in my mind, I inadvertently said out loud, "Oh. Just somewhat unpleasant." To my surprise, the dentist calmly replied, "Yes, this *is* somewhat unpleasant." We both laughed at our mutual agreement.

Even though I'm afraid of experiencing pain when I go to the dentist, it's the fear of pain that creates the most suffering: I feel anxious, my body tenses, and I dread the anticipated pain. However, the actual moments of pure physical pain are typically infrequent, if at all. Still, my fear creates avoidance behaviors, such as putting off check-ups, which leads to the suffering of judging myself, feeling shame for being scared, and feeling guilt for not taking proper care of my body's precious teeth and gums.

Because we live in sensate bodies, we do and will experience pain and unpleasantness of all kinds. To live more freely and with unshakeable confidence, we need to learn how to work with pain and unpleasant sensations, so when they arise, fear doesn't close us down and limit us.

Neutral Sensations

Let's explore what happens when we experience a sensation with a neutral feeling tone. Because the perception of feeling tone is subjective and unique to each of us, what I perceive as neutral may not be neutral for you. Right now, my sensations of breathing, sitting, reaching to pick up a pen, typing on the keyboard, and feeling my feet touching the floor all have a neutral feeling tone. Yet because neutral sensations aren't intense or dramatic, we often don't notice them. If we do become aware of them, our attention doesn't stay with them for long. The mind creates the *judgment* that the sensation doesn't matter. As a result, we disconnect and lose awareness of the body, leaving the unfocused mind free to wander in whatever direction it feels like going.

Because of impermanence, a neutral sensation may shift to pleasant or unpleasant. Sitting in the same posture can be neutral for a while, but when you realize your foot has fallen asleep or your neck aches, the unpleasant feeling tone wakes you up and brings attention back into the body and the present moment again.

The first reaction the mind always has to the feeling tone of a sensation is to judge it. That judgment leads to attaching, trying to holding onto and keep the pleasant; avoiding, resisting, or trying to change the unpleasant; and withdrawing or disconnecting from the neutral.

This Sensation Is Not "Me"

On the heels of the mind's automatic judgment is our habit of taking the sensation personally. We identify with the experience, attaching a sense of self to it. We say to ourselves, "My back is killing me. My headache is horrible today. My bad knee really hurts." Ascribing self-ownership via the all-powerful personal pronoun "me" leads to reactive stories that carry us away from what's happening in the moment. We spin an interpretation and give the sensation a meaning about ourselves. This leads to more judging and a swirl of stories further attaching us to the experience, which can increase our suffering. An ache, an itch, or a familiar pain can trigger a flood of memories, worries, and conclusions about how we are, who we are, why we are the way we are, and what will happen to us because of it.

For example, let's say you feel an odd soreness in your belly (unpleasant feeling tone) and you don't like it (judgment). The sore spot can lead to anxiety, fear, and dread when reactive thoughts arise like, "What's that funny feeling in my stomach? Maybe it indicates the beginning of an ulcer. What should I do? I must be really stressed. I'd better change my diet right now. No more spicy food. But what if it's a tumor? Maybe it's cancer! I'll have to have surgery, and then chemotherapy. I'll feel sick and horrible, and get really skinny, lose my hair, and look awful. I could die!" Now, on top of the peculiar sore spot, you feel seriously upset. These reactive thoughts happen in a split second without our conscious awareness.

Is what I'm describing familiar to you? Our minds unspool like this all the time. We get swept up in stories, reside in a painful imaginary reality, and lose connection with what is real in the present.

The habit of identifying with our experience is a root cause of suffering. It causes us to incorrectly assume we are our bodies. Body equals me and we are inseparable. This assumption is understandable because when the body hurts, it grabs our attention. Pain is often loaded with history and meaning, which automatically gives rise to judgment, identification, and reactive stories. We blame ourselves for being sick, weak, and imperfect. When the body is comfortable and working well, our attention goes to other matters. When the body is injured, sick, unable to function as it's supposed to, or does not look the way we think it should, we take the condition personally.

If we can remember we live in our bodies but they are not who we are, we will suffer less when they are hurt or not functioning well. Our bodies are simply our vehicles for living this life, and are subject to change like everything else. They get sick, become injured, and die. They also heal and recover. We have a profoundly important relationship to our bodies because their health directly affects our lives, but they are not who we are. In fact, it's easier to tend to our body wisely when we do get sick if we can learn to disidentify with it.

When I was first diagnosed with cancer, I was surprised to discover I felt shame for being ill. I felt embarrassed when I told people my diagnosis. After all, *I* shouldn't be ill. It was weak to be sick. It meant something was wrong with *me*. As I looked mindfully into my mind and heart, I realized that I, like most people in our culture, was attached to the notion that being healthy reflects a form of being perfect, and in being sick, I was not perfect. The habit of identifying with the body and being attached to a false belief that it had to be perfect created the shame I felt. Knowing I needed all of my resources and energy to heal, I let go of taking my body and the illness personally and released the false notions about perfection.

> We live in our bodies but they are not who we are.

Pain Without Suffering: Avoiding the Second Arrow

Fortunately, it is possible to learn to experience pain and other unpleasant sensations without suffering. The key is to refrain from being pulled into the habit of adding judging, attaching, and identifying to our direct authentic experience. The reactive add-ons spin us off in painful stories that create our suffering. A well-known teaching the Buddha gave to his students, illustrates this point. He said, "Imagine what it would be like to get struck with an arrow. The place where that arrow strikes your body would be very, very painful. Now, if you were to get struck with a second arrow in exactly the same place the first arrow hit you, the pain from the first arrow would amplify tremendously. This is what we do to ourselves whenever we judge, attach, and identify with our experience."

Our mental and emotional reactions to the pain, the reactive stories, are the second arrow. They add a layer of suffering on top of what is already painful. The unpleasantness from the direct and actual sensation is just that: sharp, dull, piercing, aching, or throbbing, for example. The feelings of dread, fear, panic, and the accompanying flood of sensations — rapid heartbeat, rush of adrenalin, or nausea —arise from the reactive add-on stories the mind creates.

Mindfulness is one of the most effective mind-body methods for working effectively with pain because it teaches us how to be present with the difficult sensation without suffering the strike of the second arrow. Research consistently shows that mindfulness reduces the intensity of pain, allows more physical movement, and lowers the use of pain medication. When we can simply be present with an actual sensation, exactly as it is in the moment, the direct experience of the sensation becomes workable. Even difficult pain can become interesting to explore mindfully. Learning how to work with pain is empowering and helps build unshakeable confidence.

Spaciousness

The principle of spaciousness is another key tenet for staying present without suffering from unpleasant sensations, or for staying present with anything that is difficult. Spaciousness refers to a vast, unlimited quality of acceptance. We want to hold or cradle the difficult sensation in the field of our awareness with plenty of room around it. The more unpleasant the feeling tone of the sensation, the more room or space we want to give it.

Jack Kornfield describes a wonderful metaphor for this concept. He suggests we think of our consciousness, our mind, as being like a room with ceiling, floor, walls, and two doors. One door is the In door and the other is the Out door. Experience flows into our awareness through the In door and moves out of our awareness through the Out door. The room of our mind can change in size. It can be a small, tight space, or as open, expanded, and vast as the universe, depending on our present mind state. When we're relaxed, calm, and peaceful, the room of our mind is naturally open and spacious, expanded. When we're scared, angry, or caught up in a difficult physical or emotional experience, the room of our mind, or field of awareness contracts.

> The more unpleasant the feeling tone of the sensation, the more room or space we want to give it.

Our basic job as mindfulness practitioners is to sit in the middle of the room of our mind, steady on our cushion, and note what comes through the In door, and then witness it leaving our awareness via its own timing through the Out door. For example, "Oh, here's the sensation of breathing in (coming through the In door), and the sensation of breathing out (leaving through the Out door)." Next, the sound of traffic comes in through the In door. The sound lingers a while, gradually fades away, and is gone through the Out door. In this way we notice, moment by moment, what's here as it arises, and what it's like as it eventually passes away.

When something difficult such as a sharp pain comes through the door, our reaction is to move away from it. We judge it and struggle to escape it. It hurts, so we don't like it and don't want to feel it. Ironically, by trying not to experience the painful sensation, we make things worse for ourselves. The space for experiencing the sensation, the room of our mind, shrinks because we are resisting the sensation and we're shooting ourselves with second arrows. We're on the run from the sensation and have nowhere to go because our reactions make the inner room of our mind tiny and cramped. We've created the conditions in which we're trapped and overwhelmed by the sensation.

Instead of contracting in response to what's unpleasant, we want to do the opposite: expand. We want the room of our mind to become vast and open. We want the inner field of our awareness to be big. The unpleasant experience then has plenty of room to move around in, and we can remain stable and steady in the spaciousness as we investigate the actual qualities of the sensation. Because we aren't judging, resisting, or caught up in stories about the sensation, sooner or later it subsides on its own, exiting through the Out door.

Spaciousness helps us remain stable with anything that's difficult. Amazingly, we create spaciousness by simply inviting it, by remembering it. We train ourselves to encourage softening, relaxing, opening, widening, and expanding around what is here. Learn to say to yourself, "Can I give this more room? Can I relax around this more? Can I expand even a little bit more? Can I hold this gently in my awareness? Can I soften around the edges of this?" There's no limit to how much internal room we can create. Probably the hardest part is to remember to invite it.

> Spaciousness helps us remain stable with anything that's difficult.

Power of Beginner's Mind

Cultivating beginner's mind is another powerful ally for staying steady with difficult sensations and experiences. The more we can live fully here in this moment, fresh and open, free of assumptions about ourselves or others and what is going to happen, the more we can authentically connect with what's real and true now. Beginner's mind is operating when we fall in love, visit a new city, or have any new experience that excites us. A new, unknown experience invites us to pay close attention with lots of curiosity. When we drop into beginner's mind, we are naturally spacious and open to new possibilities.

When we have pain or chronic discomfort, the mind tends to close off to new possibilities. Memory builds a history that predicts a future. Many experiences — mental, emotional, and physical — are rolled up in memory, making our relationship to the sensation complex. Chronic pain tends to generate many emotions — impatience, anger, shame, loneliness, sadness, grief, depression, and more. We carry all the things we've tried to do to fix, eliminate, treat, heal from, manage, and live with the pain. When the familiar painful sensation shows up again, the room of our mind becomes crowded with unpleasant memories, assumptions, and conclusions. We are dragged into those emotional reactions and stories once again.

In contrast, bringing fresh and curious attention to the old familiar pain reduces suffering. With beginner's mind, each time the pain appears, we ask ourselves to relate to it as if it's completely new. "What is it like in *this* moment?" We practice deliberately dropping all previous knowledge of it and invite as much interest, detail, and curiosity as we can muster for the sensation right now. "What is its size, shape, weight, texture, and temperature like right now? Does it have a center? An edge? Is it solid or hollow? Is it moving or static?" These questions invite our attention to stay with the sensation, just as it is now, rather than releasing second arrow strikes with memories, assumptions, and conclusions from the past. To stay present with chronic pain is difficult. It takes precision, energy, courage, and the willingness to treat ourselves tenderly. The payoff, however, can be transformational.

Pearl, a 74-year-old woman suffering from shingles, came to see me for help in managing her pain. She'd been experiencing severe and unrelenting sharp pain for three months. She was allergic to pain medications, and was feeling beaten down, discouraged, and at times panicked about the pain. I taught her what we are practicing here. First, she concentrated on and connected with the sensations of her breath. This helped her settle and center. I asked her to shift her attention to the sensations of pain, and find an accurate descriptor. She called it "sharpness." I asked her to notice the feeling tone, and then to take all of her attention to the sensation as if she had never experienced it before. I invited her to become really curious and interested in the actual sensation and to learn all the qualities and characteristics about it, just as it is right now.

I asked her to cradle the sensation in her awareness gently and tenderly, with lots of sensitivity and care. Encouraging her to relax as much as she could around the edges of the sensations, and to invite spaciousness by imagining she could hold these sensations in the vastness of the blue sky. She was silent through the guidance, and I continued to encourage her to relax, soften, notice if or how it might be shifting, and to keep being very gentle and tender with herself and the sensation. After a while, I asked her to notice her breath again and then to open her eyes and return her attention to the room.

As she opened her eyes, she appeared remarkably more relaxed, and when I asked her what happened, she broke into a big smile and excitably proclaimed, "Why I barely have any pain right now! It was amazing how it did change, a little here and a little there. I had thought the pain was solid and the same everywhere in my arm. But it really has a lot of variety, and it keeps changing. Relaxing around it was really helpful. And when you asked me to be tender and gentle with it, I suddenly saw how mean I've been to it. I realized all these months I'd been hating the pain. By hating it, I've been creating more pain and lots more tension in my body. Now I know what the pain needs. Now I know what I need."

Everything Is Impermanent

Remembering impermanence is another key element for helping us companion sensations mindfully. With a mindful approach to sensations we directly see the reality of impermanence. We witness how the sensations, whether pleasant, neutral or unpleasant arise and pass away on their own. Everything is changing all the time. Sometimes we are happy when change occurs, such as when a headache clears, winter changes to spring, or pregnancy ends and the baby is born. When we're happy and enjoying ourselves, we don't want the experiences to change. We want them to stay just the way they are forever. Understanding impermanence is integral to experiencing freedom from suffering.

When we resist the reality of impermanence we suffer. For many years I suffered from headaches that would sometimes last for several days. They weren't exceedingly painful, but they were a major inconvenience. During a headache, I felt a throbbing heavy veil fall between the external world and myself, and it took a lot of effort just to make it through the day. Before learning about mindfulness, my reaction to feeling the beginning of a headache was dread: "Oh no. I hate these headaches. This is going to be a real drag. What if it goes on for days? Nothing I can take or do really helps with it. Am I going to have these for the rest of my life?" Without realizing it, I was shooting myself with second arrows and making my misery worse.

> Understanding impermanence is integral to experiencing freedom from suffering. When we resist the reality of impermanence, we suffer.

The first time I brought mindfulness to the experience of the headache, I made a number of useful discoveries. By checking in on what the sensation of the headache was *actually* like throughout the day, I learned that the pain was not constant. It ebbed and flowed. Sometimes it was strong and sharp. Other times it was softer, even neutral in tone. Contrary to what I had assumed, the headache was not solid and constant. Instead, it was always changing. Discovering the impermanent nature of pain was enormously helpful. Now when a headache arises, I don't feel burdened by it. I notice the sensation with curiosity, spaciousness, and kindness, trusting that on its own, it will shift and change. I can't control the headaches, but I can choose how I relate to them. I can refrain from firing second arrows.

Center and Go Into the Pain

Happy to be finding mindfulness helpful with chronic headaches, my first challenge to applying mindfulness to acute pain came one evening when I was playing city-league basketball.

As I jumped up to catch a rebound, I crashed mid-air into my opponent, who was also going up for the rebound. As we hit the floor, she landed on top of me and I heard a strange snapping sound. In my mind's eye, I saw my left knee cap pop apart and then come back together again. Instantly, I was consumed in sharp, all-encompassing pain. My entire field of awareness was a huge, black pain. Lying on the floor, I heard my teammate Jackie, another mindfulness practitioner, say, "Mare, center and go into the pain." I knew she was right, but for a second I had no idea how to do that. Then, as if jumping off a diving board into unknown water, I dove my awareness into my knee and began connecting with the extremely unpleasant sensations with as much curiosity, kindness, and breath as I could muster. I opened to the painful sensations just as they were, breathing in and around them, holding them gently with lots of spaciousness. To my amazement, within a few seconds the intensity of the pain diminished by half. I thought, "Wow! This really does work." With a few more minutes of relating to the sensations this way, the pain dissipated enough so I could be carried off the court. I later learned I had torn the posterior cruciate ligament in my left knee.

On another occasion, I was cross-country skiing on a cold winter morning when I made the unwise decision to step out of an iced track while skiing downhill. As I stepped out, I looked down to see the middle of my femur bend unnaturally to the left. I knew I had broken my leg. While my skiing buddies helped me stay warm as I lay in the snow waiting for the emergency snowmobile team to rescue me, I felt the most excruciating pain I had ever experienced in my life. It was much more intense than the knee injury or the pains of childbirth. However, I was also grateful I had a way to relate to the pain and stay calm. I brought all my attention to the sensations, surrounding them with as much spaciousness as I could. I practiced staying steady with my breath and continued expanding around the sensations of pain. I stayed completely present, didn't go into shock, even cracked a few jokes between the waves of pain, and remembered impermanence. I was confident I wouldn't feel this pain for the rest of my life. Although it was excruciating, the pain was workable. I continued the practice through the snowmobile transport, the ambulance, the necessary x-rays, and until the emergency room doctor gave me a shot of morphine, yanked off my ski boot, and rushed me into surgery.

Practice

Meditation:
Mindfulness of Sensations

I invite to you experiment with bringing mindfulness to the sensations in your body. Although the previous examples described tending to painful sensations, as you practice you are opening to whatever sensation is predominant in the present moment, whether it's pleasant, neutral, or unpleasant. Read through the following instructions and then practice for 10–15 minutes. Please do your best to drop all expectations about what will happen so you can open freshly to what you notice. Remember to be kind to yourself, no matter what.

- Begin by practicing mindfulness of breathing for several minutes.
- After you feel connected with the breath and settled, intentionally open the field of awareness to include other sensations in the body.... Stay with the sensations of breathing until another sensation becomes more predominant.
- When the new sensation is in the foreground, let go of the breath and bring all of your attention to the new sensation. This sensation is now the primary object of your attention.

• Find a word that most accurately describes the sensation and softly note it. Avoid using the word "pain," as it's emotionally charged and not specific. Instead, describe the sensation, as in "Tightness. Pressure. Coolness. Itching. Throbbing. Aching." Note the sensation calmly and neutrally, without the personal pronoun of "my" or "I." For example, as soon as you feel tightness in your shoulder or an itch on your cheek, softly note, "Oh, here's tightness." Or, "Here's itching."

• Next, briefly notice the feeling tone of the sensation. Ask, "Is this pleasant, neutral, or unpleasant?" Accept whatever is true in this moment. Don't dwell on it, just make the observation.

• Now move your attention to wherever the sensation lives in your body and invite yourself to become curious about it, just as it is right now…. Bring beginner's mind, fresh and open attention, to this sensation just as it is…. Investigate and ask questions such as, "What is its size, shape, texture, weight, depth, and temperature? Is it moving or still? Does it have an edge? A center? Is it soft or hard? Hollow or solid?" The task is to explore the direct experience of the sensation precisely and accurately. By being truly interested in the direct experience of the sensation, we refrain from judging and being pulled into reactive second arrow stories.

• Next, accept the sensation exactly as it is right now. You aren't trying to change it or do anything to it. You are letting it be. Hold it in your awareness gently, tenderly, softly, with kindness and loving attention….

• Stay present and relax around it, concentrating on the sensation in this accepting, kind way and giving it spaciousness and room to be just as it is….

• Remain steady with the sensation until you realize it is no longer predominant. Your attention has moved to something else because the intensity of the sensation has changed and another experience has moved to the foreground. Impermanence has ruled….

• Now bring attention to the sensations of breathing again…. Your breath remains in the foreground of your awareness, until another sensation (or the same one) arises and becomes predominant.

Processing the Practice

What was the practice like for you? Could you directly experience how a sensation shifts and changes on its own? If you experienced discomfort, did you suffer less by being present with it this way? Could you be curious enough about the actual sensations to keep your attention with the sensation instead of being absorbed into judgments and reactive thoughts? If you experienced an itch, could you stay with the direct experience long enough to see how the itch subsides on its own? To realize an itch resolves on its own demonstrates a principle for practicing mindfulness and for understanding reality: every experience has its own set of causes and conditions. When we don't interfere with what's here in the moment, when we don't struggle with it, condemn it, resist it, or cling to it, or in other words, when we don't mess with the conditions, they shift and change on their own. This is the inevitability of impermanence, and it applies to every experience we have.

> When we don't struggle, condemn, resist, or cling to conditions, they shift and change on their own.

Tip for Severe Pain

When pain is strong, it takes more energy to work with it, making it hard to sustain concentration. In this case, practice alternating attention between the sensations of pain and the sensations of the breath. Focus on the sensations of pain precisely and with lots of spaciousness and gentleness for a few minutes, and then bring the sensations of the breath into the foreground and concentrate on these sensations for a few minutes. Shift to the sensations of pain for a few minutes and then shift back to the breath. Each time you concentrate on the pain, notice it with fresh beginner's mind and spaciousness. This often has the effect of replenishing energy and concentration, and can build up momentum for being able to distinguish even more details, characteristics, or layers of the painful sensation.

Mindfulness With Difficult Medical Procedures

Besides bringing mindfulness to every dentist visit as I do, you can practice with any procedure that's unpleasant, such as having blood drawn or receiving a flu shot, a pelvic exam, or an MRI. Margaret decided to practice during a mammogram, an experience that had always been painful for her. Accepting that she has a "white coat syndrome," the high anxiety-pulse and blood pressure raising-reaction to all medical procedures, she practiced mindfully breathing as she waited to be called into the exam room, and as the technician was moving and aligning the equipment to her breast. She noted all the sensations as she experienced them. When she felt cool hardness as the technician lay her breast on the machine's plate, she noted, "Somewhat unpleasant." When the pressure of the machine's plates squeezed her breast, she noted, "Unpleasant." When the pressure increased, she noted, "Yes, more unpleasant." After more squeezing and then holding her breath as the pressure released, she noted, "Ah, neutral again." When she felt relief, she noted, "Pleasant." When the technician left the room to check on the results, Margaret sat and breathed mindfully. She practiced in the same way with the other breast. After the procedure, she realized by staying mindfully present moment by moment, the mammogram wasn't horrible. It was unpleasant, yes, but not actually painful.

This Approach Takes Courage

Given our conditioned fear of pain, it's natural to feel resistance to opening to it. Please be kind and gentle with yourself if you're timid about opening to pain. The mindful approach asks you to be brave and go straight into unknown and potentially unpleasant territory. As we open mindfully to the unpleasant sensation, anything can happen — the sensation could become more intense and more unpleasant. It could also stay the same. Eventually it will diminish. If you have chronic pain, chances are you resist that pain and suffer with it. Be very gentle and start by opening to it a little and see what happens. Practice holding it gently for a few seconds, and then come back to your breath. Appreciate yourself for every foray into the unknown. You are building your courage and inner stability.

Inner Security

One of the greatest benefits of bringing mindfulness to sensations is the sense of inner stability and security it creates. Cultivating inner stability is a crucial antidote to the habit of othering. As we learn to stay present with what is unpleasant without suffering and to let go of what's pleasant when it changes, we deepen the confidence in our ability to handle whatever is here. We also increase our trust and respect for the body and its wisdom. We see how the body has its own life, its own way, and its own innate intelligence. It provides essential data we are wise to heed. We can take safe harbor by grounding our attention in the body. It provides the information we need to live and flourish, and is always doing the best it can to be our reliable home for this lifetime.

Ownwork Suggestions

Formal Meditation Practice:
Breath and Sensations

Meditate every day on the sensations of the body breathing and on other sensations as they arise in the body. Be very gentle and patient with yourself. Please notice the effect of the practice on your mind, body, and heart. Write in your journal after each meditation if that's helpful.

Informal Practice

• Continue the Dropping In practice as frequently as possible throughout the day, except now focus on sensations you can feel in your body. Practice softly noting and apply beginner's mind and spaciousness as much as you can. Please register the effect.

• Watch for othering. When you spot it, be glad you see it, and return attention to your breath and your direct experience. Ask, "What's happening for me right now? How am I relating to it? What's the wisest and kindest way to respond to myself right now?" Notice the effect.

• Watch for evidence of impermanence: how your experience changes throughout the day, how others change, and how the weather, plans, and events constantly change.

11

The Sticky Icky Habits of the Judging Mind

The judging mind has an opinion about everything. It's full of noise and old learning. It's a quality of mind addicted to maintaining an image of itself.

Stephen Levine

Judging is an important cognitive function of the mind, and it may also be the most prominent habit of the conditioned mind. Recall that every experience creates a feeling tone that the mind instantly judges. When the feeling tone is pleasant, the judging mind approves. When it's unpleasant, the judging mind disapproves, and when it's neutral, we hardly care. Beyond the primal reaction to feeling tone, we need to make conscious and skillful judgments every day. Repeatedly, we must analyze and assess situations and conditions to make intelligent and wise decisions. We couldn't function well without making discerning judgments.

The ability to judge and the habit of judging are established early in our lives. When my grandson, Joshua, was first learning to talk, because I was so excited to know him, I began asking him lots of questions. Did he like this toy better or that one? Did he like this snack more than the other one? When at first he didn't have preferences, it dawned on me I was encouraging him to make judgments. Knowing the ability to judge can be both helpful and limiting, I backed off. He was so open and fresh, still living in the precious innocence of childhood. However, it wasn't long before he began expressing his opinions spontaneously. As with all of us, the ability to judge helped him define and shape his sense of self distinct from others.

Power of the Judging Mind

Even though we couldn't function successfully without the ability to make judgments, the conditioned mind develops bad habits when judging. (I'm judging the judging mind here.) Namely, besides the primal reaction to feeling tone, we develop the habit of mindlessly, automatically judging practically everything we experience. Most of the views and opinions the judging mind expresses are internalized from our families, culture, and the world around us. Rather than being ideas we deliberately and wisely choose, they become entrenched in our unconscious minds, without our conscious consent. Over time the conditioned responses morph into beliefs that influence how we relate to ourselves, others, and almost everything that happens.

Checking in

• How's your formal sitting practice going? At this point in learning mindfulness, many women say it's hard to find time to meditate. The newness has worn off and the demands of daily life seep in. If this is true for you, don't be discouraged. It's difficult to change our routines and create the space to practice. Meditation goes against the grain in our culture because we are habituated to doing and being "productive." However, meditating is very important "doing." We're training our minds to be our friend and ally rather than our tyrant. The hardest part is showing up on your cushion. Please be kind to yourself and keep encouraging yourself to sit every day, and every time you do, notice the effect. Keep collecting data on how these practices affect you. Your rational mind needs to see if they are beneficial.

• How was it to work with sensations, on and off the cushion? Are you finding it helpful? Can you spot when you are hitting yourself with second arrows now? Many people report less suffering with chronic aches and pains. One woman, severely limited by arthritis in her lower back, pronounced mindfulness the most effective method she's ever tried for dealing with chronic pain, and she's tried the gamut. "It really, really works!" she said.

• Have you noticed any effect on your sleep patterns? Many find meditating helps them sleep. If you're someone who has trouble sleeping or who wakes up in the night, try using the practice as soon as you wake up. It's often helpful for getting back to sleep again.

The judging mind is full of evaluations, assumptions, and conclusions. It has the power to make us feel great, even on top of the world. "I am the best! That was really incredibly brilliant of me!" The judging mind also has the power to create inner hell. "I can't believe I screwed that up so royally. That was really bad. I'm so ashamed of myself!" Between these extremes, the mind carries on an almost constant prattle of approval and disapproval, nearly relentless in the habit of othering. We have opinions about what's right, what's wrong, what's good, and what's bad. We know how we are supposed to be and how the other is supposed to be. We think one idea is great, while another one is weak. We like this particular color but hate that one. The judging mind is like an inner empress sitting on her lofty throne casting declarations willy-nilly, as we, her humble subjects, mindlessly obey her. Learning to refrain from judging is integral to cultivating mindfulness, gaining freedom from othering, and living authentically.

> Learning to refrain from judging is integral to cultivating mindfulness, gaining freedom from othering, and living authentically.

Judging and Self-Criticism

Growing up, we develop definite ideas about the right and wrong ways to be, look, and live. These beliefs seep in silently and slowly, burrowing into deep neural grooves in the brain. As women, in the subordinate position, we unconsciously learn to view ourselves as unequal and judge ourselves as lesser. We believe we are not enough. As a result, our habitual judgments are directed against ourselves first and foremost. For many of us, criticizing and blaming ourselves is the constant undertone in our mind. The mighty inner empress rants disapproval and demands correction. Like bad elevator music incessantly playing in our heads, we aren't really aware of the judgments and criticisms, except for persistent feelings of anxiety, tension, irritability, or dull heaviness. If you can bring awareness to the ranting soundtrack, you'll hear variations of "What I just said was really stupid. I shouldn't be feeling that! What's the matter with me? I'm such a (weirdo, idiot, slut, pig, bore)! I am so (selfish, lazy, mean, ugly, dumb)! When am I going to (lose some weight, keep my mouth shut, get it together, stop being so pathetic) and be how I'm supposed to be?"

Othering breeds the habit of self-criticism. That critical inner voice keeps us stuck and absorbed in the belief that something is wrong with us. This underlying unconscious view naturally makes us feel bad about ourselves, unworthy, undeserving, and insecure. We don't feel safe being just ourselves. Instead, we strive to make ourselves better: more likable, generous, loving, and patient in the eyes of the other. We aim for perfection, attached to the illusion that if we can be perfect, others will like, approve, and accept us. Finally, we'll be safe, secure, and okay.

> Othering breeds the habit of self-criticism.

Judging affects everyone and everything else, although we're most hard on ourselves. When we pay attention and realize our inner tyrant is also busy piling criticisms onto others, or we slam someone with a particularly harsh judgment, we turn against ourselves with more judgments. We aren't supposed to be disapproving, petty, or unfairly critical of others. It isn't nice. It's not perfect. One judgment leads to a more caustic self-judgment in a vicious cycle. Do you ever see that in yourself? Is this pattern familiar?

Judging and Comparing

Consider the habit of comparing ourselves to others. Occasionally we come out on top, but more often than not, we land on the bottom. The first teacher on my spiritual quest, Dhyani Ywahoo, a Cherokee and highly respected Tibetan Buddhist Rinpoche who founded the Sunray Meditation Society, said that, "If there is such a thing as a deadly sin, it's the habit of comparing. Because comparing always separates us." Comparing pits me against you and results in me feeling better than you, worse than you, or sometimes the same as you. Judging and comparing keep us caught in dualistic thinking. Things are either this way or that way, and we fail to see all the variations and possibilities in between. The underlying assumption is that there is an absolute right and wrong way to be. These rigid judgmental views and our attachment to them are the root cause of war within ourselves, war between ourselves and others, and ultimately war between nations.

So-called "good" judgments keep us hooked in this pattern, too. Although positive judgments feel better than negative ones in the moment, they come from the same habits of judging, attaching to our view, and being caught in dualistic thinking. Lurking close to the nod of approval — "Good job. Everyone thinks I'm great. What I said was really clever." — are judgments that under other conditions can be the opposite. "Boy, what I said was really stupid. Everybody thinks I bombed now." It's two sides of the same coin.

Several meditation teachers have said the habit of comparing is the last vestige of the conditioned mind to dissolve before experiencing enlightenment. The first time I heard that view, I felt great relief. Although my habit of comparing has diminished through practice, it's still a conditioned response. It's encouraging to know through mindfulness practice we gradually become less caught up in comparing, and we need to be gentle with ourselves all along the way.

Judging and the World According to Me

Judging thoughts are egocentric. We attach to and identify with "my views." Judging thoughts can express an opinion of myself, about someone else, about what's happening right now, or something that's going on in the world. Judgments are expressions of the world according to me. We believe our judgments are the truth, the reality. In fact, they are self-created views and directly reflect our sense of self and our ideas about how we are supposed to be.

A dear friend did a psychotherapy session with me, wanting to get to the bottom of her ever-present chronic anxiety. My friend is one of the most thoughtful, caring, creative, and brilliant people I know. She's suffered from deep-seated anxiety for years, and has employed an array of therapeutic methods to try to heal it. After I guided her into a meditative state, I asked her to think of situations where the anxiety becomes intense. When she became aware of the feeling of anxiety in her body, I guided her into describing the precise experience of the sensations, and then into a deeper inquiry into the causes. This led her into remembering childhood experiences with her mother that especially provoked anxiety. When she asked, "What is this anxiety really about?" or "What's at the root of this suffering?" what came to her was the startling realization that "My mind critically judges absolutely everything I think, feel, say, and do. After every thought, feeling, and action, I hear, 'You shouldn't think that. You shouldn't feel that. You shouldn't do that. That's wrong.'" She said, "No wonder I think there's something wrong with me. I'm always telling myself there is!" The habit of constant criticism and judgment that tells her she's wrong provokes the pervasive anxiety she feels. Witnessing the pattern with my dear friend, I appreciated her important insight, but regretted the power of our minds to create such suffering.

Experiencing a Judgment
With Awareness and Curiosity

The first time I saw the intensity and depth of judging in my mind, I was stunned. We hurt, stifle, and oppress ourselves with the judgment gavel. The first empowering step we can take towards cultivating freedom is using the principle of awareness with curiosity. Curiosity is a powerful antidote to judgment. When we can be fresh and open, and bring the curiosity of beginner's mind to our experience, being authentically interested in seeing clearly what's happening in the moment, our mind, body, and heart naturally open. Curiosity creates internal spaciousness from which to observe our experience. From that inner roominess, we can release our tight grip on the judgment. We are inviting our inner blue sky into the field of our awareness.

When I first began to bring awareness with curiosity to the expressions of my judging mind, I was amazed at the sheer volume of judgments. Judging seemed like the main activity of my mind. I began a practice of saying to myself each time I noticed a judgment, "Isn't that interesting?" That question shifted my relationship to a judgment. Asking "Isn't that interesting?" helped me create enough space and separation so I could step out of the way of the direct hit. It shifted my position from being the target of jugement to sidling up next to it. From this different and safer perspective, I could be authentically curious and witness its effect on me. I observed the sensations the critical words created in my body, how my heart contracted, the effect on my energy, and much more. Seeing the actual impact of the judgment on my whole being — not only my mind spinning off in more painful stories, but also the uncomfortable physical sensations of my heart closing and losing energy — increased my aspiration to find freedom from the oppressive habit of judging.

> Curiosity is
> a powerful antidote
> to judgment.

Because we all need to wake up to the habit of judging, I invite you to contemplate the activities of your judging mind. Do so with sincere curiosity and kindness, understanding judging is a deeply conditioned pattern and does not reflect who you actually are. What are the habitual judgments your mind slings against yourself? Who are the frequent visitors or vultures that scare you and make you feel bad about yourself? What do you condemn in yourself? As you reflect on these questions and notice what arises, try saying to yourself each time you spot a judgment, "Isn't that interesting?"

Practice

Meditation:
Examining the Effects of a Judgment

To experience the power of judgment, I encourage you to try the following mindful experiment. Before you begin, identify a familiar painful judgment your mind makes against yourself.

- Bring your attention into this moment and drop fully into your precious body.... Invite some relaxation and softening.... Now focus on the sensations of breathing for a few minutes...noticing anything else that comes into your awareness with kindness, gentleness, friendliness.... Notice your mind-body state, just as it is right now before you zap yourself with this judgment: the sensations you are aware of in your body, the rhythm of your breathing, where you feel relaxation or ease, where you may feel some tightness or tension.... Notice what your mind is like right now: busy, calm, restless, or slowing down.... Let it all be as it is....

- Bring that familiar negative judgment into your awareness by remembering a common situation that prompts it, and let the usual scenario play out in your mind.... Deliver that judgment, saying it in the tone you usually use with yourself.... Now, with as much curiosity and sensitivity you can muster, notice exactly how that judgment affects you: what you see and hear, the emotions it provokes, and all the sensations it creates in your body. How does it affect your energy? What happens in your mind, heart, and body as a result of the judgment?

What did you notice? Did tension increase in your body? Did you feel a sense of pulling in, pulling away, contracting, tightening, or shrinking? Did your thoughts go off in other painful imaginings, other familiar complaints, or conclusions about yourself? Did your body respond with tension, such as tightness in your belly or a heaviness in your chest? Was it hard to stay with effects of the judgment, as if your mind wanted to escape from the discomfort it created?

167

Judging closes the mind and heart and creates opposition. We shut down and turn against ourselves. We get mad at ourselves. If the judgment is aimed at another, we shut down, turn against, and pull away from them. Judging creates disconnection from ourself and from the other, and from the direct experience of the present moment as we go off in stories, memories, and conclusions. Judging is the opposite of beginner's mind. As soon as we judge something, either positively or negatively, we think we know how it is. We've made our conclusion and don't need to stick around to investigate it more fully. We lose our open presence and mindfulness.

> Judging creates
> disconnection from our self
> and from the other,
> and from the
> direct experience of the
> present moment.

Bringing Mindfulness to the Judging Mind

We are not wrong to judge. Judging is a necessary function of our intellect that lets us live responsibly and make intelligent decisions. Judging is also a strong and deeply conditioned habit, one we practice automatically and unconsciously. We have no choice over conditioned habits, so those habitual judgments have the power to create tremendous suffering for ourselves and others.

Our task is to bring mindfulness to the experience of judging by observing the judgment itself clearly and with curiosity, refraining from judging it as either good or bad. Instead, we notice it with kind awareness. The basic instruction is to softly note "judging" as soon as you become aware that your mind has judged something. It's a soft and neutral noting, "Ah, judging is happening right now." Omit the personal pronoun. Instead of noting "I'm judging," note only "Judging." Experiment with adding the question, "Isn't that interesting?" to help to separate yourself from the judgment. Next, escort and shift your attention immediately to the sensations of the breath. As you connect with the breath, the automatic attachment to the judgment naturally loosens and releases.

Practice these steps with judgments you make against yourself, as well as judgments made toward other people, situations, and preferences. The more you can become curious about the action of the judging mind, the more you'll be amazed at how busy and active this habit is, and how it limits us and creates misery. With practice, you'll see how freeing it is to have more choice with judging. The judging habit is deeply engrained, so offer kindness and acceptance towards yourself when you're caught in judgment.

Lightening Up Helps

During a week-long meditation retreat, my judging mind was on a rampage, creating a painful inner hell. It seemed all I was experiencing was my mind's habit of judging. I judged everything my eyes landed on, mostly with negative critiques. I was unhappy with everything about myself, everything around me, plus I judged myself for being caught in all the terrible judging. "That woman is way too skinny. Her hair is really thick; I wish mine was like that. That woman who's always coughing should meditate somewhere else. It's so selfish of her to be disturbing the rest of us. My mind is pathetic, it's wandering all the time. I'm terrible at meditating!" The nasty banter went on and on, relentlessly, day after day, it seemed, and I was feeling very discouraged with myself.

Luckily, in a group check-in meeting with the teacher, one woman mentioned all she'd been experiencing so far on the retreat was her mind stuck in judging. As she described her experience, she burst out laughing. She was amused by the antics of her judging mind. She viewed the judgments as silly, ridiculous, and funny. Unlike me, she didn't seem to be suffering at all. Reflecting on her lightness and humor, I recognized I'd been taking the antics of my judging mind personally with grim seriousness. I was identifying with all of it, the content and the habit.

This insight freed me from the misery. I'd been holding myself responsible for my mind's habit of judging and concluded I should be able to stop it. With relief, I remembered judging is simply a conditioned habit and not unique to me. I also remembered that habits operate automatically. Our freedom from habits is born from bringing mindfulness when they arise. Rather than feeling frustrated and caught, I stopped viewing the habit as me and simply observed when a judgment arose. I'd softly note, "Ah, judging," then shift my attention to the breath and present moment, let the judgment go. I had the power to release myself from this inner hell.

Ownwork Suggestions

Formal Meditation Practice:
Mindfulness of Breathing, Sensations and Judging

Set your timer for how long you'll sit.

Arrange your body in a comfortable, dignified posture, inviting relaxing and softening.... Drop attention down into the body and concentrate on the sensations of breathing, bringing beginner's mind to the experience...tending to one breath at a time....

When you feel settled and collected, intentionally open the field of your awareness to other sensations in the body.... When another sensation is more predominant than the breath, that sensation becomes the object of attention: softly note it, and then note the feeling tone (pleasant, neutral, or unpleasant). With beginner's mind, investigate all the qualities and properties of the sensation (its size, shape, depth, weight, temperature, and texture).... Hold it spaciously in your field of awareness, accepting it and letting it be just as it is...staying with the sensation until it's no longer in the foreground of your awareness....

When you notice judgments, whether about the predominant sensation or about anything else, softly note "judging," (not "I'm judging") and return attention to the breath, letting go of the judgment....Stay with the breath, home base, until another sensation is more predominant or a judgment arises....

At the end of the sit, notice what you are like now.

Informal Practice

• Be on the lookout for judging. When you see it, neutrally note, "Oh, there's judging." Be sure to note this without a judgment, and then let it go by moving attention to the sensations of breathing. Please notice the effect.

• Watch for othering and notice if a judgment is almost always embedded in the othering. Practice saying to yourself when you see othering, "Isn't that interesting?" Notice the effect.

• Continue to practice Dropping In as frequently as you can, always remembering to ask, "Given this is what is happening, what's a wise and kind way to respond to myself right now?" Open to whatever arises. Be sure to follow your advice. Please notice the effect.

12

The Power of Thoughts: Don't Believe Everything You Think

What we think, we become.

The Buddha

Thinking, Thinking, Thinking

As I'm sure you've noticed by now, it's rare to find moments that are truly thought-free. The mind is a busy sense organ. Its main function is to think, and othering is all about thinking. We think about what the other is feeling, wanting, and needing and what might be going on with them. We think about what they are thinking. We wonder what they're thinking about us. We think a lot about ourselves, especially in relationship to others. We judge, compare, and critique as well as remember, daydream, plan, rehearse, and worry.

You may have noticed how fickle your thinking mind can be. One moment you can be exclaiming your brilliance, your creativity, or your supreme skill at performing a task, and you're filled with confidence. A few moments later, you can be thinking you're the lowliest, most wretched creature on the planet. In an instant, our thoughts can make us feel fantastic or horrible. Researchers have tried to estimate how many thoughts we think a day, and the range seems to be between *67,000 and 90,000, on average*. Further, up to 80 percent of thoughts are reruns, and the vast majority of those reruns are negative.[20] No wonder we feel exhausted at times. The Buddha said, "Who is your enemy? Your mind is your enemy. Who is your friend? Your mind is your friend." He was describing the volatility and power of the thinking mind.

Thoughts Create Our Reality

The sense door of the mind, more than any other sense door, has the greatest power to create our reality. Energy follows thought. Thoughts create feelings and emotions that lead to ideas, speech, and actions. Thoughts make the world, for good or for bad. If you look around the room you're in right now, most of what you see exists because someone first thought of it. The chair you're sitting in, the piece of art on your wall, the light bulb in the lamp, and the electricity creating the light, all began with someone first thinking of the idea to create it. Likewise, the

Checking in

• Are you catching the mind in its pervasive habit of judging? Isn't it amazing how prevalent judging is? Have you discovered how mindfully noting judging frees you from its clutches? Keep practicing and see what happens.

• What are you discovering about your mind's habits of othering? We must learn to spot the pattern because only then do we have any possibility of freedom. When seeing clearly, we can pop out of the deep groove of the habit, and for that moment we have some freedom. Each time we recognize, "Oh, there's othering," we diminish the power and momentum of the habit. Appreciate each time you spot it. Remember, no matter what the particular othering thought is, *do not judge* yourself for it. Just be happy you are seeing it.

• How's it going getting to your cushion and meditating every day? Be kind and keep encouraging yourself to practice daily. Even 5–10 minutes is beneficial. Meditating does pays off.

• Are you beginning to treat yourself more kindly? Even a little bit? Please keep practicing.

stress you feel when you imagine an upcoming meeting with your boss, or the anticipation of eating a piece of chocolate cake, or the tension you feel when your loved one is unexplainably late in returning home — all begin with thoughts in the mind. An ancient Chinese proverb says, "Watch your thoughts; they become words. Watch your words; they become actions. Watch your actions; they become habits. Watch your habits; they become character. Watch your character; it becomes your destiny."

We Can't Control Our Thoughts

We can't control our thoughts. We can't decide to think only loving, kind, beneficial thoughts. Thoughts are continuously arising out of conditions over which we have little control, and we have too many thoughts to control anyway. I used to believe we should be able to control our thoughts and change them in positive directions. Even when we know they are negative, attempting to not think those thoughts doesn't work. Once, in a workshop, a teacher asked us to practice a "negative thought fast" throughout the entire three-day training. My instant reaction to her request was, "Ha! I won't be able to do that for even one minute." I was shocked and humbled at the intensity of my negative thought habit.

> By becoming mindfully aware of our thoughts, we can choose how we want to respond to them.

Through mindfulness, we attune to the different kinds of thoughts we are experiencing. We see which thoughts contribute to our clarity, depth, and well-being, and which thoughts undermine it. By becoming mindfully aware of our thoughts, we can choose how we want to respond to them. Mindfulness enables discernment with our thoughts. We can let go of the ones that create suffering and enjoy and benefit from those that take us in the direction we want to go.

Types of Thoughts

The mind creates many kinds of thoughts. Some thoughts are fleeting and random, more like momentary images and memories that arise and pass away rapidly, seeming to express no particular message or emotional charge. Some thoughts entertain us. When we're feeling bored, disconnected, or uncomfortable, the mind finds something to land on to keep us busy. It spins fantasies, daydreams, and plans, which offer us some distraction, a kind of comfort when we're feeling uneasy. Unfortunately, this type of thinking rarely leads to greater calmness or ease. Instead, it tends to stimulate and agitate us, leading to more thoughts.

As we've learned, many of our thoughts are "add-ons." They are reactions to our direct experience, rooted in our conditioning, and usually arise from a feeling we're experiencing. These reactions take us abruptly away from our present moment experience into the mind's stories. For example, imagine you're looking out the window, thinking about the fun picnic you've planned for later in the day. You spot one little dark cloud in the sky. You think, "Oh no. What if it starts to rain? Everybody will get wet, the food will be ruined, and the kids will get all muddy and dirty. I'd better cancel the picnic. Everybody is going to be bummed and upset." Or, perhaps you feel a strange ache in your back and think, "Uh-oh. What if this ache is spinal stenosis like my mom had. That means more pain, surgery down the road, and eventually I'll be in a wheelchair." The habitual "what-if's" are powerful add-ons, imagining a reality that doesn't actually exist.

Belief Thoughts

Some levels of thoughts are insistent and repetitive, such as painful memories, images, conversations, and events we habitually play over and over in the mind. Many of these thoughts are rooted in deeply conditioned negative beliefs outside of our conscious awareness. Beliefs such as "I'm not good enough" or "I don't matter" trigger familiar feelings of unworthiness, fear, and shame. Hopeful thoughts that try to guarantee a future for us often arise repetitively in reaction to fearful thoughts. At times we are trapped in the same thoughts, memories, and feelings running in a continuous loop in the mind. Like a broken record stuck in the same neural groove, we become lost in these stories.

Wise Thoughts

Fortunately, many thoughts reflect the mind's great and wonderful capacity to investigate, inquire, and reflect. These thoughts are creative and help us delve deeply into what we don't know, and give birth to new ideas, insight, understanding, compassion, and intuition. Creative thoughts express our wisdom and deep intelligence, helping to enliven and awaken us. These kinds of thoughts are profound and healing. We are inviting ourselves to open to these thoughts each time we ask, "What's the wisest and kindest way to respond to myself right now?"

What's the wisest and kindest way to respond to myself right now?

Mind and Body Are Connected

We know the mind and body are interconnected. What we are thinking, whether we're aware of it or not, affects the body instantly. We experience the connection when we get butterflies in our stomach thinking about an upcoming event. Or at the doctor's office when our heart races and palms get clammy when our name is called. How we experience stress, of course, depends primarily on how we react mentally to the conditions of the situation.

There is a fun and impressive experiment you can do to demonstrate the mind-body connection. The method, called muscle testing, is a simple and direct way to receive feedback on the body's energy, power, and strength in response to specific thoughts.

Power of Thoughts Experiment

Work with a partner, with one person serving as the tester, the other as the subject.

1. Find your partner's muscle-strength baseline. Standing, have your partner raise an arm straight out to the right, parallel to the ground, palm facing down. Place your hand on top of your partner's wrist and press down firmly as they resist your pressure. Push down hard and hold the pressure long enough (5 seconds) so you both can clearly measure their strength. Release your pressure and ask your partner to drop their arm. You've established their baseline strength.

2. With their arm relaxed, ask your partner to say the following phrase to themselves, repeating it three times (in their mind): "I'm weak. I'm confused. I don't trust myself," and then immediately raise their arm for testing. Press down on their raised arm (as hard as with the baseline), as your partner resists. Notice the effect.

3. Next, with their arm again relaxed, ask your partner to repeat the following phrase three times, "I'm strong. I'm clear. I trust myself," and then immediately raise their arm for testing as you press down (applying same amount of pressure) as they resist. Notice the effect.

4. Now reverse roles and repeat Steps 1–3.

Okay, what happened? Did you find you lost strength when you said you were weak, confused, and didn't trust yourself? What happened when you said you were strong, clear, and trusted yourself? Did you regain your strength? Isn't this experiment amazing? Negative thoughts can instantly deplete the body's power and strength, while positive thoughts amplify it. Consider the thousands of thoughts you think each day. What percentage of those thoughts tend to be positive and what percent are negative?

Impressed by this experience, one woman decided to try the experiment with her 16-year-old son, who was suffering from depression and anxiety. She knew he had a habit of bombarding himself with negative thoughts, but he had little awareness of how the thoughts were affecting him. Although he first resisted the experiment, when he finally agreed to do it, he was stunned and encouraged. He saw for the first time how his negative rants were draining him of energy, keeping him depressed and anxious. He began a practice of bringing awareness to the negative thoughts and then shifting out of them by moving attention to his breath. He told his mom for the first time he now had hope he could feel better.

Considering that thoughts are so powerful, we can be happier and live with more ease by being precisely aware of what we're thinking. Remember, the mind is continuously creating thoughts based on ever-changing external and internal conditions over which we have limited control. Only by becoming aware of exactly what we're thinking can we discern whether a thought supports our energy or depletes it. Then we can *choose* how to respond: we can agree with it and follow it, or we can choose to let it go and move attention to something more beneficial.

> We can be happier and live with more ease by being precisely aware of what we're thinking.

Conditioned Reactions to Our Thoughts

Cultivating discernment is not easy because conditioning has trained us to be ruled by thoughts. Even though the mind is a thought factory, continuously spewing ideas and stories, we assume what we are thinking accurately reflects reality. We are extremely attached to our thoughts and don't question them. We could even say we are addicted to our thoughts. They certainly hold us hostage at times.

We Think We Are Our Thoughts

One reason we are ruled by thoughts is that we strongly identify with them. We take them personally. Descartes, the great seventeenth-century philosopher, famously said, "I think. Therefore, I am." This statement clearly captures our experience, doesn't it? When we begin to pay close attention to thoughts, we realize we are the primary subject in most of them. In fact, our ego, or sense of self, is completely created

We have a personal movie theater in our heads.

by our thoughts. As the central star in our imaginings and inner dramas, the mind spins unending stories about a Me. The story of self is told to us over and over through the opinionated inner commentator of the judging mind. Some stories are about the "good me," the "successful me," the "how I'm supposed to be me." Some are about the "bad me," the "imperfect me," the "how I'm not supposed to be me." It's like we have a personal movie theater in our heads. Some films are short takes, others are longer dramas, but the star is always us. Sometimes we play the heroine, sometimes the villain, other times the victim. Given so many of our thoughts center on ourselves, the illusion that we are our thoughts is logical.

We Believe Our Thoughts

Another misunderstanding in our conditioned relationship to thoughts is we believe whatever we think. Incredibly, we don't question our thoughts. We take them as facts, the truth, and real events in our lives. The worries, assumptions, memories, plans, judgments, imaginary conversations, imagined catastrophes and successes — we believe them all. For example, we see a certain look on someone's face and assume we know what they are thinking, or before walking into a meeting, the mind creates a scenario about how the meeting will go, which biases perception, and we behave from those imagined assumptions. Our mind spins a story about what's going on, and we act in response to those stories without realizing they're made up.

Because othering trains us to avoid conflict, I used to assume I didn't experience much conflict with others. During a meditation, I observed a pattern of believing my thoughts that made me question that view. I was remembering a conversation during which I felt anxiety because of a disagreement. As I recalled what happened, my mind cleverly slipped in a better ending without any conscious intention to change the memory of the conversation. In my new altered version, I skillfully said everything I wanted to say, and the other person responded just as I wanted them to respond. My story was so lovely. Observing this remake of the event, I realized the imagined change gave me a sense of resolution and relief from the actual difficult conversation. Without seeing that I made up a story, I would have fooled myself into believing everything was fine between us. Obviously, whatever was unresolved would have remained so, and I would have been less aware of what was genuinely real between us. The conditioned mind can be tricky.

I Think, Therefore I'm Not Here

Thoughts abduct us from the present moment. When we habitually attach, identify, and believe our thoughts, we lose contact with the here and now. We disconnect from what is real. Sometimes the abduction is so complete it's like a mind train zooms up next to you, a door opens and sucks you in, and off you go on a trip to who knows where. At some moment, the door opens and you're plopped out, back here in the present moment again, wondering where you've been and what's happened while you were gone. Ever experience anything like that?

When you start paying attention, you realize thought abduction happens all the time to all of us. Perhaps you're listening to a dear one tell you something important, and you're with them for a while, but at some moment you realize you didn't hear the last few words they said because your mind took you off on an inner trip. This habit is most alarming to me when I drive home from work and suddenly wonder, "Was that last traffic light I just drove through green or red?" I really can't remember because I was so absorbed in a story. Further, I now can't even remember what I was thinking about. Buddhist writings call this experience "living in the dream." Through mindfulness, we are learning to wake up from the dream, the altered reality the mind creates, and reside instead in our real, present moment, sensate experience.

Thoughts are Essentially Empty

Because we're conditioned to believe, identify, and attach to our thoughts, they seem lifelike and real. However, as an object of our attention, they are light, changeable, and empty. They have no true substance of their own, especially as compared to the other sense doors. Sensations in the body are dense, more substantial, and lingering. Sounds are distinct vibrations that have their own timing. The sights we see with our eyes stay with us as long as we are looking at them, and smells and tastes have their own definite life. In contrast, when we choose to remove our attention from thoughts, they dissolve instantly. Much like the way thoughts are depicted in cartoons, our ideas, words, and images create a thought bubble. As soon as we see them clearly and remove our attention from them, the bubble pops, and the thoughts simply dissolve into space. We could say mindfulness is like a giant needle that pops the thought bubble and lands us back in reality.

Deeper Understanding and Insight

During one of my early meditation retreats, the teachers were explaining what thoughts are, how they continuously arise and pass away beyond our control, and emphasizing we are not actually our thoughts. I felt excitement and relief from this new understanding. At the end of one sitting practice, I was mindfully walking out of the meditation hall when a surprising thought arose in my mind. To appreciate the

183

thought, you first have to imagine the physical setup. Two narrow curving hallways lead in and out of the meditation hall, and at the end of every meditation, we walk out single file through the hallways, keeping our eyes down so as to not interact with anyone, staying mindfully with our own direct experience. As we were walking out of the hall, in a single file, through the narrow hallway, I imagined deliberately tripping the woman in front of me and watching a domino-like effect of all the bodies in front of her falling down. My first response to that image was to laugh (silently, of course) at the outrageousness of the imagining. My next thought was, "Okay. Right now I am really glad I know I am not my thoughts. Because if I weren't aware of that right now, I would instead be thinking, 'What does that thought mean about me? What kind of a person am I? Do I have some hidden inner aggression? Do I have some deep desire to hurt people? Did my mother do something to me?" Without mindfulness, I would have taken that thought personally, causing my mind to spin various interpretations and then form a conclusion about what it *meant* about me. Instead, I enjoyed the humor of the goofy thought and let it go.

From this freeing experience, I realized I judge myself for my thoughts a lot, telling myself I'm awful for thinking a particular thought. Ever noticed that habit in yourself? The understanding that *we are not our thoughts* is radically good news. Thoughts are only one aspect of experience and not any more important than what we are actually seeing, hearing, smelling, tasting, or feeling in this moment.

> We are 100 percent responsible for what we do with our thoughts.

We cannot be responsible for the thoughts that arise; they just happen. Thus, it's a misunderstanding to charge ourselves with responsibility for what the mind thinks. However, we are 100 percent responsible for what we *do* with those thoughts. How we respond to them makes all the difference in the world.

Othering Is Fed by Our Thought Stories

When we're othering, we are immersed in the thinking and story-making mind. We're constantly imagining what's going on with others. We make assumptions about what they're thinking, feeling, sensing, needing, and wanting, including what they are thinking and feeling about us. Through our judgments, fears, assumptions, and conclusions, we predict their reactions and then we respond accordingly. This mental activity is rooted in deeper conditioned belief thoughts that are born from our gender position in the patriarchy, telling us we are not enough. Our belief in not being enough, or that something is wrong, inadequate, or missing within ourselves, propels us to strive to be more perfect and pleasing for the other. Striving for perfection stimulates an exhausting escalation of judging and comparing thoughts that often lead to more self-doubt, self-negation, and self-loathing. These reactions fuel more obsessive thoughts, as we get caught up in second guessing ourselves, reviewing what we said or did, and worrying it wasn't good enough. This cycle can go on and on, until we are far away from reality, caught up in our dream, which may feel more like a painful, crazy-making nightmare.

> When we're othering, we are immersed in the thinking and story-making mind.

Othering also breeds numerous thoughts about control, where we plan and rehearse, imagining exactly how to present ourselves so the interaction will go just the way we want it to. We imagine the whole conversation, back and forth: I say this, and then they say that, and then I respond, and they say this, on and on, imagining the conversation going exactly right. Yet, when it comes to finally having the conversation in real life, it rarely goes as we imagined it. Do you sense how lost we can become, how much suffering we experience due to our conditioned reactions to thoughts?

Changing Our Relationship to Our Thoughts

Fortunately, we can wake up and realize we are making up thoughts all the time, and they may or may not be true or helpful. We can also stop identifying with our thoughts and understand we don't have to believe everything we think. To do so is deeply freeing. Further, instead of being trapped in imaginings about the future and memories about the past, we can realize what we're thinking may have nothing to do with what is actually happening in the present moment. Wisdom is knowing a thought is just a thought, nothing more, and we can choose how we respond to our thoughts. Making those choices is truly liberating and revolutionary.

We don't have to believe everything we think.

Bringing the discerning light of mindfulness to thoughts transforms our relationship with them. Being aware of the exact thought or story we're thinking right now enables us to *discern whether this thought serves me or not.* We learn to ask ourselves: Does this thought reflect reality as it is now, and is it accurate and true? Is it about what's actually happening in the present moment or is it an add-on? Is it about the present moment, or the past or future? Does it support or enhance my energy, or deplete my energy? Does this thought serve my well-being, or does it create suffering? When it's clear it does not support our well-being, we can release our attachment to it and choose to let it go.

Method for Freedom with Thoughts

The first step is awareness: we realize when a thought or story has grabbed our attention and is predominant. We observe thinking is happening and *softly note* it as, "Thinking, thinking." We don't note it as "*I'm* thinking," because the personal pronoun keeps us identified with the thought.

The next step is to *intentionally discontinue being carried along in the storyline*. We refrain from continuing to think the thought, and instead purposely move attention to the sensations of the breath. By shifting attention away from the thought and reconnecting with the sensations of the breath, the thought or story is naturally released. The air goes out of the thought bubble and it dissolves. In that moment, we can catch a glimpse of the true nature of thoughts: without attachment, identification, and agreement, they are empty, light, and without substance of their own.

In making the shift in attention from the thought to the breath, incite curiosity about *this* breath with beginner's mind. Remind yourself to take sincere interest by asking, "What's this breath actually like right now?" This question reestablishes full connection with the present moment, and creates a gap while resting in the sensations of the breath before another thought arises.

As you bring attention to the thought that's here now, it may be

Mindful Inquiry: Does This Thought Serve Me or Not?

• Is this thought or story accurate and true?

• Is it about what's happening now, in the past, or in the future?

• Does it support my energy or deplete it?

• Does it support my well-being and lead me in the direction I want to go?

obvious what kind of thought you're thinking. It may be a memory, fantasy, worry, or judgment. The mind may be planning a project, rehearsing an imaginary conversation, solving a problem, or visualizing something you want. You may be caught up in various forms of othering. In this case, you can softly note the kind of thought it is: "Planning...remembering...daydreaming...problem-solving...wanting...othering." If you have to consider what kind of thought you are having, then just note "thinking."

In her book *Real Happiness*, Sharon Salzberg suggests a helpful metaphor for mindfully observing thoughts.[21] Each thought is a visitor knocking on the door of your house. The thought doesn't live in your house, it's just visiting. You can greet the thought at the door, acknowledge it (softly note it), and then let it go. You may also choose to invite the visitor in (if it's a useful thought) and let it stay awhile. In this way of mindfully observing, we can see how one thought leads to the next and to the next. When our thoughts are leading in a direction that's not useful, or likely to cause suffering, we can change course.

Practice

Meditation:
Mindfulness With Thoughts

Please try the following short meditation to bring mindfulness to your thoughts. Set your timer for five minutes.

• Begin by moving into your sitting posture, making sure your body feels stable, aligning your spine, and inviting everything to relax and soften. Focus on the sensations of breathing this breath...letting it be just as it is right now.

• As soon as you notice that a thought is predominant and you've lost connection with the breath, softly note, "Thinking, thinking." Discontinue being carried along in the thought and instead, gently and firmly shift attention to the sensations of the breath.

• Bring lots of curiosity to the actual sensations of the breath. As you bring attention to the breath, observe what happens to the thought. Continue practicing, being attentive to every thought that's predominant, shifting back to the breath each time. If it's immediately obvious what kind of thought it is, experiment with naming the thought exactly, as in, "Planning, remembering, fantasizing, judging, or rehearsing."

What was that practice like for you? Did you notice as soon as you noted "thinking, thinking" and shifted your attention with curiosity to the breath, the thought vanished or dissolved? Isn't that amazing? Did you notice the little space or gap before the next thought arrived? Could you enjoy a moment of resting in the breath, freed from the thought story? Did you feel some relief?

Understand that we are not trying to get rid of thoughts. Thinking is what the mind does. We wouldn't ask the nose to stop smelling, the ears to stop hearing, the eyes to stop seeing, or the body to stop feeling, so we don't ask the mind to stop thinking. The mind with all its thoughts, perceptions, and emotions is the sixth sense door of our direct experience. If we struggle and try to get rid of a thought, we are fighting with our experience. The struggle results in more frustration, creating even more thoughts about the experience. Instead, we are exercising choice about how we relate to the mind's thoughts. We are *choosing* not to dwell in the thought, but to focus attention on the breath instead. We are making an intentional decision. We choose where we want our attention to be, and by choosing to shift to the breath, the thought dissolves on its own.

Please remember the basic and kind principle of nonjudging. Regardless of the content of the thought or the volume of thoughts you're noting as you meditate, practice not judging your experience. It doesn't matter how many thoughts arise as you practice. What does matter is choosing to note and pop out of the thoughts by shifting to the breath, over and over. Each time you do shift, you're strengthening your mindfulness muscles.

After you've had some practice, you can add further clarity and precision to the practice by noting the exact thought story in more detail. For example, when you realize a planning thought is here, instead of noting "planning," you can note, "Planning the _____" (dinner, new work project, garden). Instead of noting "rehearsing," you note, "Rehearsing the_____" (conversation with Dave or the boss). The more detailed noting gives you more information about what's on your mind, while refraining from being carried away by it. Notice whether the expanded noting is helpful to you.

At times, the softly noting method doesn't release attachment and we remain trapped in repetitive or obsessive thoughts. Perhaps you can't stop going over a plan to make sure it's right, or you keep remembering something you said to a friend and regretting it, or you realize you're caught up in trying to figure out the right thing to wear to an important event. You may be aware these are othering thoughts, and still they keep occupying your attention. In these cases, an underlying emotion is most likely connected to the thoughts. Perhaps a feeling of anxiety, fear, sadness, or self-loathing is connected to the stories. You can't release the thought because your system is asking for more skillful, healing attention. Because the story is energized by the underlying emotion, it does not dissipate as easily as thoughts with little emotional energy. We'll explore how to work with these kinds of thoughts and the emotions they create in Chapter 14.

By cultivating awareness of exactly what we are thinking and by recognizing our habits with thoughts, we can bypass a lot of suffering. Renee, a student in a recent class, reported a new experience with her husband during an argument, due to being aware of her exact thoughts. They were having a familiar conflict trying to make plans for the weekend. They each wanted to spend time in different ways, and he especially wanted some time by himself. Because Renee now recognized the mind's habit of spinning stories, she was aware of what her husband was wanting and her mind's fictional interpretations. She realized that she often didn't accept what he said he wanted, but instead believed her mind's stories, which were full of negative assumptions and judgments. Her mind's interpretations of "what he really means" had always been hurtful, and because she believed these interpretations, she often got mad and ended up fighting with him. This time, though, mindful of what was happening in her thoughts and realizing they were all made up, she spotted the stories, let them go, and simply accepted what he wanted. They could make plans with much greater ease and had a fun weekend, together and apart. This was a major insight for her, and she was hopeful about finding more ease in her relationship with her husband.

Developing the ability to choose how we want to relate to thoughts is a powerful skill. We are not trying to stop thinking or control thinking, but rather to not be bothered by thoughts and to choose how we relate and respond to them. Over time (meaning months and years), as your mindfulness skills develop, your whole mind-body-heart system will become more calm, and you'll have more moments of resting in stillness and quiet. The quality of your thoughts will gradually shift to being more kind and gentle. I've noticed over the years I've been practicing that the speed of thoughts moving through my mind has slowed, the volume of judging thoughts has declined significantly, and the accepting and loving thoughts have increased.

Ownwork Suggestions

Formal Sitting Meditation:
Mindfulness of Breath, Sensations, and Thoughts

Decide how long your sit will be, perhaps now stretching the time to 15–20 minutes. Make the amount of time one that's kindly possible for you.

Arrange your body in a comfortable sitting posture, with your spine aligned, feeling upright and stable...and sense your whole self sitting here: body, mind, heart.... Slowly sweep your attention through your body inviting relaxation and softening.... Receive yourself as you are, noticing whatever you are aware of with acceptance and kindness: sounds, sensations, thoughts, smells, tastes, images....Drop attention to the place in the body where it's easiest to directly feel the sensations of breathing.... Anchor your attention there, concentrating on each breath as it occurs, letting it be as it is, relaxing around the sensations....

When a sensation arises that is more predominant than the sensations of this breath, let go of the breath and bring your attention to the sensation. Softly note it: "Pressure, aching, tightness, itching, coolness, or throbbing." Investigate the actual qualities of the sensation exactly as it is with beginner's mind: shape, size, depth, weight, temperature, color, and texture.... Hold it in your awareness with spaciousness, relaxing around it, staying with it as long as it's present.... When attention shifts to something else, bring attention to the sensations of the breath again....

When a thought becomes predominant, pulling you away from the breath (or sensation), softly note, "Thinking, thinking," or name the kind of thought it is (if it's obvious): "Planning, fantasizing, rehearsing, othering, judging." Discontinue being carried along in the storyline and shift attention to the sensations of this breath (releasing attachment to the thought).... Stay with the breath until another thought or sensation is predominant.... Continue practicing this way until your practice time is up.

Notice the effect of this practice.

Informal Practice

• Bring mindfulness to your thoughts: Be aware of when you're othering, worrying, judging, assuming, fantasizing, or making up a story, and practice noting it as "Thinking." Remind yourself that it is only a thought. Ask yourself whether this thought is serving you. Is it accurate and true about what's happening right now? Does it take you in the direction you want to go? If not, move attention to your breath and mindfully breathe for several breaths. Notice this with curiosity and kindness.

• Do ordinary activities mindfully: We can do everything with mindfulness, and when we do, it improves the quality of the experience because we are completely present. We also give our busy thinking mind an opportunity to rest in the present moment. The activity (such as brushing teeth, washing the dishes, hugging your loved ones, chopping carrots, or walking down the hallway) becomes the primary object of attention. Concentrate with beginner's mind on the activity. When attention wanders away into thoughts, note that, and then return your attention to being present with the activity again. Notice the effect.

• Dropping In: Continue to train yourself to pause and bring your attention fully to the sensations of your body breathing many times throughout the day. Especially remember to practice this when you realize othering is happening. Notice the effect.

13

The Wanting Mind and the Four Noble Truths

*At the base of
the conditioned mind
is a wanting.*

Stephen Levine

I Want What I Want, But What Do I Really Want?

If we look more deeply into our experience, we see that most thoughts are based on either wanting or not wanting something. This is a universal human condition. Wants and desires lead us in all directions: to nourishment, creativity, fulfillment and freedom, and also to destruction and the deepest suffering. Thich Nhat Hanh, a Vietnamese Buddhist monk and wonderful teacher of engaged Buddhism, suggests that both our original desire and original fear are born at our moment of birth and very first breath.[22] He says when we're in our mother's womb, all of our needs are met and we are very content. She breathes and eats for us, and we are warm and safe, completely dependent on her body. The shock of birth, bright lights, loud sounds, unfamiliar cold and motion, creates our first experience of fear. Instantly, we have to take our first breath or else we'll die. Thus our first desire, the desire to survive, is born. So from the very beginning of our birthed life, desire and fear are linked inseparably, and perhaps all our subsequent desires and fears stem from this experience.

Desire, or wanting, and the fear of not getting what we want, are natural impulses and give energy to our life. Desire is the juice of life. It not only keeps us alive, it's what gets us get out of bed in the morning, curious about a new day. Wanting is both natural and a conditioned urge in the mind. Ironically, if we look closely, we realize wanting can never be completely satisfied. When one desire is satisfied another one appears. Sometimes what we think we want turns out not to be what we want. In addition, our wants, like everything else in nature, are always changing. Being human, living in these physical bodies, having these amazing minds and hearts, we continually want and need so many things. Remember Maslow's hierarchy of needs? It always made a lot of sense to me. We have basic needs for food, water, shelter, and safety that must be met in order to survive. We want to feel secure, and have comfort and ease. Beyond these basics, we are also motivated to fulfill other needs such as love, connection, self-respect, and ways we can give, help and contribute. We also want to be authentic, whole, and fully ourselves. Yet the force

Checking in

• So how is it going paying mindful attention to your thoughts? Are you noticing the amazing stories the mind spins? Have you been able to exercise some choice and freedom with them?

• Have you observed that sometimes when meditating a great idea comes to you, such as plans for a new project, but you're reluctant to stop thinking about it because you're afraid you'll forget it? When this happens, just note it as a great idea, bravely choose to let it go, and trust it will occur to you again later. This is another practice at exercising kind discipline.

• How's your sitting practice going? Please do the best you can to sit some every day. The hardest part is actually getting to the cushion. The best advice I've discovered on this common problem is to make the agreement with yourself to put your body in the sitting posture once before the day ends. That's all. Once there, it's easy to shift to the breath and begin practicing, even if it's for only a few minutes.

• What was it like to do ordinary activities mindfully? Please do experiment with this because it can make a humdrum task, such as washing the dishes, interesting and even enjoyable.

of wanting often obscures what's happening in the present. We can get completely lost in planning, trying to secure what we want. When we're caught in worry we're absorbed in fears about what we don't want.

Othering is deeply tied to wanting. We want a lot from others. We want the other to be how we want them to be. We want them to be happy, and to respond to us in just the ways we imagine. We want them to love, accept, and approve of us, and ideally think we are perfect. We want ourselves to be our version of the perfect me. Fundamentally, we want things to be the way we want them to be, all the time. We can feel pretty unhappy — grumpy, miserable, sad, disappointed, mad, scared, despairing — when we don't have what we want.

Othering is deeply tied to wanting.

What creates the real trouble for us, however, is that the mind habitually attaches to what we want. The problem isn't wanting or desire per se — it's *how we relate* to what we want that makes all the difference. Our conditioned habit is to grasp, cling, and grip onto what we want, sometimes so intensely it feels like we'll die if we don't get it. Our culture, entrenched in consumerism, exploits the wanting mind, encouraging us to want more and more. I remember a cartoon where a dashing looking woman is carrying a shopping bag full of purchases, and the caption read, "I shop. Therefore, I am." We develop specific wants for clothes, cars, better furniture, better appliances, newer cell phones, vacations, special foods. We want better and more perfect bodies that show no signs of aging; we want the perfect marriage, kids, job, friends and on and on. The more intensely we are attached to what we want, the more we experience agitation and restlessness in the mind and body. Because desire is creative energy that spurs us constantly toward something to get, have, or be we aren't peaceful or calm when we're in a state of wanting. Instead, we feel unsettled, even off balance, energetically leaning forward, unconsciously reaching for what we want.

A television advertisement I saw for a new car powerfully depicted how wanting consumes us and obscures our present moment. The first clip shows a dad around the dinner table with his family, eating, talking, and having a good time. He is engaged in the conversation, and there's a tiny car stuck to his forehead. Nobody else apparently sees the car. In the next scene, it's the same situation at the dinner table, but the car on his head is slightly bigger, and he's more withdrawn from the conversation. The successive scenes show the car getting bigger and bigger and he interacts less and less with his family. Finally, the car on his head is gigantic. He is thinking only about the car he wants, oblivious to anything else. In the closing scene, he's at the dealership happily buying the car he wanted. The car on his forehead is now gone. This is how it is with wanting. We become so preoccupied with what we want that we really aren't here at all. Familiar?

> Wanting consumes us and obscures our present moment.

We Don't Know What We Want

As women, gender conditioning warps our relationship to our needs and wants. Because we're so focused on the other, we typically know more about what they want and need than we know about ourselves. The habit of disconnecting from authentic experience as we focus on the other blocks our access to vital information about ourselves. Consequently, many of us don't have a clue about what we really want. Psychologists studying girls' development say this pattern consistently shows up around the age of puberty.[23] At this age, when asked "What do you want?", girls react with, "I don't know. What do *you* want?" We turn the question back on the other person because we've stopped asking ourselves. It's become more

> Gender conditioning warps our relationship to our needs and wants.

important to find out what the other wants. We may also feel anxious when we consider what we want.

I had a "light bulb moment" in my early thirties, standing in my kitchen when my husband and friend were both asking me in a pressing way, "Mare, what do *you* want?" It felt as though they were energetically pointing their fingers at me, demanding to know what I wanted. Although I don't recall what prompted their question, I do remember realizing I had no idea what I truly wanted, about anything. My standard operating mode was to find out what the other person wanted first, and then I'd figure out what I wanted. On my own, separate from anyone else, I never really knew or inquired. I was stunned to recognize that I couldn't answer the question of what I wanted.

Besides not knowing what I wanted, except in response to others, I felt unknown to myself in other essential ways. I made a deal with myself to investigate. I decided to ask myself whenever I possibly could: "What do *I* want? What do *I* need?" Because asking these questions provoked anxiety, I kept my discoveries private at first. I began asking the questions numerous times a day over a period of months, about all kinds of things, big and little. As I did, I learned a lot about my desires, values, and opinions. I also realized my basic motivation for not knowing was safety. It was safer to not know what I wanted. Because we're in the subordinate position in society, conflict is scary. We're trained to avoid conflict. If I knew and expressed what I wanted and it was different from what the other person wanted, we would be in conflict. I assumed we'd fight and I'd lose. Still, I knew I needed to learn about what was true for me, so I pushed forward slowly.

Ask, But Don't Tell

Asking and discovering what I wanted built connection with myself. It was empowering to be more knowledgeable about my own desires and opinions, whatever they were in the present. Directly expressing what I wanted required a big leap into the unknown. As women we're taught to drop hints rather than state what we want clearly and specifically. Fear that we'll be ridiculed, criticized as selfish, shamed or rejected keeps us silent. I remember a moment in my childhood when my father told me if I asked for what I wanted directly, then I definitely wouldn't get it. I was perplexed by his message, as it seemed backwards. I'm sure he was reacting from his own unexamined conditioning, perhaps afraid I'd become brash or greedy, not demure or "ladylike." Thus I learned to subtly imply, suggest, or simply stare at things I wanted in the hopes someone would notice and remember. As I recognized all this oppressive conditioning I gradually began to express what I wanted more directly.

What's true for you? What happens when you realize there is something you really want, especially when what you want affects another person in some way? You might pause for a moment and just notice your habitual reactions. When I ask this question in class women commonly say:

• *I assume I won't get it. I stuff it. I repackage it so the other person will hopefully say "Yes." I scale it back so I'm less likely to be disappointed.*

• *I second-guess myself: why do I want this? I feel shame and think I'm selfish and shouldn't have a need.*

• *I immediately feel tightness and anxiety. I feel vulnerable. My throat tightens and my heart races.*

• *This is the biggest issue in my life. I'm scared to ask and I assume I shouldn't have it because I asked for it. I have to earn it. I apologize for wanting it.*

• *I feel angry and defensive. I try to manipulate the situation so the other doesn't realize I want it.*

• *I get it for myself and then feel guilty. I feel selfish and self-centered. I try to talk myself out of it.*

• *I only know what I want when I'm alone. As soon as someone else arrives I disappear. It's automatic and I don't even notice I'm gone.*

It's Self-Responsible to Know What We Want

Contrary to what we've been taught, it's not selfish but rather self-responsible to know what we want. I used to believe that if my spouse really loved me, then he'd know what I wanted. I thought this was a sign of deep and true love. However, that kind of wishful thinking leads to disappointment because none of us are mind readers. Not knowing what we want or being afraid to express it when we do know causes enormous suffering. Suppressing our desires doesn't make us happy or our relationships easier. Discovering what we want is part of knowing ourselves. It's essential for cultivating our inner authority and authenticity.

> Discovering what we want is essential for cultivating our inner authority and authenticity.

Being blind to our wants and needs doesn't make them go away. We still have them — they are part of being human. When we aren't aware of them, we often say "Yes" when we really mean "No," and vice versa. Have you ever found yourself doing something you've said yes to and then realize you're feeling grumpy, resentful, and wish you weren't doing it after all? Chances are you've bumped into a "No" you didn't know you had.

Further, we have to know what we want before we can discern if it's wise to want it, or even possible to have it. We might yearn for events that may never happen, or want things we can have only once in a great while, or achieve things that only last for a short time. Sometimes we're so attached to wanting something, we're miserable because we don't have it now. What's happening in the present isn't good enough for us. We think, "If only I had the right partner. If only my spouse would finally change. If only I had more money. If only my boss would understand me. If only I'd lose more weight. If only the weekend were here." We assume when the "if only" finally arrives, then we'll be happy, at last. Only by knowing what we want can we distinguish how we're relating to it right now. Do I want it so badly I'm rejecting what's happening now? Am I holding onto what I want because I think it is the only thing that will make me happy? Bringing the wise light of awareness to observe what we want and our relationship to it can relieve a lot of suffering.

Judy, a client and mindfulness student in her late thirties, grew up in a family beset by chaos and misery, caused by her parents fighting much of the time. To cope with the stress as a child, her mind developed an effective strategy of distracting and soothing herself through daydreams. In her daydream, everything was how she wanted it to be, and all her desires were completely met. As she grew older, daydreams became the default reaction to stress or discomfort. Every time she felt upset, her mind shifted her into her perfect fantasy, where everything was just how she wanted it to be. In her adult daydream she enjoyed a wonderful career and plentiful income, a loving partner, a house, dog, children — the perfect life. Unfortunately, in her actual life things weren't going so well. Her job wasn't great, she wasn't making enough money to buy a house, and prospective partners paled compared to her ideal imaginary guy. She felt increasingly angry and disappointed, believing life was unfair because she wasn't getting what she wanted.

Through mindfulness practice, Judy began to recognize her attachment to these desires, the tenacity of the pattern, and how pervasively it was affecting her. She came to realize this neural groove, though temporarily soothing, was actually creating misery and limitations in her real life. Understanding that her attachment to the "perfect life" was unrealistic, she began to reexamine her wants, update and shift them to more realistic goals. With intentional practice to spot the pattern of escape, mindfully shifting to her breath and to what was true in the moment, she gradually began to discover real satisfaction and happiness in being herself, living her real life.

The Wisdom of the Four Noble Truths

The teachings called the Four Noble Truths help clarify our understanding of the wanting mind, as well as provide a philosophical framework for the entire practice of mindfulness. These are the first teachings the Buddha gave after experiencing enlightenment, and they address the root issues and challenges of daily living. They point directly to how the mind creates our suffering and how we can transform it to find true freedom and happiness. I felt such relief when I first heard these teachings. They validated my experience and inspired me to explore my mind and inner life more deeply.

First Noble Truth

The *First Noble Truth* essentially says that even though life is amazing, wonderful, and precious, it also involves suffering. There's a basic unsatisfactoriness to life, a kind of uneasiness. The Pali word for this is *dukkha*. No one escapes dukkha. No matter how perfect someone's life appears on the outside, every single being, without exception, experiences suffering. We can see the reality of suffering in all dimensions and aspects of life. On a global scale, our world suffers from the terrible violence and destruction of wars, homelessness, poverty and starvation, global warming, and all kinds of distress, injustice, chaos, tragedy, and loss. On the individual level, we all struggle to make our lives "successful." We want to be happy, and yet we cling to hopes and fears. We want security though it seems impossible to find it. We strongly prefer pleasure and comfort over pain and discomfort, so we strive to make our lives satisfying and under our control.

Moreover, we want our happiness, satisfaction, and security to be ever-lasting, permanent in fact. Perhaps the desire for permanence is a basic primal desire, possibly rooted in the safety and contentment we felt in our mother's womb. The problem is that permanence is impossible to achieve. Impermanence is a basic law of nature. As we know, everything exists in a process of change. From the tiniest subatomic particle to the most spectacular mountains in the world, from the oldest government institution to a fledgling new mom's group, impermanence is continuously at work. Change is constant. We see this truth easily in the changing weather and seasons, as well as in the seasons of our bodies. They are growing, aging, getting ill, injured, recovering, and eventually will die. Relationships too are continuously changing, and eventually every relationship we have will come to an end. Nothing in this earthly realm is permanent, ultimately stable or secure. We don't like impermanence. We want predictability and control. We want to know what's going to happen so we can be ready for it. We don't like the unknown. We want guarantees that we will be okay.

Though the teachings say life is full of both 10,000 joys and 10,000 sorrows, the Buddha taught there are actually just four unavoidable realities in being human that cause pain and potential suffering. These are the pain and potential suffering of being born (we've done that one), of being ill, of aging, and of dying. All the other ways we suffer are due to the habits of conditioning and our misunderstanding of the way things really are — our inability to perceive reality clearly. I find this observation encouraging and optimistic. The more we understand how to work with our minds and hearts to become free from conditioning, to perceive reality accurately and tap into our true nature blue sky mind, the less we will suffer. Even with the "unavoidables" we can learn to work with pain, distress, and loss more skillfully so we're less caught in suffering when those difficulties arise.

At a retreat with Pema Chödrön, she explained that the western mind takes it personally that everything is changing and unstable. This misunderstanding amplifies our suffering. Because we don't really accept impermanence, we assume it's a personal failure that we can't get everything under control and keep our life in order. We strive to make life predictable and secure. When it all shifts or even falls apart, we blame ourselves. Until we accept reality as it is, always changing, we may spend our whole life trying ever harder to get things just right, and thinking something is wrong with us because we can't. Can you relate to these thoughts? I remember a very clear moment on a June morning some years ago thinking, "Okay. Now everything is just the way I want it to be. All the pieces are in the right place. I have everything so together!" The next morning, something major changed, and I realized I had forgotten impermanence. I laughed out loud at my silliness in thinking everything would now stay just how I wanted it to be. This is dukkha, the fundamental uneasiness of our worldly existence.

Second Noble Truth

The *Second Noble Truth* says the root cause of all of our suffering is craving and attachment. Clinging to our desires. We grasp and hold onto what we want, what we yearn for, and we resist what is actually happening in the present moment when it isn't what we want. We tend to think, "I *must* have this object or state in order to be safe, successful, or happy." We believe this without question, and keep our attention riveted on what we think will make us happy, permanently. When we do get what we want, we're afraid we'll lose it so we keep clinging to it so we will always have it. Ultimately, we're looking for permanent relief from dukkha.

Because of this misunderstanding, we try to find happiness in external conditions we believe will give us lasting satisfaction and pleasure. We think, "When I get a different job, then I'll be stress free. When we remodel the kitchen, we'll have happy, family meals together. When my knee stops hurting, then I'll be able to run again and I'll be happy. When my family (child, boss, spouse, friend — other) finally appreciates me, then I'll be happy." We completely forget that happiness is only experienced in the present moment. Now.

A client, Sara, a wonderful woman and dedicated high school teacher, suffers terribly because she is convinced she can't be happy until she finds a partner. Although she's been in several important relationships, none of them have worked out long-term. She is now in her fifties and believes the possibility of finding someone and finally being happy is rapidly diminishing. She feels lonely, hopeless, and depressed about her prospects. Yet, she cannot see that by being so attached to finding someone, and believing someone else is the only thing that will make her happy, she creates misery for herself right now. She focuses on what she doesn't have, misses the sweet things that are happening in her life, and suffers deeply.

We also create suffering by clinging to our views and opinions. We develop very fixed ideas and beliefs about just how things should be. We have judgments about everything. We approve of this and don't approve of that. Essentially, as my father put it many times, our basic assumption is, "*My* view is the right view." In its extreme form, attachment to our view is fundamentalism: the belief that my way of thinking, believing, perceiving, and behaving is the only right way. We see the tragic effect of this conditioned attachment in the violence in our communities, politics, and wars all over our poor aching world.

> Attachment to self is said to be the root of all suffering.

The Buddha taught, however, that at the root of attachment to view and to external conditions is attachment to the idea of self. Attachment to self is said to be the root of all suffering. The conditioned mind takes everything personally, believing there is a permanent "Me" that must be promoted, defended, and protected. This sense of self evolves from conditioning as we unconsciously attach to beliefs and ideas about how we're supposed to be, not supposed to be, and what's supposed to happened to us. As we've been discussing, women's subordinate position in society naturally trains our minds to believe the self we are is less important and worthy. For many of us, our sense of self is distorted and wounded, and we grow up with deep beliefs that we aren't okay.

Further, because the mind is constantly spinning stories, mostly repetitious variations of the conditioned views our mind holds of ourselves, we labor under the illusion that we are unchanging. This illusion also promotes the sense that we living in our own little world, completely separate from others. The Second Noble Truth encourages us to see beyond this distortion to recognize we are all connected and interdependent, and to realize our actual direct experience of ourselves, like everything else, is fluid and impermanent. To release our attachment to a wounded fixed separate self and become less identified with the story of "Me," we need to remember our basic goodness and true nature, and through practice develop a healthy sense of ourselves that is trusting, accepting, and respectful.

Third Noble Truth

The *Third Noble Truth* says there is a remedy to suffering. We can free ourselves by learning to let go of whatever we are clinging to that isn't happening, and instead accept what is actually happening in the moment. This truth is so simple and so profound. As one student said, "Really, it's let go or get dragged." When we recognize everything is changing and impermanent, including the experience of ourselves, and

> We must be attentive to how we relate to our goals and desires, holding them with clear intention yet without clinging.

when we cling we suffer, we realize it's only sane and wise to loosen our grip on whatever we're holding on to, accept the truth of the moment and live in harmony with the way things actually are. This doesn't mean we can't work for change within ourselves or in the world. Rather, we must be attentive to how we relate to our goals and desires, holding them with clear intention yet without clinging. This realization is what actually creates peace and stability within ourselves, and brings our highest and sustainable happiness.

Fourth Noble Truth

The *Fourth Noble Truth* is called the Eightfold Noble Path. Also called the Middle Path, it describes eight aspects of living in harmony with the way things actually are. It emphasizes cultivating wise understanding, wise intention, wise livelihood, wise speech, wise action, wise effort, wise concentration, and wise mindfulness. Although all the aspects are interrelated and cultivated together, mindfulness is fundamental. If we don't realize when we are suffering, then we can't change our relationship to it and have no way of finding our way free.

What's so radical about these teachings, at least to the western mind, is they assert that in order to find freedom from suffering we must first recognize it, and then move mindfully into the direct experience of it. By exploring the difficult experience skillfully, we can discover what we're wanting, realize how we're relating to it, see our habits and misunderstandings clearly, which then allows us access the wisdom to release our grip. This seems to be the opposite of what our culture teaches. We're taught mostly to get away from stress and suffering as soon as we can. We habitually and automatically distract ourselves from it. We numb out by having a drink, buying something, eating something, or doing whatever we can do to get away from what's uncomfortable. Certainly, we are not taught to move closer to it, right?

The Four Noble Truths

1. There is suffering in life: dukkha.

2. There is a cause to this: clinging to our desires:

3. There is a way out of suffering: let go of clinging.

4. There is a way: The Eightfold Noble Path.

The Four Noble Truths encourage us to recognize suffering, accept it, open to it, get to know it really well, and stay steady with it. When we do, we access our wisdom and find our way through it. The only way out is through. The obstacle is the path. Transformation then occurs organically, naturally. Clearly opening to suffering takes courage. Yet we're developing our courage each time we practice. We're being brave every time we open to our authentic experience with curiosity, kindness and acceptance,

The only way out is through.

The obstacle is the path.

not knowing what the next moment will bring. We are learning to stay with ourselves, and through that staying we discover our wisdom, which deepens our trust in ourselves.

Working Mindfully With the Wanting Mind

To apply the lessons from the Four Noble Truths, the first step is to become aware of our wants. Only by knowing what we desire can we discern how we're relating to it, which then allows us to respond wisely. As we've been discussing, knowing what we want isn't always easy. Othering has trained us to know what others want, not what we want. So to learn this crucial information about ourselves we may have to prime the pump.

Consciously knowing what we want is self-responsible.

I encourage you to begin asking yourself directly as I did, "What do *I* want? What do *I* need?" Ask these questions as often and in as many situations as you can. Notice whatever you discover without judging or discounting it. Remember, to consciously know what we want is to know ourselves better. It is *self-responsible*, not selfish. It is being authentic, and gives us essential information to bring to our lives and relationships. It's not uncommon, though, to have no answer when you first begin to ask the questions. It may be years since you've been honestly interested in discovering what you want. You may have many conditioned fears about it. Please be kind and patient with yourself, and keep asking with lots of tenderness and curiosity for whatever emerges.

As you sincerely open to discovering your desires, be on the lookout for conditioned reactions. They will surely come up, and it's helpful to acknowledge them so you can respond wisely. For example, your mind might decree you are selfish for wanting to know yourself, or it might criticize what you want, leading you to feel guilty or anxious. Practice noticing these reactions with curiosity and gentleness. Keep

209

reminding yourself these are conditioned reactions, *not the truth*, and not wise or beneficial. Each time we can be aware of habitual reactions and respond skillfully, the oppressive neural grooves diminish a little.

Beyond the initial inquiry, the basic practice is to softly note wanting, desiring, or longing when we're aware of something we want. This includes noting "not wanting" as well. In fact, sometimes we're more aware of what we don't want than what we do want. When that's true, we may discover what we actually want by asking, "I don't want this, but what do I want instead?" It's powerfully helpful to delete the personal pronoun "I," and simply note "wanting." This naturally gives some space to release identifying. Softly noting with a neutral and kind voice, also gives rise to acceptance. Rather than judgment, we're accepting the truth about ourselves in this moment.

The second step is to inquire more deeply by asking questions such as, is what I want achievable right now? If not now, when? What control do I have over it? Is it wise and beneficial to want this? As you make this assessment, please do it with kindness and understanding towards yourself.

After you discover what you want and assess its plausibility and wisdom, notice how you are *relating* to it. Are you clinging to it for dear life, gripping and clutching on to it, feeling you must have it or else? Or can you be aware of wanting it without your knuckles turning white? Can you hold it in your awareness with some room around it by relaxing your grip? Even if what you want is indispensable, it helps to invite yourself to loosen your grip on it. Desperation is suffering.

If you discover what you want is healthy, in your best interest, and achievable right now, then respect your desire and if possible give it to yourself. If what you want involves someone else, then do your best to muster up your courage and express it as clearly and directly as you can. Stay connected to yourself as you state your desire and allow yourself to experience your desire fully, being mindful of all your thoughts, feelings, and reactions. Remember, you are being self-responsible, not selfish.

If what you want isn't possible now, or doesn't serve you, then bow to your desire, and encourage yourself to let it go. Kindly invite yourself to soften, relax, and release your grip. If you've been attached to the object of your desire a while, you may have to repeat the releasing steps a number of times. Stay with yourself completely through the letting-go process, being fully aware of all your thoughts feelings and reactions. Please practice not judging anything you experience.

Relating to Wants Mindfully:

• When aware of a desire or want: Softly note, "Wanting."

• Inquire: Is this achievable right now? If not now, when? Is it under my control? Is it wise and beneficial to want this?

• How am my relating to this? Clinging, gripping, clutching? Can I relax my grip and hold it spaciously?

• If having this is beneficial and possible, give it to yourself. If it's not possible or in your best interest to want this, encourage yourself to loosen your grip and let it go.

Looking More Deeply Into Desire

Examining our wants mindfully to see if they really serve us can save us a lot of suffering. Some years ago, after a difficult challenge in my relationship with my partner, I headed off to a week-long meditation retreat at IMS. Although still feeling a little shaken, I felt encouraged when Pam sent me off with a packet of eight notes tied together by a pink ribbon, with the instruction to open one each day on retreat. I was touched and encouraged, thinking, "Oh goody. A love note for each day."

Deciding I'd open one each morning after breakfast so I'd have a little love message to carry with me through the day, I eagerly opened the first one. I read it and thought, "Hmm. That's nice", set it on my windowsill and went off to my yogi job. The next morning, I opened the next note and thought, "That's sweet", and again went off to my job. The third morning, as I opened the next one with noticeably with less anticipation, I read it, and again thought, "Hmm. Yes. Nice."

As I was about to go off to my yogi job I paused and noticed I hadn't had much reaction to these little notes so far. Curious, I took several mindful breaths and then asked myself, "What am I actually experiencing right now?" It took a few moments for the feeling of disappointment to rise to my awareness. Yes, each morning I'd been eager to read Pam's note, and yet each morning without being aware of it I brushed the feeling of disappointment away and distracted myself with my yogi job. Accepting this, I asked myself, "Well, what had I really been hoping for? What was I wanting in those notes?" The answer bounded up quickly. I wanted them to be passionate love notes, affirming her great and boundless love for me. Instead they were offerings of kindness, like, "May your day be peaceful." Or, "Remember to see the blue sky". I realized because I'd been so attached to wanting them to be fervent and adoring, I'd shrugged off the kindness and couldn't receive what she was offering.

Now clear of the difference between my desire and the reality of what was given, I asked myself if I could cradle my disappointment, accept my desire, and loosen my grip on it? Could I then accept and receive what was actually being given with an open heart? Thankfully, I was able to accept what was actually true, and release the attachment. On the remaining days I enjoyed the kindness of these notes, and didn't make myself wrong for what I had wanted, or make my partner bad for not fulfilling my desire.

Because desire drives our experience, creating our thoughts, emotions, words, and actions, it's really helpful to discover our deepest wants and needs. Often, without awareness we are drawn into wanting a particular person or event to be a certain way. We get caught up in trying to control the surface details, and miss the deeper desire that's fueling it. When the event or response doesn't turn out the way we want, we can feel disproportionately frustrated or disappointed. To understand our reaction, it's often helpful to discover the root desire that's fueling it. I encourage you to try this experiment to explore a want mindfully to find the root of your desire. Through this inquiry, which is like peeling an onion, when we get to the core desire we may realize there could be many ways to meet that particular need, besides the one we were banking on.

Practice

Meditation: Exploring a Want

• First, settle into your sitting posture and connect with the sensations of breathing. Let your whole mind-body system relax a bit and drop into a calmer, quieter space.... Now, think of something you really want in your life right now: something that's important and matters to you. Let your imagining of this flow: notice the story, the images, all the thoughts, emotions, and sensations that arise as you imagine what you want.... Now imagine actually getting what you want. Imagine this as vividly as you possibly can.... Imagine what it feels like to really have this. Notice what it sounds like, looks like, feels like, and what your life is like now that you finally have this....

• Now, staying with the imagining of having exactly what you want, ask yourself, "What does having this give me? What need is met by having this?"....Open to whatever occurs to you, and experience what it's like with this need being met, for several minutes.... Now ask yourself, "With this need met, what does that give me?".... Open to whatever comes, and rest with that need being met for a few minutes....

• Now ask again, "With this need met, what does that satisfy or give me?".... Open to whatever arises.... Keep inquiring in this way, going deeper underneath each need until you sense that you've come to the root need or desire... Experience this being fully met for a few minutes.... Return to your breath for a few minutes.

What was that like for you? Were you surprised at what you discovered? Often in the exploration, I discover that my surface want — the specific thing I'm most attached to having be the way I want it to be, such as a successful dinner party, a relaxing vacation, a strong and healthy body, publishing this book — has ultimately to do with a truly basic and core need. I realize I can meet the need in many ways, not just the one way I'd pinning my hopes on. I find desires like feeling connected and loving, being safe and stable within myself, or wanting inner peace are often at the root of many wants. This discovery can be freeing and help us relax with how things are working out (or not) in the moment. It helps us be more flexible and cling less rigidly to the more superficial aspects of life.

Ownwork Suggestions

Formal Sitting Meditation:
Mindfulness of Breath, Sensations, and Thoughts, and Wanting

Decide how long your sit will be and set your timer. Arrange your body in a comfortable, stable posture, with your spine aligned.... Open to yourself just as you are with kindness, curiosity, and acceptance.... Slowly sweep your attention through your body inviting relaxing and softening....Drop attention down into your body, and concentrate on the sensations of breathing this breath.... Open to each breath as it occurs with fresh attention.... Letting the breath be as it is....

When you realize some other sensation is more predominant than the breath, shift your attention to this sensation: softly note it, "Aching, or pressure, or tingling." Note the feeling tone: neutral, pleasant, unpleasant.... Now investigate the actual qualities of the sensation just as it is right now.... Let it be just as it is.... Stay with it until it's no longer predominant, and return attention to the sensations of breathing....When a thought/story is predominant, softly note "Thinking," or name the kind of thought: "Planning, remembering, judging, rehearsing, wanting." Instead of continuing to think the thought, shift to the sensation of the breath, letting the thought story go....

When you feel settled in yourself after some minutes of practicing, intentionally ask yourself, "What do I want? What do I need?" Open to whatever comes into your awareness.... Ask the question again and open to whatever arises.... Repeat this a number of times, discovering whatever emerges without judgment.... Stay open and accepting of whatever you notice....

Return attention to the sensations of the breath and to being mindfully aware of other sensations and thoughts until your practice period is complete. Notice the effect of this practice.

Informal Practice

• Ask yourself repeatedly throughout the day, "*What do I want? What do I need?*" Notice whatever occurs to you without judgment, and with lots of curiosity and appreciation. You are getting to know yourself better.

• Experiment with directly meeting your wants and needs, and be receptive to your reactions. Remind yourself this is self-responsible. This is not selfish.

• Dropping In: Return your attention to your breath many times throughout the day, and notice yourself with kindness and curiosity, just as you are in the present moment.

14

The Wisdom of
Our Messy Emotions

You calm your feeling
just by being with it,
like a mother tenderly holding her crying baby.
The mother is your mindfulness...

Thich Nhat Hanh

We Are Emotional Beings

We humans are fundamentally emotional creatures. We can be swept away into passionate states of joy and delight, or plunged into deep sorrow or fear. We can be hijacked by resentment, anxiety, shame, guilt or depression. We like our happy and pleasant feelings, but dread the painful ones. Painful emotions can leave us feeling vulnerable, shaky, raw, and unsafe. Because most of us haven't been taught how to relate to our emotions skillfully, we can react in ways that create further suffering. When we're caught in a painful emotion, our reaction to it is the problem, not the emotion itself. By learning to explore our emotional landscape mindfully, we can bring greater depth, vibrancy, healing and freedom to our lives.

When we're caught in a painful emotion, our reaction to it is the problem, not the emotion itself.

Wanting Generates Emotions

Emotions are a natural part of our experience and arise directly from our desires. Whenever we want something emotions quickly follow. When we're not calm, content, or happy, it's because a want or desire has been activated somewhere in our mind-body-heart system. It may be something as simple as starting to feel hungry for lunch, the sense of boredom arising, or an undercurrent of longing for connection with another. As we imagine getting what we want, we might feel hope, eagerness, or anticipation. Even if we aren't consciously aware of having a want, it still drives our energy, thoughts, emotions, and our actions. Gender conditioning also trains us to believe we shouldn't have wants, don't deserve what we want, and to fear it will create conflict. So wanting may easily provoke guilt, shame or anxiety. Emotions also emerge when we don't get what we want, when our feelings get hurt, when our safety and security feels threatened, or when something pokes old emotional wounds.

Checking in

• What has it been like to ask yourself, "What do I want? What do I need?" Hard or easy? Any guilt or anxiety coming up in response? Remember these are just conditioned reactions and it's essential to spot them. Have you been surprised by what you're learning about yourself?

• How about when you gave yourself something you wanted? What did you experience? Uncomfortable reactions, a sense of relief, some satisfaction, or a feeling of empowering yourself?

• Please keep asking yourself what you want and need. This helps us learn so much more about ourselves and reminds us to pay attention with self-respect.

• How is your sitting practice? Please try to sit even a little bit every day. When you can't, be kind rather than harsh with yourself, and renew your intention to sit tomorrow.

• Keep practicing Dropping In to your breath as often as you can throughout the day. This is a stable and concrete way to build connection with your authentic experience.

When we do get what we want, satisfaction is usually short-lived though, because conditions change, and new wants show up. For example, a client who often suffers from anxiety and depression, said she was encouraged about her relationship with herself because she was finally being able to spot her mind's habit of nasty self-criticism. She also realized that she simultaneously raised her bar so that just being aware of self-criticism is not good enough; now she expects herself to stop the criticism altogether. This expectation leaves her dissatisfied and still trapped in judgment. Have you seen this in yourself? It's a common pattern for us. Because we're often so attached to perfection, when we keep adjusting its definition we set ourselves up to feel chronically dissatisfied.

What Are Emotions, Anyway?

As reflections of fulfilled or thwarted desire, emotions offer vitally important information about us. When our wants and needs are satisfied we feel the lovely, preferred, "positive" emotions: we are happy, calm, grateful, at ease or content. When we're feeling upset, they are like a stop sign that says, "Hold it. Something is going on that matters. I'm not getting what I want. Pay attention." These emotions point to where we may be grasping and clinging to some desire, or where we have wounds that are asking for healing presence. They point to where we may need to give ourselves compassion, kindness and love. They point to where we may need to bring discerning wisdom to see through false conditioned beliefs or unmet desires that need to be released.

Emotions offer vitally important information about us.

As part of the sense door of the mind, emotions are created by our thoughts, perceptions, and beliefs. Though in the moment we're swept up in an emotion we may not be consciously aware of those thoughts. Basically, we experience an emotion whenever the mind creates a story that is dramatic enough or sufficiently energetic to create a corresponding sensation in the body. We call emotions "feelings" because they create sensations in the body. We feel them. Eckart Tolle calls emotions "the body's reaction to the mind."[24] For example, when the mind creates a story that's intense enough to generate butterflies in our stomach, we call it "anxiety." When the story is scary enough to make our heart beat rapidly and our bloodstream flood with adrenaline, we call it "fear." When the mind creates a story gloomy enough to make our heart and chest feel heavy, we call it "sadness."

Emotions are created by our thoughts, perceptions, and beliefs.

As internal experiences, emotions are different from purely physical sensations or the mental formations of thoughts. They are more amorphous. They lack the clear boundaries, or distinct beginnings and endings that thoughts have. Emotions aren't as tangible as simple body sensations, nor are they as clear and light as thoughts. Although some emotions, such as anger and fear, can erupt quickly, others roll in more slowly like a cloudbank quietly shifting our internal weather. It may take a while to realize, "Oh, I'm feeling kind of grumpy and irritable today."

Emotions often occur in clusters or layers. I may be aware of feeling angry, but as I explore the emotion mindfully I may realize that within the anger is hurt, sadness, or disappointment. I might be aware of feeling guilt, but as I pay attention to it, I may realize that along with the guilt is anger, fear, and loneliness. Nearly any combination of emotions can be connected to each other and happening at once. This is part of what makes emotions especially challenging to work with skillfully.

Like every other experience we have, emotions are impermanent. They arise when the right conditions come together, and pass away when those conditions change. Emotions are our inner weather, transient conditions that affect our experience temporarily, but don't alter our essence. Sometimes, our emotional weather can be so intense that we forget that our stable true nature, like the blue sky, is always beyond the thick clouds or the dark scary storm. In her book, *My Stroke of Insight*, Jill Bolte Taylor points to evidence that the natural lifespan of any particular emotion

221

is only 90 seconds.[25] Because our habit is to get lost in the story, which feeds the unpleasant sensations, we're often swept up in the emotion for much longer. We sometimes fear an emotion will last forever, which ironically only serves to keep it going.

Science Validates the Importance of Emotions

Emotions have a deeper impact on the body beyond the present moment sensations they create. They affect our physical health. We know that neuroscience has firmly established the validity of the mind-body connection. Neuroscientist Candace Pert, an internationally recognized scientist, is credited for discovering that small protein-like molecules, called neuropeptides, are the intercelular messengers that connect our thoughts and emotions to our nervous, endocrine, and immune systems.[26] Her breakthrough work began the field of psychoneuroimmunology, or mind-body medicine. The existence of neuropeptides proves that what we think and the emotion those thoughts create directly affect our health. These molecules relay our thoughts and feelings to our bodily systems, where they affect our energy level, body weight, pain and pleasure reception, memory, problem solving, mood, and immune response. It is clear that what we think and feel can make us well or ill.

> What we think and feel can make us well or ill.

Our Conditioned Reactions to Emotions

Emotions are born from both our desires and the intensity of our attachment to them. Some of our wants are superficial and our attachment is minimal. Perhaps you had plans to go on a walk with a friend and they cancelled because their child was sick. You might be slightly disappointed, but it's not a big deal. Yet, we may be deeply attached to other desires. For example, perhaps you've had a long day at work and as you drive home you imagine having dinner and spending an enjoyable evening with your sweetie. If you arrive home and discover they're tired, grumpy, and don't want to connect, your emotional response will depend on how attached you are to your imagining, and what meaning you give to their behavior. If you create the story that you have a problem in your relationship because they don't want to connect, you'll likely feel worried or discouraged. If you have an underlying belief that goes something like, "I don't really matter and therefore people aren't interested in being with me," you'll likely feel quite up-

> Emotions are born from both our desires and the intensity of our attachment to them.

set, rejected, and hurt. On the other hand, if you aren't that attached to having a connection this evening, or you don't overlay a story about your partner's response, or don't take it personally, then you're better able to accept it and roll with it.

Conditioned Beliefs Shape Our Emotions

Psychotherapist and mindfulness practitioner Miriam Greenspan, in *Healing Through the Dark Emotions,* sees our Western culture as primarily emotion-phobic, where societal messages train us to suppress, shame, punish and neglect our emotional experiences.[27] Greenspan posits that the patriarchy views emotions as weak, female, and childish. Thus, men are trained to dissociate from them, which severely limits their abilities to connect in relationships, or to perceive their own or anyone else's feelings. Women are expected to be emotionally sensitive and vulnerable, but at the same time we're discounted for these qualities. Although we are generally better able to access our emotions than men, we are also shamed for it. This is quite a Catch-22.

This cultural view requires us to keep our emotions in check. So the emotional range we women are allowed is limited. We're called hysterical if we're "too upset." If we're grumpy or angry, or assertive or even aggressive we may hear, "She's such a bitch." Some of us get labeled "too sensitive," meaning we are able to access and feel emotions easily, but those around us feel uncomfortable and don't know how to respond. They want us to chill out, calm down, or grow a thicker skin.

When my marriage was beginning to come apart, my husband and I would unskillfully flail around trying to communicate our conflicting desires and concerns. I remember feeling tremendous frustration with our inability to connect on an emotional plane. I would move quickly into expressing a feeling I was having while he would assert his intellectual view, arguing that my emotions were irrational and thus held no weight. I'd feel dismissed by his judgments and we'd continue on, blindly attached to our positions. It felt like we were trying to communicate on different dimensions, and were hopelessly missing each other. This gap in emotional literacy was frustrating and profoundly sad to me, a pattern I continue to see again and again in the psychotherapy I do with my clients and their male partners.

As we know, through the training to other our minds develop painful and incorrect beliefs about ourselves that color our experience and negatively affect our relationships. Although we may not be consciously aware of them, these powerful beliefs fuel emotions that can play over and over. Beliefs such as, "I'm not good enough, I can never really trust anyone, I'm always left out, I'll never belong, or I don't matter," are common for many of us. By bringing these beliefs into the light of awareness we can assess their accuracy and helpfulness, and then choose how we relate and respond to them.

Othering Requires Disconnecting From Our Emotions

Even though we are more in touch with our emotions than men generally are, gender conditioning makes us mistrust our feelings. Besides being painful, they can be disruptive and get in the way of othering. Consequently, to varying degrees, we learn to disconnect from emotions. We certainly don't view them as bearers of good news, even though they hold invaluable information for us. Instead, we view our unpleasant emotions as problems. The effect of disconnecting naturally breeds anxiety and depression. We become chronically worried about ourselves, self-conscious and full of doubt about whether we're okay. When self-doubt turns into self-blame and loathing, we sink into depression. Because feeling anxious and depressed isn't how we're supposed to be, we shoot ourselves with more second arrows by blaming and judging ourselves for feeling that way in the first place. All of these habits of thinking can keep us caught in terrible suffering.

Family Training

Our relationship to our emotions is shaped most profoundly by our families of origin. Our parents projected their unique conditioning onto us, and so certain emotions and ways of expressing them have been nurtured and practiced more than others. Because the family was our first training ground for shaping our emotional landscape, it's useful to reflect on this training.

In my family of origin, my parents basic style was to exert tight control over emotions. They used suppression, threats of punishment, and sometimes actual punishment, to keep our emotions under wraps. For example, when I'd get upset I was told, "There's nothing to be upset about. You shouldn't feel that." Or, "You're okay, so stop crying now." Though the biggest distortion and insult was, "That's not what you're feeling," Consequently, I quickly learned to tuck in my emotions. This created a narrow emotional terrain, where we were never outwardly upset, never allowed to argue, but also we were rarely ever blissfully joyful. When others would ask how I was, I'd respond with a habitual smile, saying, "I'm fine." Growing up in the "Fine Family", as near as I could tell, I mostly did feel all right. Later when taking psychology classes in college, I realized the "Fine Family" approach was oppressive and unhealthy. It kept me on the surface, and I was longing to know myself. As I came to know myself better I realized that under the surface of "fine" was a rather steady state of low grade anxiety. These realizations led me to teachers and experiences that gradually helped me find my full emotional palette.

The opposite of my family's style is exemplified by our next-door neighbors. We call them the "Yellers" because their habit is uncontrolled expression of emotions, especially the difficult and angry ones. Although they've mellowed over the years, we've witnessed numerous episodes of severe distress: screaming, yelling, swearing, shaming, sobbing, doors slamming, and sometimes the sound of glass and furniture breaking. They'd be swept away by their emotional state with little ability to do anything other than act out of it, leaving a lot of emotional and sometimes physical damage in its wake.

Both the "Fine Family" and the "Yellers" reflect unhealthy and unskillful ways of relating to our emotional lives. Suppressing emotions leads to anxiety, depression, and numbness from habitually shutting down when painful emotions arise. The inability to regulate emotions at all wreaks pain and havoc to everyone involved. Both styles create toxic residues that require a lot of emotional clean-up and healing in order to truly recover. Every day I work with people whose hearts and minds have been severely hurt by parental emotional and physical abuse, and the deep misunderstanding about how to relate wisely to our emotions.

What's true for you in your family of origin? What did your parents model and teach you about emotions? How did they respond when you were upset? I urge you to contemplate your unique training, because identifying and understanding our own habits not only helps us work wisely with ourselves, it helps us to be more accepting and compassionate relating to others when they're caught up in difficult emotions.

Judging

Beyond the beliefs we form from our families and society that create our specific neural groves with emotions, we have other habitual reactions to emotions that amplify our suffering. The judging mind jumps in right away and adds to the challenge. Our automatic reaction to feeling an emotion is to judge it as "good" or "bad." We declare it as appropriate or not. It's right or wrong. If we're experiencing something pleasant, we call it a "good" feeling: happy, excited, eager, calm, joyful, blissful, and so on. If the emotion is unpleasant, we label it "bad": sad, disappointed, angry, anxious, jealous, lonely, guilty, and so on. Basically, the judging mind concludes certain emotions are okay to feel, while others are not. Again gender bias is at play, dictating the emotions we should and should not feel. For example, it's generally more acceptable for women to feel scared than angry, and for men to feel angry rather than scared. When men do feel afraid, it is acceptable for them to react with anger and violence.

Identifying

After the automatic judgment, we take the emotion personally by identifying with it. We attach that first person pronoun to our momentary experience by thinking, "*I'm* so mad. *I'm* outraged." Or, "*I'm* depressed. *My* depression is so heavy." Or, "*My* anxiety is horrible right now." By attaching a sense of self to the emotion, we add to the story of Me and to the illusion that we are a solid, fixed self. This habit leads directly to painful second arrow thoughts such as, "What's the matter with me? I'm really messed up and wrong/sick/ weak to feel this way." Or, "I'm going to be depressed and alone for the rest of my life. My flaws are so obvious. No one will ever want to be with me." These reactions keep us stuck in the story and absorbed in the emotion. We fail to realize that emotions are universal. We all have the potential to experience their full range. When conditions are right, we will naturally experience anger, sadness, joy, delight, fear or longing. Each emotional experience is a transient state, not belonging to anyone, and not unique to anyone.

> Each emotional experience is a transient state, not belonging to anyone, and not unique to anyone.

Resisting

On the heels of judging and identifying comes resisting. Difficult emotions are unpleasant in feeling tone, and we don't like unpleasant. We attempt to not feel them by employing various resistance strategies. Avoidance is the strategy of trying to escape what's painful through distraction. We all have our favorites: we have a drink, smoke, eat something, buy something, gamble, exercise, binge on our devices, work more or harder, and of course, we other. Othering can be a powerful distraction that pulls us away from what we don't want to notice within ourselves. Most addictions are fueled by our desire to escape from what's unpleasant.

Othering can be a powerful distraction that pulls us away from what we don't want to notice within ourselves.

Another method of resisting painful emotions is to dominate and over power them. Denial is domination, and a favorite of the "Fine Family" style. "Nope, I'm not upset. I'm fine." We suppress, pushing the feelings down and hopefully out of our awareness. What are we pushing the emotions down into? The body. The body becomes the vessel for holding the uncomfortable energy. The negative consequences for this strategy can show up as chronic headaches, back pain, and unexplained physical symptoms. Denial can reflect a kind of anti-identification where our conditioned sense of self refuses to accept the fact that we are capable of feeling the emotion. It doesn't fit our ideas about ourselves. A long-time student said that until recently, she had believed she never got angry, and was, in fact, incapable of experiencing anger. Not surprisingly, she has also suffered from chronic back pain most of her adult life. Through mindfulness practice, she's discovering that she does indeed feel anger at times, and not surprisingly, her back pain is diminishing.

Another strategy is to overpower the emotion by any combination of demanding, minimizing, or projecting it onto others. This can show up in thoughts like, "Stop feeling this way. Get over it right now!

This is nothing to get upset about. I'm not the one who is upset, you are." Paradoxically, attempts to resist experiencing the emotion only serves to entrap us. We become negatively attached to it, like Velcro. Though our exit strategies may give us momentary relief, they don't address the emotion in a healthy or effective way. Sooner or later, because it's unresolved and hasn't been given wise attention, the emotion will arise again.

Bringing Mindfulness to Our Emotions

Mindfulness is the most effective and empowering method I've found for working with challenging emotions. It can bring about deep and transformational healing. Over years of practice, mindfulness has radically changed how I relate to difficult emotions. Although never pleasant, I no longer fear them because I have the confidence I'll learn something useful about myself, I know it's a temporary mind-state, and I can remain steady as it moves through. I use this method every day in my psychotherapy practice, and in teaching it to women in class I've witnessed its effectiveness over and over. Remember that the difficulty we have with emotions and the havoc they can bring to our lives is not due to our emotions per se. Our suffering is caused by our conditioned reactions to them. Our habits to fear, judge, personalize, and resist emotions keep us trapped in an adversarial, hostile relationship. We haven't learned how to relate to emotions skillfully. Mindfulness teaches us how to make friends with our emotions and live with them in harmony.

Mindfulness teaches us how to make friends with our emotions and live with them in harmony.

Neuroscientist Richard Davidson has been studying the effect of mindfulness meditation on the brain. His research suggests emotions can be regulated through mindfulness. Examining the neural activity of long-time meditators, as well as people newly trained in meditation, Davidson observed brain activity both while subjects were meditating, and when bringing mindfulness to emotions. He discovered that when mindfulness is brought to a difficult emotion, the neural activity in the amygdala, the part of the brain that's activated by the emotion, actually decreases.[28] In essence, mindfulness acts like a dam that slows down the flow of a raging river. Just a few moments of mindfully noting, "Here's anger. What's it like? How am I actually experiencing it right now?"

We start to regulate an emotion the moment we become mindfully aware of it.

shifts neural activity to the prefrontal cortex, where common sense and intelligence are activated. This enables the practitioner to respond to the emotion with more presence and wisdom, rather than habitually reacting and being swept away by it. This indispensable research suggests we start to regulate an emotion the moment we become mindfully aware of it.

Mindfulness creates a stable safe place or container from which we witness and learn from the emotional storm. The basic view we take is whenever an emotion surfaces, something important is happening for us and we are wise to give the emotion our skillful attention. Psychologist and Buddhist teacher, Tara Brach, in her wonderful book, *Radical Acceptance*, says that when an emotion is here, especially when it's a difficult one, it's good news because it provides an opportunity to respond to yourself in a new and healing way.[29] The emotion is a sign that something has been triggered and is asking for your wise presence.

Comforting the Crying Baby in Your Living Room

The basic approach we want to take in relating to difficult emotions is described beautifully by a metaphor offered by Thich Nhat Hanh. He says that when you're upset, it's like having a crying baby in your living room.[30] As a good parent, when you're in the kitchen chopping vegetables for dinner and you hear your baby crying in the living room, you don't ignore your crying baby, or yell at them, or tell them to get over it and stop crying. You don't slip out the back door to go for a walk. Instead, you drop whatever you're doing and go into the living room and pick up your crying baby. You hold your baby gently and tenderly in your arms and give her all of your presence and kind attention because you love her and you're concerned that she's so upset. Soon your baby will sense your presence and begin to calm down a little. When she's calmer you can inquire about what's causing her upset.

This is exactly how we want to treat ourselves whenever we're upset. Rather than turning against, abandoning, or running from our experience, we stop what we are doing and bring our mindful kind and tender attention to our direct experience. We mindfully breathe and hold what we're noticing gently, with as much steadiness as we can muster, and with lots of curiosity, compassion, and acceptance, precisely because we are hurting and upset right now. We can think of mindfulness being the mother we truly need in this moment. Instead of turning away or against ourselves, we practice being good mothers, staying with and opening to the pain and what it's trying to let us know. Being kind, compassionate, present, and loving with ourselves is just what we need when we're hurting, isn't it?

The First Steps in Working With Difficult Emotions

Although we will delve more deeply into transforming emotions in Chapter 18, there are some basic first steps that help us be the mindfulness mother we need when we're upset. This method can be applied both in formal meditation practice and on the spot when upsets arise as we're living our lives.

The first step is to recognize that you are experiencing a difficult emotion. You might just say to yourself, "Yes. Here's feeling upset right now." This is very helpful because by simply naming that you're upset, you've already begun to shift your relationship to the experience.

Next, choose to *Drop In* fully to this moment by breathing several breaths with full awareness and attention. This helps you ground in your body, come fully into the present, and gathers your wits about you.

Turn towards your direct experience and name what you are feeling by "*softly noting*" it: "Here's anger/fear/shame/guilt/sadness." This step is crucial because it involves both a level of acceptance — "Yes, this emotion is here" — and also promotes dis-identification by noting the emotion as "anger/fear/shame, etc." not "*I'm* angry, *I'm* afraid, *I'm* ashamed." Softly noting the emotion instantly creates some space and releases resistance.

The first steps to relate mindfully to a difficult emotion:

1. Recognize that I'm upset right now.

2. Drop In – mindfully breathe three breaths.

3. Accept – turn towards and softly note it.

4. Be curious – exactly what and how am I experiencing this?

5. Offer compassion and gentleness – "I'm so sorry this is painful."

6. What's the wisest and kindest way to respond to myself?

Bring *curiosity* to your experience by asking, "What is this? How am I actually experiencing it? What am I thinking, imagining, or telling myself? What story is my mind creating? Is there something I'm wanting that isn't happening right now? Has some an old wound or painful belief been poked? What am I feeling in my body, what are the sensations of this emotion?" Encourage yourself to relax around the sensations, letting them be however they are, giving them a lot of space.

Hold all that you're noticing with *gentleness and compassion*. No judging allowed. You just want to know and understand what's truly going on for you right now. Compassion is essential because being present with the emotion is hard and painful, so to stay present your heart needs to remain open. I've found it helps to literally say to myself, "I'm sorry this is so hard right now."

Because emotions are fluid and based on ever-changing conditions, it's likely that by now, the intensity has subsided some, and you may have a better sense of what the emotion is really about. It's helpful to ask, "Well, given that this is what's here, or this is what it's about, what's the *wisest and kindest* way to respond to myself right now?" We are intending to discover what we truly need in this moment. Listen to yourself deeply, and open to whatever occurs to you.

Softly noting the emotion instantly creates some space and releases resistance.

Watch Out for Second Arrows

Because of conditioning, it's easy to create additional layers of distress by shooting ourselves with second arrows when we're caught in emotional storms. We blast judgments, blame, criticism, and add-ons by forming conclusions such as, "I shouldn't be upset right now! I should be bigger than this! When am I going to grow up? This always happens to me!" The habits of taking the experience personally and turning against ourselves deepen and complicate our suffering. We want to be aware of this reaction, refrain from judging ourselves for it, and choose to let it go by shifting attention to the breath and our actual direct experience.

It's All About Practice

Learning to work skillfully with emotions takes practice. At first, begin by opening to an emotion when it arises during formal meditation practice. Be very gentle as you learn to utilize this process with emotions. Over time you will gain confidence in staying with yourself when painful emotions strike, you'll see more clearly the temporary nature of emotions, and what happens when you apply mindfulness. Gradually you'll increase your ability to respond with kindness and wisdom.

The informal practice of recognizing, Dropping In, and softly noting is an essential core practice as well. As I've experienced and many women report, the practice of softly noting on the spot, saying, "Here's feeling jealous. Here's uncertainty. Here's anxiety," is enormously helpful. This simple practice puts you upright after succumbing to a wave of emotion. You can stand steady on your own two feet as the wave swirls around you, and then passes away.

A young mother, Heather, described an experience she had applying mindfulness on the spot as she was shopping in a department store with her four-year old during the winter holidays. As she was paying for her purchases, she realized she'd lost track of her daughter. Feeling panic rising, she Dropped In, breathed several breaths mindfully, observed her mind racing with scary thoughts, felt her belly in knots and her heart pounding, and then asked herself for a kind and wise response. It then occurred to her to concentrate on the color of the jacket and hat her daughter was wearing. She took another mindful breath, and began calmly scanning the store. She found her daughter within a few minutes and all was well again. It would have been easy to be overwhelmed by her initial mind's panic, shoot multiple arrows of self-blame and add-ons. Instead, mindfulness helped her keep her wits about her and find her daughter with ease.

Cultivating Courage

Remember that every time we are mindful, we are developing courage. We are cultivating unshakeable confidence. The practice asks us to be open, moment by moment, to the unknown and the unexpected. Bringing mindfulness to our difficult emotions requires special bravery simply because we've been trained to fear them. Our emotions can be messy, inconvenient and sometimes terrifying. As you'll discover when you venture into the emotional territory with the tools of mindfulness, our imagined fears — the scary stories we create — are far worse than the actual reality.

Many of us are reluctant to know ourselves because we're afraid something is wrong with us, or we'll discover a horrible flaw or secret that will be unbearable. This is conditioned fear. In all my years of working mindfully with myself, clients, and students, I have never found an unbearable secret. Certainly, we do learn information about ourselves that we didn't know, realize, or remember. Yet, even if the information is surprising or painful, mindfulness provides a safe, accepting container and skill set to stay steady, wise, and kind with whatever turns up. To discover it's possible to open to our emotions and learn, heal, and grow from them is powerfully freeing. We build deep trust and faith in ourselves as we find our own wisdom and learn we can handle whatever challenges we face. With growing security and self-confidence, we learn to relax with ourselves just as we are. As a result, we lose our need for the other to validate that what we're feeling or how we are is okay. Gradually, through mindfulness, we learn to accept and validate ourselves.

> Through mindfulness we learn to accept and validate ourselves.

No matter where you are in your practice, whether a beginner or an experienced practitioner, take heart that each time you practice matters. Every time you softly note, "fear is here" or "anger has arisen," and you notice your experience with even a tiny bit of acceptance and curiosity, you are having a direct impact on your brain and conditioned neural grooves. By interrupting those habitual neural pathways, you are weakening them and building new pathways of awareness. You are gaining access to your natural wisdom, your true blue sky nature. Even if right now you only remember to practice mindful awareness once a day, or even once a week, it matters, it makes a difference, it counts.

Ownwork Suggestions

Formal Meditation:
Mindfulness of Breath, Sensations, Thoughts, and Emotions

Decide on how long you'll sit, and arrange your body in a stable, comfortable posture.... Slowly sweep attention through your body inviting relaxing and easing.... Drop down into the body to concentrate on the sensations of breathing.... Allow the field of your awareness to be, open, and spacious, creating plenty of room to remain steady as experience shifts and changes.... Stay with the breath until some other experience is more predominant... Practice relating to other sensations in the body, thoughts arising, sounds being heard, in the ways we've been practicing....

When you realize an emotion is predominant, first softly note it ("Here's fear/sadness/ irritation") and accept it just as it is. Breathe several breaths mindfully, and then investigate with curiosity: How am I experiencing this emotion right now? What's the story? Do I want something that I'm not getting? What sensation(s) does this story create in my body? Describe the sensations to yourself and relax around them, giving all plenty of room, just as it is.... Stay steady and open to all you notice.... Offer compassion to yourself, saying, "I'm so sorry this is painful right now" to help your heart stay open... At some point you may want to ask, "Well, given this is here, what's the wisest and kindest way to respond to myself right now?....

Open to whatever arises. Remember you can shift back to the anchor of the breath at any time.... At the end of the sit, reflect on what you noticed and appreciate yourself for your practice.

Informal Practice

• Track your emotional landscape throughout the day and practice softly noting it ("Here's irritation. Here's loneliness.") Notice how much your emotions shift and change throughout the day. Note the habits of judging and shooting second arrows — with kindness and curiosity.

• Whenever you realize you're upset: Drop In and mindfully breathe several breaths; softly note your experience ("Here's feeling mad"); bring curiosity to it ("What was I just telling myself? Am I attached to something that isn't happening the way I want it to? What's the sensation? Where do I feel this in my body?"). Offer compassion and kindness to yourself — the crying baby in the living room. Ask, "What's the wisest and kindest way to respond to myself right now?" Notice the effect.

• Keep watching for habits of othering, especially when you feel emotions. Invite yourself to be very curious about this.

15

What Am I Truly Responsible for? The Power of Resistance and Acceptance

The curious paradox is that when I accept myself just as I am, then I can change.

Carl Rogers

Controlling? Who, Me?

Have you ever been accused of being controlling? Ever feel like you're a control freak? If so, take comfort, because control is a big part of the conditioning to other. Othering trains us to be overly responsible for others and under-responsible for ourselves. We take on the responsibility for meeting the other's needs and maintaining their happiness and well-being. We assume we're the only one who can do the job correctly, so we put ourselves in charge. What about our own needs? We tell ourselves that we'll take care of ourselves later.

> Othering trains us to be overly responsible for others and under-responsible for ourselves.

Often, later never comes. Assuming over-responsibility can lead to painful consequences, and trains us to behave at times like a bossy, intrusive, nagging busybody.

Signs of over-responsibility include habits of directing, advising, correcting and commenting on the way the other person acts. It's the habit of jumping in to do most of the work rather than an equal share of the tasks, and being the first to volunteer to help. Over-responsibility is behind assuming we know what the other is thinking and adjusting our behavior accordingly. It's not asking for what we need and want because we're afraid it will upset them. It's the tendency to feel guilty when the other person is upset, as well as when we feel angry with them.

One of the most common patterns of over-responsibility occurs when the other person is upset. We presume it's our job to make them feel better. We take on their problem and try to solve it for them, offering advice, stepping in to do tasks for them, or do all we can to cheer them up. While the desire to help another is certainly kind and compassionate, we often go overboard. We can spend enormous mental and emotional energy worrying about them, dreaming up schemes that would fix their problem, and figuring out exactly what they should think and do to stop being upset. Does this strike a familiar chord?

Checking in

• How's your sitting practice going? I hope you're feeling more confident in your ability to practice. Now that you're paying attention to sensations, thoughts *and* emotions, you may be finding the practice more challenging. At this point, I often hear women say, "I liked meditation better when we were just concentrating on the breath. It made me feel calmer." If that's true for you, remember you can't go wrong by simply practicing mindfulness of breathing. However, what's so beneficial about learning to be present and stable with emotions is we gradually understand, accept, and trust ourselves more.

• Have you noticed the effect of softly noting the emotion? "Oh, here's fear," or "Here's feeling down." This shifts our relationship to the emotion and helps free us from being so trapped in it. We're honing our skills to relate to all we're experiencing with steadiness, kindness, and wisdom. Please keep at it. If it feels possible, increase your sitting time.

• What about spotting the story that created the emotion? Remember, the mind is continuously spinning stories, explanations, conclusions, and predictions, and our job is to see them and not judge or take them personally. Keep asking yourself, "What was I just imagining? What was I just telling myself?" When we can see the story, and remember it is a story and not necessarily true, we create instant freedom.

• When you ask, "What's a wise and kind way to respond to myself?" please remember we are not searching for a strategy to fix the situation. We're accessing our true nature, our wisdom about how to support ourselves in this moment. Listen for your wise counsel: some genuine encouragement, intelligent common sense, or your loving attitude.

But It's Our "Job"

Taking responsibility for others is our traditional gender role in the patriarchy. Historically as subordinates, it's always been our job to care for the growth and development of others. We take care of everybody — not only our children if we have them, but also our partner or sweetie, parents, other relatives, friends, friend's children, neighbors, and colleagues. Certainly our biology contributes to this role. We value connection, so relationships are critically import-

> Taking responsibility for others is our traditional gender role in the patriarchy.

ant to us. They are central, in fact. We are relational beings. However, othering makes us not only feel responsible for what's going on in the relationship, but we *need* the relationship to feel secure. As a psychotherapist, almost every woman I've worked with names relationship challenges as the primary reason she's seeking help. Most assume they are responsible for repairing what's wrong in the relationship.

The work of Carol Gilligan,[31] Jean Baker Miller,[32] and others at The Stone Center at Wellesley College, contend that a woman's conditioned sense of self is developed in the context of relationship and connections. An inner sense of connection to others is, in fact, the central organizing feature for developing our sense of self. Thus, our sense of who we are is grounded in our ability to make and maintain relationships. As girls we're encouraged to center our attention on others, be aware of their feelings, develop empathy, and create relationships that benefit and support the growth of others. Miller contends that this behavior is both natural for us as women, but is also required by our culture because we're trained and expected to perform the caretaking roles.

In contrast, boys and men are generally encouraged to center on themselves, to focus on their own experiences and needs, rather than be empathic and concerned with others. They are conditioned to believe they must figure out how to succeed in the world, strive to be on top, and achieve independence. For men, the prevailing cultural view is that a healthy sense of self means being autonomous, rational, separate, and in control of emotions. Rather than making relationships central as they are for women, independence and separation are viewed as "manly" and are highly valued. Further, Gilligan found that women's morality is primarily organized around the ethics of responsibility and care. We must never cause another person pain, directly or indirectly, so we bend over backwards to not upset the other. In contrast, morality for boys and men is focused more on impartial justice, rights, and reliance on laws and their fair application.

Looking at these patterns in the context of patriarchy and the power structure of domination, it makes perfect sense that relationships are central for women. Because subordinates have less power, it's simply smart to focus on the other and the relationship, and to the best of our ability do what we can to make sure they are happy, and especially, happy with us. If trouble disturbs our relationship, particularly if our own needs are creating conflict, then it's in our best interest to do whatever we can to take care of the problem. Frequently, however, the solution means discounting, dismissing, or denying our own needs.

Our sense of self is deeply tied into feeling responsible for others. When someone is upset or needs help, we feel compelled to help. When we can't fix their problem or can't respond, we often feel inadequate or guilty. Besides believing it's our job to relieve the other's distress, we may even think it's our fault that they're upset to begin with. "If only I had said or done _____, then this wouldn't have happened and they wouldn't be upset now. I should have done something different and then everything would be okay." Have you ever thought this? It's so common, yet wildly irrational. It's natural to feel compassion, empathy, and discomfort when another is suffering. It's part of our true nature to care and want to relieve another's suffering. As women, our gender conditioning takes us overboard by creating the *habit*

> Our sense of self is deeply tied into feeling responsible for others.

of taking care of others without regard to our own needs and well-being. This is ultimately unsustainable and irresponsible.

Interdependence Is Reality

Interestingly, if we step back from conditioning and gender conventions and look at the ultimate nature of reality, we see that relationships are, in truth, central. It's a law of nature that everything exists in relationship to everything else. Nothing can exist independently. Interdependence is the reality of life. Growth and survival depend on relationships. Even though men are raised to value independence, in truth their lives depend on relationships. What's the old sexist adage? "Behind every successful man is a woman." We can more accurately expand that to behind every successful man *and* woman is a multitude of beings: parents, teachers, children, friends, partners, lovers, colleagues, grandparents, ancestors, and helpers of all kinds, including non-humans, and all those microscopic beings inside and outside our bodies.

> It's a law of nature that everything exists in relationship to everything else. Nothing can exist independently. Interdependence is the reality of life.

The reality of interdependence is a cornerstone of Buddhist philosophy. Often referred to as "co-dependent arising," the view is that literally nothing on this earthly plane has an independent existence, but rather, everything is created by innumerable other elements, causes, and conditions coming together. This interdependence is also called emptiness, which means that all forms of existence lack an independent life, or an independent permanent "self." For example, this physical book that you are holding didn't come into existence by itself. All the ideas I've written on these pages have arisen from innumerable conditions, teachers, students, and a myriad of resources and experiences I've had in my life. The paper and its physical form didn't appear out of nowhere. Rather, the paper is made from a tree which began as a seed, that was dependent on the soil, water, sun, and air to grow. It's also a result of the machines that cut down the tree and turned the wood into paper. The machines were invented by people who were raised and fed by other people, and on and on it goes. Interdependence means that no one is an island, ever. How we each are in this moment is a product of a innumerable conditions and factors coming together, reflecting the influence of countless people, relationships, and experiences through the course of our entire life up to this very moment.

It's helpful to contemplate and study the reality of interdependence. It helps us develop clarity and wisdom regarding the actual range of our responsibility, and puts a more accurate perspective on what we are truly able to control and influence.

We All Want to Be Loving, But...

According to the Buddhist view, the desire to love is the basis of our true nature. We are naturally loving, caring, compassionate beings. It is part of our natural wisdom, intelligence and basic goodness. We flourish when we receive and give loving attention, affection, appreciation, support, and acceptance. Loving and being loved is a fundamental need that can only be experienced in the context of relationships, including our relationship with ourselves.

Yet the habits and effects of conditioning for both men and women, to varying degrees, distort and block our access to experiencing our genuine loving nature. Women tend to lose themselves in the relationship, and connection with self becomes distorted and submerged by the attention we give to the other. Men have been taught to devalue relationships, causing them to miss out on intimacy and real connection with others. Often, I hear women complain that their husbands don't have many friends and rely on their wives to provide the social connections for the couple and family.

Being Overly Responsible is Exhausting

The controlling pattern of over-responsibility arises out of a core unconscious tenet embedded in othering: "Because I have to please you in order to assure my security, I must control both myself and you. I have to control myself to make sure I please you and make you happy. I have to control you so you respond to me in the ways I want you to respond. When I trust you're okay, and especially when you're reacting favorably to me, then I can feel secure." These beliefs propel us to go overboard with responsibility. We take on the task of doing whatever we can to assure their needs are met. This may include giving support when we don't have the energy to give it, having sex when we really don't want to, doing tasks that aren't ours to do, and repeatedly dismissing our own needs for the sake of the relationship.

Consequently, we do and do and do until we're exhausted. You know the drill. Even if we have a career or job, we typically carry most of the responsibility and work for running our home. Though our partner may help with housework and family tasks, we still feel it's our job to hold the kite strings for all that's happening for everyone in our family, every day, around the clock.

At some point in our effort to take care of everyone and everything, we extend ourselves too far and we collapse, numb out or shut down. Seeking relief from the unrelenting stress, we indulge in an exit strategy to find some respite. We visit the refrigerator, pour another glass of wine, or hide out in bed. Sooner or later, guilt, arising from believing we're not doing our job or being the partner/mom/friend/worker we're supposed to be, gets us up and going again. We step back into the over-responsibility trap and the cycle continues. Over time, because mind and body are connected, stress related illnesses may have their toll on our bodies.

In the book *Too Good for Her Own Good*, family therapists Claudia Bepko and Jo-Ann Krestan explain that women's gender conditioning creates an unconscious "Code of Goodness" that directs our lives and entraps us in over-responsibility.[33] The five rules of the code are: (1) Be attractive: a woman should always look good. (2) Be a lady: a woman should always be in control. (3) Be unselfish and of service: a woman should always be giving. (4) Make relationships work: a woman should always be devoted to the relationship first. (5) Be competent without complaint: a woman should do it all and never appear overwhelmed. Bepko and Krestan say the Code of Goodness trains us to give our power away, strive to be perfect, fear losing control, become cut off from our feelings, and have unclear boundaries. The more we are caught in the code's rules, the more we're likely to feel chronically out of balance, anxious and depressed.

When I talk about the Code of Goodness with the women in my classes, I always ask if they can relate to these rules. Do they think the code still applies, given that the authors wrote it in 1991? Sadly, despite the wide age range of women in my classes the response is always "Yes. It's still this way!" In the book *Wonder Women: Sex, Power, and the Quest for Perfection*, Debra Spar also confirms that not much has changed over the past 50 years.[34] Women are still firmly stuck in the trap of believing we have to do it all perfectly, or else we aren't okay. We've upped the ante, believing we should do everything we've always done, *plus* be CEOs and board and college presidents.

What's true for you? Do you feel our culture still requires us to exhibit traditional female qualities? To be attractive, polite, unselfish and al-

---

The Code of Goodness

1. Be attractive; always look good.

2. Be a lady stay; in control.

3. Be unselfish; always be giving.

4. Make relationships work; relationships come first.

5. Be competent without complaint; do it all easily.

ways giving, the one holding the primary responsibility for the relationship. A super woman who does everything without grumbling about it?

Being Overly Responsible Is Disrespectful: Pain Is a Teacher

Constantly monitoring our partner, kids, friends, or co-workers on how to be, or what they should do — cheer up, calm down, don't think that, don't feel that, stop being afraid, get to work, stop working and relax — is tiresome for us and for them. Despite all our guiding, suggesting, and demanding, we cannot control another's thoughts, feelings, or actions. Unsolicited managing and correcting can provoke resentment, and we may be rightly accused of nagging, being bossy or controlling. We may also grow resentful of the other, weary of tracking and making sure everything is getting done, and getting done in the exactly the way it *should* be done.

> Our attempts to control others can interfere with their growth and learning.
> Distress and pain are signals and teachers for each of us.

Further, our attempts to control others can interfere with their growth and learning. Distress and pain are signals and teachers for each of us. They point us to where we need to be paying closer or more skillful attention. By solving their problems for them, we take away their opportunity to learn and develop confidence in their own ability to handle the challenges of life. Instead, we may be reinforcing their dependence on us, and possibly encouraging them to view themselves as limited. Thus, it's not always an act of kindness to help, at least without the other's permission.

We Can't Be Responsible for Another's Happiness

Rachael, a social worker, married for twenty-eight years, with a son and daughter in college, sought therapy because her marriage was in crisis. In the past year, both her sister and a dear friend had died of cancer and she had a brief affair with an old boyfriend. She was feeling lousy about herself, guilty and stuck in self-blame. She said she didn't know how she really felt, why she had the affair, or what she really wanted. She felt lost to herself, shut down and confused. Her main experience was a heavy current of tension, worry and a pervasive dull numbness. To me she seemed anxious, moderately depressed, and disconnected from her authentic experience.

> Happiness is a personal responsibility, an inside job.

As she began to connect with herself through therapy and learning mindfulness, she realized that for all the years of her marriage, she'd operated under the belief that her job was to make sure everyone in her family was happy, especially her husband. He was prone to mood swings, overusing alcohol, and erratic behavior. A fun family outing could easily shift to a crisis when her husband's mood would suddenly flip. When she couldn't cajole him out of his ugly mood and make things okay again, she'd blame herself and feel like a failure as a wife and mother.

When she realized she had made herself responsible for his happiness all those years, she was stunned. She'd been bending over backwards trying to do something that was impossible. Happiness is a personal responsibility, an inside job. It's created by our own specific thoughts, perceptions, and feelings in response to what's happening around and within us. At the same time, because we are interdependent we do affect each other and contribute to the conditions of the present moment, so we need to be mindful of our thoughts, perceptions and conduct. However, it's not possible to control another's thoughts and make them happy. Clearly, Rachael's guiding dictum, "I'm responsible for your happiness" is deeply conditioned in many of us. It reflects a deep misunderstanding of how things truly are and distorts responsibility and power.

Finding Balance in Our Responsibility for Others

What are we responsible for in our relationships with others? This is an essential question and the answer is fluid, and based on changing situations and conditions. First and foremost, though, we need to be responsible for ourselves. We need to take 100 percent responsibility for our authentic experience. We need to know the exact thoughts we're thinking, the emotions we're feeling, what's happening in our body, and

> We need to take 100 percent responsibility for our authentic experience of the moment.

what we're needing and wanting. In order to respond to the other's request or mood appropriately we need to first know our own internal data. This is being self-responsible. Choosing to mindfully Drop In is the simplest and surest way to find yourself. Breathing several breaths with full awareness, inquiring into what you're actually experiencing, gives you the essential information you need.

Then, we must let others take responsibility for themselves. As Bepko and Krestan wisely suggest, never do something for the other that they are capable of doing for themselves, unless they ask for help directly, and we honestly want to, and as long as doing so won't negatively affect us or them. This means that we are not automatically responsible for anyone else's problems, needs, feelings, meals, clothes, homework, headaches, stress, worries, things they can't find, decisions, jobs they don't finish, appointments, or transportation. Obviously, these guidelines must be adjusted for developmental age and abilities, but they form an emancipating list. When I share the list with the women in class, they voice a huge surprise, "Really? Not responsible?" and then an equally huge expression of relief. Many put the list on their refrigerator door so their whole family can see it and be encouraged to adopt a healthier balance of responsibility.

Maggie, a mother of two teenage sons, realized she'd always done everything for them, and had felt pride in that. Now her oldest son was about to go off to college and he didn't even know how to do his own laundry, let alone clean or cook for himself. Upon realizing her over-responsibility habit, she sat down with her boys and told them that she'd been unwise in doing it all, and her job now was to teach them how to be independent so they could take care of themselves. She didn't want her sons to expect their girlfriends to do these chores for them. After some grumbling, they got it and agreed that taking care of themselves was actually their own responsibility.

> Never do something for
> the other that they are
> capable of doing for themselves,
> unless they ask for help directly,
> and we honestly want to,
> and as long as
> doing this won't negatively
> affect us or them.

Because our sense of self is tied up in care giving and being dependable, it can feel risky to begin respecting our own boundaries and say "No" when we don't have the time, energy, or desire to help. We may fear we'll be judged as selfish, unreliable, or family and friends will stop asking for our help. We may fear they will stop needing us. However, by being authentic and truthful, others will come to trust us more. They'll realize that we too have limits and boundaries, and when we do say "Yes" we are there 100 percent. More importantly, we will be aligned with our own energy and won't have to push ourselves beyond our limits.

The Habit of Resistance

When we delve more deeply into the pattern of over-responsibility, we see that it is rooted in the conditioned mind's habit of resistance. Whenever something is happening that we don't like, we resist it. The judging mind zooms in with an immediate "No." Whatever we resist creates suffering. Most of our habits of correcting, cajoling, and criticizing stem from our feeling uncomfortable with what the other is feeling or doing. So we step in, trying to dominate, control and change things so they're how we think they should be. Yet, when we resist by trying to dominate and correct we create a power struggle, and a fight may ensue. The nature of resistance creates more disconnection than connection in relationship. The irony is that whatever we don't want to experience just becomes more solid the more we resist it.

I had a remarkable wake-up to the power of resistance a few years into studying mindfulness. I attended a nine-day training program that Jon Kabat-Zinn offered to professionals who wanted to teach mindfulness as a method for reducing stress. The training was held in July at the Omega Institute in upstate New York. Because one of the housing options was camping, I decided to bring my tent and have the delight of sleeping outside while learning more about mindfulness from one of the country's most important mindfulness teachers. I was excited about the whole event. Studying with Jon Kabat-Zinn, learning more about mindfulness, camping in the summertime, nothing could be better. I pitched my tent near the small lake in the campground and went off to the first evening's session. When I slid into my tent at the end of the evening, I discovered the lake was filled with a zillion bullfrogs — all enthusiastically croaking chaotically and loudly. My instant reaction was "Oh no!" as I imagined a difficult sleepless night ahead.

Instantly, I began strategies to not hear the bullfrogs: I pulled my sleeping bag over my head, but it was a steamy July night and after a few minutes I flung it off. I tried putting my pillow over my head, but that didn't work either. Nothing really worked. After what seemed like hours of tossing and turning I finally feel asleep. In the morning, I complained to a camp mate who hadn't heard the frogs at all, and she offered me her earplugs for the next night. I hopped into my tent the next night, hopeful my problem would now be solved with ear plugs. However, the frogs were as loud as ever.

This struggle continued each night. I was trying not to hear the frogs, tossing and turning, and taking forever to fall asleep. During the day, feeling sleep-deprived, I began to worry that I might get sick, and even considered skipping the evening sessions so I could fall asleep before the frogs began their incessant croaking.

Finally, on the fifth night of the nine-day training on mindfulness, as I was lying in my tent trying not to hear those frogs, I thought, "Wait a minute! I could bring mindfulness to this experience!" Ironically, practicing mindfulness had not even occurred to me. I had only wanted to not hear those frogs. Now, at last remembering mindfulness, I invited myself to become really curious about what I was actually hearing. I coached myself to open and listen precisely and spaciously to *all* I could actually hear in the moment.

The next thing I knew, I was waking up to a beautiful morning, having had a good night's sleep. I was flabbergasted. I realized all those nights I'd been trying not to hear the croaking, it was resisting those sounds that made me so tense and anxious that I couldn't fall asleep. Fighting with my experience, trying to exert control over something I had no control over had created my suffering. It wasn't the frogs' croaking that kept me awake, it was my resistance. As soon as I brought mindfulness to my experience by inviting myself to accept and really listen to the sounds with curiosity, opening to them just as they were, I relaxed and fell asleep. This was a huge and important insight: what I resist persists. What I am able to accept and open to changes on its own.

Impressed with the power of resistance and acceptance from this experience, I wondered what else I resisted without even knowing it. As I brought the question into my awareness, I soon realized, sure enough, I resist many things, from the mundane to the consequential: a green light turning yellow as I approach. I have to stop. Rats! I'm happily writing away on my computer when the phone rings. Somebody wants my attention. Ugh! It's early morning and I want to remain sleeping but my dog gets up and barks to go outside. Grr! I'm all packed and ready to go on a long-awaited meditation retreat and I come down with a nasty virus and can't go. So disappointing. Although these are all ordinary life events, the habit of instantly resisting them creates various degrees of physical tension and emotional stress that are actually avoidable when we're mindful of them.

Acceptance Is the Key to Change

Wanting things to be different from how they are in this moment creates our suffering. It's really that simple. Mindfulness asks us to accept whatever is happening right now regardless of whether we want it or not, like it or not. We open to the whole shebang of our experience — the difficult and unpleasant, the neutral as well as the pleasant. We relate to whatever is here with sensitivity, curiosity, the freshness of beginner's mind, and always with kindness, compassion, and spaciousness. Doing so isn't easy, however. We'd rather not have contact with what feels uncomfortable. It's against our instinct. So acceptance requires bravery because as we open to what feels unpleasant we're also opening to the unknown, and we're often afraid the unknown will be filled with even greater discomfort.

> Wanting things to be different from how they are in this moment creates our suffering.

However, accepting what's here right now is transformative. Carl Rogers, the psychologist credited with starting the client-centered humanistic psychology movement, discovered that when we accept our experience fully, just as it is, then paradoxically, it changes on its own. Acceptance is being willing to suspend judgment and simply open our mind and heart to what is happening in the here and now: the anger I'm feeling, the pain in my belly, the disappointment I feel because my friend let me down, the light turning red, the croaking bull frogs.

Acceptance Requires Relaxing With What Is

When we can accept and open to our experience with curiosity, letting it be as it is, we naturally bring spaciousness to it. The field of our awareness expands. This inherent relaxation allows room for impermanence to have its effect, and the experience shifts and changes on its own. When we react by resisting, we actually contract the field of our awareness, which makes whatever we are feeling more solid, rigid, and predominant. Spaciousness not only creates room for the experience to shift and change, it also creates the conditions whereby wisdom, insight, and new possibilities can easily emerge. This deepens our understanding of ourselves, and grows our compassion, self-respect and trust.

Acceptance Is Active Investigation, Not Passive Resignation

When we accept our present moment experience we aren't going belly up, giving up, or collapsing into powerlessness. It's not, "Well then, whatever." It's also not permission to indulge or flail around in the difficult emotion, either. We certainly are not asking ourselves to endure any treatment or situation that is not healthy for us, or to accept an abusive relationship. Rather, acceptance brings us closer to our experience. It informs us. It is an active investigation into our direct authentic experience. Acceptance deepens our intimacy with ourselves because we are investigating *exactly* what is happening right now. It enables us to know our experience with clarity. When something needs to be said or done regarding ourselves or others, like stating a boundary, because our mind is open and spacious there's room in our consciousness for

Accepting what's here right now is immediately transformative.

that wise action to come into our awareness. We discover a wise and skillful response.

Applying Mindfulness to Resistance

The basic approach for bringing mindfulness to our habit of resisting is to train ourselves to ask, "How am I *relating* to what's happening right now?" Am I accepting, curious, open and letting it be? Or am I judging it, trying to control, change or fix it? Am I being overly responsible here? If so, I'm resisting and increasing my suffering.

When we realize we're resisting, we softly note it, and then apply curiosity. "What's this resistance like? How am I actually experiencing it? What's the story? What's the feeling of it in my body?" As we explore kindly and gently, we're accepting it and learning about it. Then we can ask, "What am I wanting that's not happening right now?" When we learn what we're wanting, we can ask, "Is this something I actually have control over?" This exploration can help loosen our grip on what we've been clinging to when it's not achievable now. As we continue to follow our experience, we may find it's now possible to open to what we've been resisting. "Okay, yes, here's disappointment and sadness." We keep inviting ourselves to relax, soften, and give everything we notice plenty of room.

How am I relating to what's happening right now? Am I accepting it or resisting it?

Joseph Goldstein, one of the country's first Vipassana teachers, who along with Sharon Salzberg and Jack Kornfield founded IMS, suggests that when we're caught in resisting, it can helpful to use the phrase, "Let it be. Let it be. Whatever it is, it's okay. Just let me feel it."[35] This naturally invites our mind to relax and lets the field of our awareness become more spacious. We don't have to do anything to our difficult mind state — we just have to let it be. When we can release our resistance by letting our experience be, things shift and change the way they naturally do on their own.

A client, Dorothy, wanted to work on the anger and resentment she felt towards her mother-in-law. She didn't want to be upset. She wanted to be loving and kind towards her, because after all, that was how she *should* be with her. It was clear she was stuck in resistance. After guiding her into her body, the sensations of breathing, and settling into her internal experience more, I invited her to open to all those uncomfortable feelings with lots of curiosity and kindness. While refraining from judging all that she noticed, I asked her to observe her mind's stories, and then feel and investigate the sensations of these emotions in her body. As she connected with the sensations I suggested she gently say to herself, "It's okay that I'm feeling this. Whatever it is, it's okay. Just let me feel this." Within a few minutes of practicing, the difficult feelings softened. She could now accept and understand the anger and resentment she had felt. Her spacious relaxed mind opened to her wisdom and true kindness, first towards herself and then towards her mother-in-law. She experienced the healing and transformative power of mindful acceptance.

> It's okay that I'm feeling this.
> Whatever it is, it's okay.

Self-Responsibility: Healthy Boundaries

By accepting our present moment experience, we relate to our lives from a balanced, informed place. We're aware of our own needs, thoughts, and feelings — all the authentic data about ourselves — and we bring that information to the circumstances at hand. When a situation with another provokes the desire to leap in to help or fix, inciting our over-responsibility habit, we can respond skillfully. We can drop into the present moment, mindfully breathe, accept and open to our exact thoughts and feelings, noticing it all with curiosity, kindness, and without identifying with it. This creates the room to choose how we want to respond to what's happening. It affords us the space to ask the pivotal question, what's the wisest and kindest way to respond right now?

If we're confused about finding a skillful response, it's sometimes clarifying to breakdown the word "responsible" into its root parts: *response-able*. We then ask, "What am I actually *able to respond* to right now?" Do I have the time, energy, and ability to respond now? Beyond being "able," it's also self-respecting to ask, "What do *I want* to respond to right now?" Clarifying what we want up front can avoid resentment arising later when we hadn't even considered what we wanted. These questions and their answers enable us to take appropriate responsibility for our own self, and our relationships with others.

Establishing healthy boundaries is spiritual warriorship. It takes courage to open to what's difficult with ourselves and the other, to stay balanced in our awareness of self and other, and to not abandon ourselves in habitual ways. When you've arrived home from an exhausting day and your kids come in the door yelling, "Hey mom, we're starving! Can you make us something to eat?" you can Drop In and mindfully breathe to learn what's true for you. If you discover, yes, I'm tired, really tired, and I don't have the energy right now to feed anyone anything, then you can lovingly reply, "Hey kids, I'm really beat right now and need fifteen minutes to recover. Please go to the fridge and find something to tide you over until I make supper." Taking appropriate responsibility for ourselves is important for all our relationships. In this way, we teach our loved ones that we have needs and boundaries, too. This lesson ripples out and encourages everyone to take healthy responsibility for themselves.

> Accepting our authentic experience creates the room to choose how we want to respond to what's happening. What's the wisest and kindest response right now?

Accepting ourselves and others is not easy. It takes practice, patience, and trust. It means letting go of our agenda. It means listening to ourselves and the other and accepting what is true in the moment. Acceptance is healing and empowering because it cultivates compassion for ourselves and for others as we learn to companion our difficult experiences with our wise open heart and mind.

Ownwork Suggestions

Formal Sitting Practice:
Choiceless Open Awareness —
How Am I Relating to What's Here?

Decide how long your sit will be. Arrange your body in a comfortable, stable posture, making sure your spine feels aligned.... Feel your whole being sitting here.... Open to yourself just as you are in this moment with kindness, curiosity, and acceptance.... Slowly sweep attention through your body inviting softening, relaxing, releasing....

Connect with the sensations of breathing.... Enjoy being with each breath as it occurs.... Expand the field of your awareness to allow plenty of room to relax around these sensations.... When something else becomes more predominant than the breath — a thought, a sensation, a sound, a smell, or an emotion — softly note it.... Pay special attention to how you are relating to this experience: are you open to it just as it is? Accepting it with curiosity and kindness? Giving it lots of spaciousness? Letting it be? Or are you resisting it by judging it, trying to change it, fix it, or caught in stories about it? If so, softly note: "Here's resistance," and bring curiosity to how you're experiencing it... Invite yourself to relax with it, let it be as it is right now.... Notice the thoughts and stories.... Investigate the sensations.... You might inquire about what you are wanting that isn't happening.... Relaxing with all you notice.... Encourage yourself to accept whatever is here by saying, "It's okay. Whatever it is it's okay. Let me just feel it."

Finally, remember it's always helpful to ask, "What's the wisest and kindest way to respond to myself right now?" Opening to whatever occurs to you.... Always return to the sensations of breathing...or to whatever is most predominant in the moment, staying present, steady, receptive until your practice period is complete.

Please notice the effect of this practice.

Informal Practice

• Pay special attention to the habit of assuming over-responsibility for others: fixing their upsets and problems. Ask: How am I relating to what's happening? Notice with lots of kindness and curiosity.

• Practice asking: What am I truly responsible for right now? What do I actually have control over? Am I response-able? Notice what it's like to let go of assuming responsibility when it's not yours.

• Pay special attention to the habit of resisting your experience, wanting the experience to be different from how it is. Softly note, "Resisting". See if you can let your experience simply be as it is. Ask, "What am I wanting that isn't happening right now?" Encourage yourself to let it be.

• Continue to experiment with doing ordinary activities mindfully. Notice the effect.

• Keep teaching yourself to Drop In and come back to your breath and your direct authentic experience numerous times throughout the day. Notice the effect.

16

Healing Self-Hatred: The Power of Loving Kindness

You can search the whole world over and never find anyone more deserving of your love and affection than yourself.

The Buddha

Self-Loathing Is "Normal" for Us

I'm sure you've noticed your mind's habit of comparing yourself to others, putting yourself down, and dishing out cruel slams against yourself. Most of us, if we're honest, have had moments of hating ourselves. For many of us, the negative barrage is a constant background noise in our mind. Self-criticism can become so familiar we grow numb to it. We don't like to admit to self-loathing, though, because to be perfect, we're supposed to feel good about ourselves. To feel bad about oneself is viewed as a weakness, and so we prefer to hide our low self-esteem, even to ourselves. Hiding our feelings adds to our shame and self-loathing, creating a nasty vicious circle.

Self-hatred is intrinsic to othering. Low self-esteem and self-doubt are the natural and unavoidable consequences of being in the subordinate position. Women have been historically defined as the lesser sex as long as the patriarchy has been in power. Aristotle, considered one of the most foundational thinkers and philosophers, writing in the fourth century, B.C., believed women were inferior, "deformed males." He said, "The female is a female by virtue of a certain lack of qualities. We should regard the female nature as afflicted with a natural defectiveness."[36] We're viewed as weak, dependent, passive, less intelligent, and less valuable than men. Such deeply held societal views, primarily unconscious, creep into our psyches whether we want them to or not.

The effect of viewing women as "less than" men has permeated our consciousness for so long that it's firmly embedded in the perceptions of both genders. Well into the nineteenth century, it was a common belief that because women's heads are smaller than men's, we are less intelligent. All of the world's dominant religions are historically biased against women, including Buddhism, where the traditional teachings hold that

> Low self-esteem and self-doubt are the natural and unavoidable consequences of being in the subordinate position.

261

Checking in

• What's it been like to spot the habit of resisting? I hope you're seeing its prevalence and the tension it creates. Whenever you spot it, simply note, "Oh, here's resistance," and bring some curiosity to it. See if it's possible to open to what actually is happening: the traffic light turning red, your children fighting, the feeling of anxiety rising up. Gently invite yourself to *let it be* and accept what's here in this moment. Remember impermanence. Even when what's here isn't what you want, when you can accept it as it is, it won't last long, and certainly not forever.

• What about the habit of assuming responsibility for others? I hope you're spotting it and are experimenting with setting wise and respectful boundaries. How are others responding? Sometimes they like us doing everything for them and prefer that we keep up our over-responsibility habits. Ultimately, it's not healthy for either of us.

• What about bringing mindfulness to ordinary activities? Washing the dishes, brushing your hair, chopping vegetables, hugging your loved one? Please remember to practice mindfulness during your day. It's simple and profoundly satisfying.

• How is your sitting practice going now? Please keep sitting even a short while every day. It makes a huge difference in helping these teachings sink in more deeply.

you must be male to become enlightened. Misogyny and violence against women continue to be very alive. In many places around the world, it is commonplace for girls and women to be abused, exploited, kidnapped, enslaved, and murdered. In the United States, a woman is sexually assaulted every two minutes, one in four women experience domestic violence in their lifetime, and one-third of women murdered are killed by their intimate partner.[37] We have a long, long way to go in turning around misogyny, and its impact on our psyche is profound.

We Feel Shame for Being Female

Even though we have made strides to bring more equality between the genders, we are still reminded all too often that being female is valued less than being a man. When we offer an idea at a meeting that's ignored until our male colleague suggests it, or we're left cleaning up the dishes and managing the kids while our husband retreats to do "more important things," or we're left in poverty after a divorce, or we have to endure sexual harassment at work, we continue to get the message that we don't matter as much. We're unconsciously reminded that something is wrong with us, we're less valued, and naturally, our sense of worth diminishes. If we look deeply and honestly into this reaction, we may discover that we actually feel shame in being female.

Shame is a sense of inadequacy as a human being. It's feeling defective, unworthy, disgraced, embarrassed, and diminished as a person. In her extensive research on shame, author Brené Brown defines it as, "The intensely painful feeling or experience of believing that we're flawed and therefore unworthy of love and belonging."[38] Though shame, like all emotions, is universal, it's generally provoked when we make a mistake and feel judged for it. Because shame is born from believing we're inadequate, it's conditioned remedy is to strive to be perfect. The shame we feel in being female is so embedded in our minds we're often blind to it. I invite you — challenge you — to see if this belief isn't lurking somewhere deep in your psychic bones.

Natalie, a 36-year-old woman in a recent class, married with a young daughter, had taken many women's studies courses in college, and had always prided herself in being a feminist. Because she intellectually understood gender oppression and the importance of equality, she thought she had cleansed herself of these biased and untrue societal views. However, when she faced herself honestly with the penetrating clarity of mindfulness, she was shocked to discover deeply buried feelings of female shame. She was dismayed and alarmed by the pervasive power of our conditioning.

As a young girl, I wasn't very drawn to traditional girl activities. I preferred to run around and play outside, and remember thinking that boys had a better deal than girls. It seemed like they were allowed to have more fun and didn't have to care about how they looked. Later, as a young wife with two little children and at the beginning of my professional career, I preferred socializing with men rather than with other moms. I found women with children rather uninteresting because they were always talking about what was happening with their husbands and children. With men, the talk was about more worldly, intellectual subjects. Reflecting on these preferences later, I clearly saw my bias against the female gender. I diminished our traditional roles and thought the man's world was more interesting and valuable. It wasn't until I understood my own internalized oppression more deeply, coupled with compassion for the pain it causes, that I could grow in sincere respect and interest for my sister women and myself as a woman and mother.

A conversation with my granddaughter when she was four affirmed these deeply held cultural views. We were playing with her two older brothers when she started singing a made-up song about penises and how she wished she had a penis. Her brothers rolled their eyes as if to say, "Oh yeah, we've heard this before." With my curiosity piqued, I asked her why she wished she had a penis. She replied, "Because then I'd be a boy. And I wish I was a boy. Boys are better than girls. They get to do more awesome things." Her kind brothers joined me in quickly reassuring her that she could do just as many great and fun things as boys. Still,

I was astonished. Although today my granddaughter lives in a world of much greater opportunity for women, I was amazed at what she was perceiving and believing already.

When my daughter was in college, she made a troubling discovery about her internalized shame. She was having a hard time selecting a major. She was confused and uncertain about what was right for her. She was smart, loved science and for a while she majored in pre-med, then she switched to anthropology, and then to sociology. After reading a book about feminism and conditioning, she called me one night, upset, angry, scared, and sad. She realized that her difficulty selecting a major was due to her belief that she wasn't smart enough to be what she really wanted to be, which was a doctor. Her opinion had been unconsciously shaped through classroom behavior. When the teacher or professor would pose a question, it was almost always the male students who raised their hands first and were called on to answer. From experiencing being overlooked over and over, she was stunned to realize she had unconsciously concluded she wasn't as smart as the male students and therefore couldn't make it as a doctor. Finding her clarity and determination, she went on to major in pre-med, discovering she was indeed smart enough to pursue her dream.

How Does Self-Hatred Evolve in Us?

A landmark study by Lyn Mikel Brown and Carol Gilligan explored how we insidiously internalize cultural views as we grow up, giving up our relationship with ourselves in order to be in relationship with others, and turning against ourselves in the process.[39] These researchers wanted to see how girls sense of self changes over time and in relationship with others. Their five-year longitudinal study followed 100 girls in a school in Ohio. They conducted in-depth interviews with girls in first, fourth, seventh, and tenth grades, and then followed each of these girls through an annual interview for five years. The interviews focused on the girls' feelings about themselves, their friends, their school, their parents, the world, their hopes and dreams, and their relationships. As the girls grew older, the results showed a progressive silencing of authentic self, increased referencing to others, and the continuing internalization of oppressive cultural messages.

At the beginning of the study, the girls in first grade demonstrated a strong and clear connection with their direct experience and authentic self. They could assert themselves when necessary, handled conflict directly, and expressed amazing and creative ideas about the world, the nature of life, and what they thought could and should be. They were open and expressive. The girls in fourth grade showed signs of beginning to hold themselves back, less willing to confront conflict directly, and more concerned with others' view of them. The seventh grade girls were even more detached from their authentic self and primarily focused on pleasing others, especially their peers, wearing the right clothes, jewelry, hairstyle, and so on. More important than being true to themselves and operating from their iternal authority was the need to fit in and be how they perceived they were supposed to be.

> Girls are culturally taught to disconnect from their own authority in order to conduct relationships "successfully."

Othering was clearly and firmly established. Sadly, at this age the researchers began to see clinical signs of depression, anxiety, and eating disorders. The girls in tenth grade were even more crystallized in their disconnection from self and focused on the external other for validation and approval.

This remarkable study clearly documented that our connection with authentic self goes underground, often never to be found again, as we move into and through adolescence. The researchers concluded that girls are culturally taught to disconnect from their own authority in order to conduct relationships "successfully." Further, they saw this loss of relationship to authentic self as fundamental in causing many of the core psychological problems women experience in adulthood.

In another important study, Mary Pipher, clinical psychologist, saw this same progression of losing connection with authentic self in her clinical practice with adolescent girls.[40] She saw adolescent girls experiencing tremendous conflict between their authentic self and their need to act feminine, and a sustained cultural pressure to split from their true selves into false conditioned selves. She refers to the change that happens for girls during adolescence as similar to planes flying through the "Bermuda Triangle": their self-worth goes mysteriously missing as they lose their true selves to the cultural prescriptions for being female. Because self-worth is based on authenticity and the acceptance of all our thoughts and feelings, it follows that girls lose confidence as they disown themselves. Pipher observed girls developing patterns of negative self-judgment in order to stop expressing thoughts and feelings they assumed were unacceptable, coupled with losing connection with their authentic voice.

Psychologist Stephen Hinshaw reports seeing these patterns for girls continuing, but now with added pressures.[41] He says today's girls are caught in a "triple bind." They are expected to achieve the traditional goals to be feminine and "act like a girl", meaning look attractive and be pretty, and be sensitive and devoted to others. In addition, they must also be competent in traditional male pursuits, "boy goals," such as academics, athletics, and promising professional careers. Thus, complete perfection with everything is now required.

Becky, a 13-year-old seventh grader, came to work with me because she was suffering from an acutely painful disconnection from her friends, to the extent that she began having panic attacks and strong feelings of not belonging and not being "good enough." She said that these feelings erupted one day when she realized she didn't enjoy being with her friends anymore. They had changed. They didn't want to play anymore. Instead, they spent their time texting and standing around together talking, not doing what they used to enjoy doing together. Because she couldn't find anything to talk with them about, she blamed herself, assuming she wasn't interesting enough to earn their attention. She felt painfully out of place, alone, and awkward. She concluded that something was really wrong with her.

I'm sure most of us can relate to 13-year old Becky. I remember feeling horribly inept and incredibly self-conscious at that age. I doubted myself, and compared myself constantly to others. The first time I heard Gloria Steinem speak in person, she said, "Girls become female impersonators by the age of 13." This stuck me as so true. We're trying so hard to figure out how we're supposed to be as a woman that we completely submerge our authentic self. It is a very difficult, anxious, and confusing period in our lives.

Low Self-Esteem Is Not a Pathology

Because low self-esteem, self-doubt, and deep-seated feelings of shame are habits of thinking born from cultural conditioning and *not* because something is "wrong" with us, we need to bring the healing power of mindfulness to these painful patterns. This means clearly seeing the painful beliefs that negate ourselves as conditioned, and not the truth. They arise as a normal response to gender oppression. Because we're taught that a normal healthy sense of self is supposed be one of confidence, trust, and ease, more like how boys and men *seem* to be, it's easy to slip into the view that something is wrong with us when we consistently doubt ourselves. The view that something is wrong with us is a conditioned lie. We must not blame ourselves for feeling bad about ourselves.

> The view that something is wrong with us is a conditioned lie. We must not blame ourselves for feeling bad about ourselves.

Historically, women's psychology has often been pathologized when it's been different from men's. Women were drugged, given lobotomies, electrical shock therapy, and often institutionalized as mentally ill because of their "hysterical" behavior. Over the years countless women have been, and continue to be, marginalized, or worse, by chronic anxiety and depression that arises from their real life oppressive and abusive situations.

If we label ourselves as "sick," or think something is wrong with us because we feel bad about ourselves, then we continue the same oppressive rap we've been taught. We end up feeling worse and more stuck in the conditioned lie. Make no mistake here, feeling shame and hating ourselves is deeply painful and creates great suffering. These feelings are not life promoting, and benefit no one. We must work diligently to spot these incorrect beliefs when they arise, clearly see the suffering they create, and work to free ourselves from them. To be fully responsible for ourselves, we need to view the beliefs for what they are — painful conditioned lies and patterns — and choose to give authority for ourselves back to ourselves.

As one of my teachers, Christina Feldman, author and co-founder of Gaia House in England says, "Authenticity and subordination are incompatible!"[42] When we connect with our authentic experience, knowing and accepting whatever we're experiencing in the moment, it's difficult to remain subordinate. As our relationship with ourselves becomes more accepting and trusting through mindfulness, we become less caught in the oppressive patterns and our behavior naturally changes. We see our conditioned beliefs and patterns more clearly, and are held hostage by them less. Increasingly as connection with our authentic experience grows, we become less likely to react in automatically subordinate ways.

Mindfulness of Our Conditioned Self-Hatred

To use mindfulness to free us from these painful wrong views, the first step is to recognize when it's happening. As soon as you're aware of turning against yourself through criticizing, shaming, condemning, belittling or any form of self-loathing, softly note it. "Oh, here's shame. Here's telling myself I'm stupid. Here's discounting myself. Here's thinking I'm disgusting/selfish/ugly, etc." This first step is huge because by naming the feeling or judgment, we instantly create some separation from the pattern. We've popped out of the old nasty conditioned thought bubble. We're *seeing* the thoughts *instead of being* the thoughts.

Because we're so deeply attached to these old incorrect beliefs it can be challenging to remember that these are only stories. Remember that thoughts may not be real or true and may not serve us. In addition, by naming and observing what's happening without using the first-person pronoun "I'm," we disidentify with the experience, which naturally creates more internal room and helps release our attachment to it. Now we aren't so caught in the hostile lie.

Next, we bring curiosity to the actual sensations these thoughts and stories create in the body. Cradle the sensations without aversion, and accept them just as they are, with kindness and gentleness. Invite yourself to relax and expand around them, giving them lots of space. Treat yourself like the crying baby in your living room and practice being a good mother to yourself. Be patient and stay as steady as you can. At some point as you're exploring the sensations this way, you can ask, "Okay, given my mind's been creating these self-condemning thoughts, what is the wisest and kindest way to respond to myself right now?" In other words, what do you really need from yourself right now? Pause then, and open to whatever occurs to you. Remind yourself these self-hating beliefs are not true, they are only a pattern in your brain. You might remind yourself of what is actually true: you are as worthwhile as everyone else, you do matter, you are inherently good and loving, exactly as you are. Be as receptive to yourself as you can. You are opening now to the wisdom that's available from your true nature blue sky mind.

The process I've described is most useful in formal meditation practice when you have sufficient time to explore your experience deeply.

Each time you sit and explore, you are interrupting the heavily worn neural groove of self-hatred, and creating a new path of self-acceptance and love. When you practice in this way, the old groove gradually fills in and loses its pull, and the new path becomes more established, easier to find and follow, as it grows in depth and strength.

Off the cushion, informally, you can practice a shortened three-step version of this method. First, when you spot self-hatred, softly note it, and recognize it as conditioned self-hatred. See if you can spot the exact condemning thought and realize it's just a *story*, all made up, really old, and doesn't serve you. Next, shift attention to your breath and pause long enough to feel your body breathing. Breathe at least three full mindful breaths. The third step is to remind yourself of what is true: you are enough, you are perfect just as you are, you are worthwhile, or any other life-enhancing belief you'd like to teach yourself. The more you practice these steps, the more you'll shift away from the self-hating habit into accepting, loving, and respecting yourself. This in turn, helps water the seeds of unshakeable confidence in yourself, just as you are.

On-the-Spot Mindfulness for Self-Hatred

- Softly note: "Here's self-hatred." Recognize it as conditioned and not true.
- Breathe three breaths mindfully.
- Remind yourself of what is true: "I am enough just as I am."

The Power of the Loving Kindness Practice

Sometimes, however, the groove of self-hatred feels as deep as the Grand Canyon, and mindfulness isn't strong enough spiritual medicine to keep us from falling into the abyss and hurting ourselves. In this case, the practice called "Loving Kindness" can be powerfully helpful and transformative. The Buddha taught this practice as a companion practice to mindfulness specifically for those times when the mind is stubbornly caught, stuck, or dead-ended in severely negative mind states. It's very useful for when we're trapped in self-hatred and shame, as well as fear or panic, guilt, anger, longing, depression, loneliness, despair, grief, or sadness. Loving Kindness creates a release from the vise grip the mind is caught in; a respite and safe place for our attention to rest so the mind, heart, and body can relax. Once relaxed, the mind's frozen torment has a chance to naturally melt and dissolve.

Also called *Metta* in Pali, and *Maitri* in Sanskrit, Loving Kindness means bringing unconditional and unrestrained friendliness towards ourselves and others. It's the sense of true unconditional love. This love is not bound to desire or to owning or possessing. At the core of the practice is the deep understanding that all beings, without exception, want to be happy and free from suffering. Yet, as the Four Noble Truths remind us, no one can live a life that is free from suffering; everyone suffers

> Loving Kindness
> is a spiritual balm that helps
> heal the wounded self,
> and moves the hurting
> mind into a safe place.

at times. When we are caught in suffering, we often feel isolated and alienated from others, not a member of the family of all beings. To intentionally turn towards ourselves when we realize we're suffering and remember that, "I, like all beings everywhere, want to be happy and free from suffering," is an inclusive act of love. This reconnects us not only with ourselves, but also with the understanding that we're all in this together. It reminds us of our interconnectedness with all beings, with all of life. By remembering that we are all in the same boat, the feelings of separateness and isolation diminish.

Practicing Loving Kindness is not adding anything new to our heart and minds. Rather, it opens us to the energy of love and kindness that has always been a part of us, but has become less accessible due to conditioning. The ability to love, to be kind, compassionate, generous, joyful, and peaceful is a part of our true nature. Conditioning and the painful circumstances of our lives trained us to shield and close our hearts trying to protect ourselves from pain. Over time, this protective shield grows thicker and harder, making it difficult to authentically love, especially ourselves. Metta helps gently soften, moisten and open our precious hearts so we can feel our love, tenderness and kindness more easily. Loving Kindness is a spiritual balm that helps heal the wounded self, and moves the hurting mind into a safe place. It helps us embrace all parts of ourselves — the painful and the lovely.

> Loving Kindness helps us embrace all parts of ourselves — the painful and the lovely.

Concentration Practice

To practice Metta, we concentrate on repeating three or four phrases that express our heartfelt wish to be happy and free from suffering. Traditionally, the phrases center around wishes to be safe, healthy, happy, joyful, and free from suffering. You create a set of phrases that feel right to you and then use them as your basic set. The phrases I've been using that I find helpful for addressing othering and self-hatred are:

  + May I be safe and protected.
  + May I be peaceful.
  + May I trust and accept myself.
  + May I live with ease and with kindness.

By deliberately concentrating on repeating the phrases over and over, disregarding whatever else might catch our attention, such as thoughts, sensations, sounds, smells, or emotions, we keep attention focused on the phrases. The power of this deliberate concentration causes the agitated mild to calm down and drop gently into a more stable place. Neuroscience shows us that such concentration shifts neural activity from the amygdala in the brain's limbic system where we're revved up in our painful emotions, to the prefrontal cortex where we naturally activate our wiser, calmer, more logical thoughts. Concentration also activates the parasympathic nervous system, which releases soothing hormones such as oxytocin and dopamine that help the whole mind-body system slow down and relax.[43]

Metta is practiced both as a formal meditation practice and informally, off the cushion. We offer the phrases first to ourselves, and then to others, in ever expanding circles so that eventually we're offer loving kindness to every being on the planet, without exception. We give the phrases first and foremost to ourselves, because the foundation of this practice is rooted in learning to be our own friend. For many of us, this first step can feel strange and awkward, if not wrong. Perhaps you've noticed it's easier to give love and kindness than to receive it. For many women, it can feel uncomfortable, and certainly unfamiliar, to be on the receiving end of kindness.

Before waking up to the habits of othering, I resisted every compliment and tribute that came my way, thinking that person's view was inaccurate at best. I would immediately give an accolade back because the interaction felt uncomfortable. Is this familiar to you? Resisting praise is born from believing we're not worthy of deserving loving attention from others. Contrary to our conditioned view, the Buddha said, "You can search throughout the entire universe for someone who is more deserving of your love and affection than you are yourself, and that person is not to be found anywhere. You yourself, as much as anybody in the universe, deserve your love and affection."[44]

> We must learn to truly love and respect ourselves, and become a stable and trustworthy friend to our self.

We must learn to truly love and respect ourselves, and become a stable and trustworthy friend to our self. When we love others without the foundation of loving ourselves, we lose our boundaries, we cling in unhealthy ways to the other, searching futilely for intimacy with the other that cannot be found because we've left our most important intimate relationship: our relationship with ourselves. Giving Metta to ourselves first before offering it to others is like the emergency instructions we hear before the airplane takes off: "Put the oxygen mask on yourself first before assisting others." Until we can truly love ourselves, just as we are, our ability to truly love others is limited.

How to Practice Loving Kindness/Metta

To benefit from the many fruits of Metta, it's best to practice it first as a formal meditation. This helps you learn the phrases, and then they'll be easily accessible when you need to use them on the spot in your life. Formal practice also gives you direct experience of some of the positive effects, it builds your concentration muscles, and works away at transforming those deep patterns that cause suffering.

Practice

Meditation:
Offering Metta to Ourselves

First, find three or four phrases to express love and kindness that feel right to you. It's best to make them general enough to cover everything, but specific enough so they address what's most important to you. Besides the ones I've suggested they can be as simple as, "May I be safe. May I be healthy. May I be peaceful." Don't struggle to find the perfect phrases, just trust that what you start with is good enough.

- Arrange your body in a comfortable posture. Comfort and ease are the rule in this practice, so if you want to lie down or sit in a chair, please do so. It's perfectly fine to move your body or change positions at any point, too. Next, connect with the sensations of your breath and practice mindful breathing for a few minutes.
- When you feel more settled, let go of the breath and move attention to your heart center. This is the heart energy center, or chakra, not your

biological heart, located right in the middle of the chest. You might place your hand over your heart center to help your attention stay anchored here. Now, invite yourself to be surrounded by and filled with the energy of kindness and love, any way you can imagine it. You might imagine being infused with soft, gentle, nourishing, friendly energy. If it feels foreign or awkward, just note that without judgment. You might instead imagine being held in the arms of a being that loves you unconditionally, and simply open to what that's like. (I sometimes imagine my wonderful old dog Millie is holding me, only I imagine her the size of "Clifford the Big Red Dog.")

• Next, recall the intention of this practice: all beings, including you, want to be happy and free from suffering. We are all the same. We all get caught in habits of conditioning and painful mind-states.

• Now, with the sense of cradling yourself in your heart center, begin offering your phrases to yourself, one phrase at a time, with as much heartfelt warmth and sincerity as you can muster. "May I be safe and protected." "May I be peaceful." "May I trust and accept myself." "May I live with ease and kindness."

• Whenever you realize your attention has slipped away, focus right back on the phrases again. Because Metta is a concentration practice rather than a mindfulness practice, the goal is to wholeheartedly attend to the phrases. It's helpful to allow a little space between each phrase so you can receive it fully. Let the pace you're saying the phrases be slow. If an image or a feeling emerges that reflects the phrase, go with it. This can deepen your connection to the words. For example, you might imagine what it looks or feels like to be "safe and protected," or "peaceful," and so on. Simply open to whatever occurs to you.

• Keep practicing like this, offering your Metta phrases to yourself, over and over, concentrating with fresh attention on each phrase. As you come to the end of your formal practice, gently shift attention back to the sensations of the body breathing. When you're fully out of the meditation, pause for a few moments to notice the effect on your heart, body, and mind.

The first time I was introduced to Metta I thought it was supposed to make me feel in love with myself. However, I didn't feel much of anything. In fact, the practice felt contrived and boring initially, and I had significant resistance to giving these phrases to myself. It was helpful to learn the intention of Metta is not to create a particular feeling. You may feel happy and relaxed, or sad, angry, tense, or emotionally dry or like nothing is happening. That's all okay. It's best to simply bring

> The power of Metta lives in the intention to offer kind and loving wishes.

beginner's mind to the practice and not be attached to any particular experience or effect.

The great power of this practice lies in the *intention* to offer kind and loving wishes to ourselves. Because shame and self-hatred are so deeply internalized I urge you to confine your Metta practice to yourself for a substantial period of time before offering it to others. Because each time we practice we're purposely treating ourselves kindly and lovingly, over time the effect of Metta seeps in. Gradually our relationship with ourselves grows more loving.

Practice

Meditation:
Offering Metta to Others

Once you feel well established in giving Loving Kindness to yourself, you can expand to including others in the formal meditation. The sequence that's traditionally followed is: benefactor, dear friend, neutral person, difficult person, and all beings everywhere.

- A benefactor is someone who supports, encourages, and helps you. This can be someone you know personally, or it can be someone you don't know, but who is a role model or inspiration for you. Bring that person to mind, imagining they are right here with you. Hold them in your heart-space of kindness and love. Recall how they support or inspire you, and then, calling them by their name if you like, offer the phases to them with as much warmth as possible. Repeat the phrases as many times as feels right for you.
- Next, bring to mind a dear friend. It's best to select someone you care about deeply and with whom there is currently no disturbing conflict. Imagining they are here with you, reflect on their friendship, and then offer the phrases lovingly to your friend.
- Now select a neutral person, someone you have neither positive nor negative feelings about. Usually this is someone you don't know at all, such as the clerk at a store or the person who delivers your mail. Reflect on the truth that just like you, this person experiences suffering at times and wants to be happy and free from suffering. Cradle them in your heart space and offer them your Metta phrases.

- The difficult person comes next, traditionally called "the enemy." This is someone you have negative feelings towards, or for whom some conflict or pain is alive in you. Remember that even though the difficult person is associated with conflict and possibly hurt, anger, fear or even hatred, still this person, just like you, wants to be happy and free from suffering. Be gentle with yourself, offering the phrases with as much kindness as you can genuinely muster. We are simply practicing opening our heart to them, even just a little. As you imagine the difficult person, be curious about how close you want to bring them to you. However close you bring them, no judging, please.
- Finally, expand your field of awareness and open your heart to all beings everywhere on the planet. This includes all the humans, without exception, even your most despised person or terrifying groups of people. It includes all of the living creatures of our planet: the animals, birds, beings that live in the earth, oceans and water. Imagine cradling all of these beings in your expanded heart space, and offer the Metta phrases to all beings everywhere for several minutes.

At the end of this meditation, pause to notice the effect on your mind, body, and heart.

Informal Practice: Offering Metta to Ourselves

Practicing Metta informally is a wonderful way to encourage our hearts to expand, grow more open and receptive, and continue to transform self-hatred. Once you've learned your phrases, you can give yourself doses of Metta throughout the day. Because it's impossible to overdose on Metta, the more you offer it to yourself the better. It's best to figure out a system that works for you so you can more easily remember to bring it lavishly into your day. Coupling it with the Dropping In practice is an easy way to offer yourself Metta. After you mindfully breathe three breaths, repeat the Loving Kindness phrases to yourself. Whenever you spot the habit of negating or condemning yourself, Drop In, mindfully breathe, and then sincerely offer yourself Metta. It's also lovely to practice Loving Kindness for a few minutes before you fall asleep at night and then again as soon as you wake up in the morning before you get out of bed. This practice helps to reset our mind and heart as we end and begin the day. Try finding a variety of ways to offer Metta to yourself because the more we're watering these seeds of love and kindness, the better.

Lately I've been offering myself Metta when I'm doing ordinary activities like walking my dog or driving the car. It helps my whole being rest in a softer place than if my mind is running on automatic. Liz, who has been practicing mindfulness and Loving Kindness for several years now, offers Metta to herself every time she washes her hands. She delights in the fact that while she's doing something great for her physical health by thoroughly washing her hands, she's also "cleaning" her mind of old grimy toxic beliefs that have kept her oppressed and suffering.

Remember, too, that Metta is helpful whenever you realize you're abducted into a difficult mind-state and your other mindfulness tools aren't cutting it. Concentrating on the Metta phrases helps move mind and body out of that stressed state so we can gather our wits about us again. This is one of its great benefits. One student, Mary, gets extremely anxious driving in intense rush hour traffic, so she offers Metta to herself whenever the fear escalates. She says it helps her remain calm and present. It's effective for moving from panic or disentangling from a worry. A dear friend who is a breast cancer survivor gets easily caught in health fears, especially when she's waiting for mammogram results. She relies on Metta for keeping herself sane during these uncertain periods. Whenever we feel overwhelmed by any difficult emotion offering Metta creates a safe respite and path to inner stability.

Whenever we feel overwhelmed by any difficult emotion offering Metta creates a safe respite and path to inner stability.

Informal Practice: Offering Metta to Others

We can offer Loving Kindness to others anytime, anywhere, as a practice to developing a more open heart. Kathy does an informal Metta practice when she takes a walk during her noon lunch break. She silently offers Metta to each person she passes, regardless of their demeanor. She says the effect is amazing. Instead of her mind habitually reacting to people, creating judgments and stories, especially about the people who look different from her, with Metta her heart stays open. By remembering we're all in the same boat, she feels a connection with the people she passes. She finds people smile at her more often when she silently offers them Metta.

Metta also teaches us how to love without attachment, and thus is the perfect antidote to the "good" part of othering: the desire for the other to be happy and free from suffering. When our important other is hurting, othering provokes our overly responsible reaction. We take control to make them feel better, or to manipulate the situation so they "see the light" and change. Clearly, this habit causes suffering for both of us and it rarely works. With Metta, we send heartfelt wishes for the person to be happy and free from suffering. We offer a simple blessing for their well-being from our heart, rather than our head. We accept them as they are, trusting and respecting their integrity, rather than demanding they be different. Sending Metta doesn't involve controlling, fixing, or manipulating because it's offered freely from the heart without strings. We keep our own heart open to them even though they're suffering, or behaving in ways that cause suffering. This doesn't mean we tolerate abuse or aren't authentic with them. We still must exercise wise boundaries, but we do it with an open rather than closed heart. Consequently, our own suffering is less.

> Metta teaches us how to love without attachment.

When someone is suffering and we feel powerless to help, we bring that person into our awareness, imagine holding them in our heart space, and sincerely offer our phrases to them. Sometimes it's helpful to say their name. "Diana, may you be safe and protected. May you live with ease and with kindness." Although we can't know what effect our loving wishes have on that person, the effect on our own mind-state is usually immediate: our mind and heart relaxes. Metta keeps our heart open as we witness their suffering. This allows us to remain compassionately present with them through their difficulty.

On one occasion right before I left for a meditation retreat, my son's fiancé broke up with him and he was heartbroken. When I tried to fall asleep that first night my mind was swept up in worry about him. "What's going to happen to Dave? Will he be all right? What if he decides never to love again? Will he fall into a big depression?" As soon as I spotted these stories, I mindfully breathed and then sent him Metta. Within a few minutes of practice, I let go of the fretting, relaxed and fell asleep. Sending the phrases helped me to remember to trust that we each have ability to find our way through our challenges.

Metta Directly Addresses Our Wounded Self

Because the root cause of all our suffering is attachment to the idea of a self, formed from conditioning, we refrain from using personal pronouns as we note our experience. This encourages less identification and attachment to self. With Metta, the intention is different. We're addressing the wounded sense of self directly. We say, "May *I* be safe and protected. May *I* be peaceful and joyful." Othering is based on the belief that we aren't good enough, we're flawed. These beliefs turn us against ourselves in shame and hatred. Metta stops us from turning against ourselves, and instead, love every part of ourselves. By offering "May *I* be safe and protected. May *I* be peaceful. May *I* trust and accept myself. May *I* live with ease and kindness," we cradle our poor hurting sense of self in the energy of unconditional love. We stay on our own side — even though we may feel scared or full of shame. We practice loving ourselves even though we believe we aren't okay. It's inclusive. With practice, our relationship with our conditioned self transforms. When we are no longer worrying about whether we're okay, lovable, attractive enough, or anything enough, we can rest in our direct, genuine, authentic experience, just as it is.

> Metta stops us from turning against ourselves, and instead, love every part of ourselves.

Metta Softens Deep Neural Grooves

The first time I directly experienced the deeply transformative power of Metta was during a weekend retreat with Sharon Salzberg. We were intensively sending Loving Kindness phrases to ourselves, others, and all beings, both formally and informally. At the end of second day when bicycling home from the retreat with a group of friends, also attending it, my partner Pam asked me if I'd be willing to go home and let our dog out while she biked on with them for a while. I said sure, happy to do so. As I was sitting on our back porch watching our dog, a very familiar pattern took over my mind: "See. Here it is again. I don't belong. I'm always the one left out, not included. I'm always excluded. The odd one. It's because I'm not how I'm supposed to be." As I felt myself beginning to spiral down into the familiar dark lonely pain of not belonging, my mind suddenly gently and firmly said, "But you're really okay right now and you don't have to believe this old stuff anymore." Instantly I popped out of the groove and was back in the present, feeling open, light and enough. I was very surprised and very impressed. I had never before moved out of that painful pit so easily and swiftly and I knew it was the effect of practicing Metta.

Please remember, then, if it seems like nothing is happening when you practice Loving Kindness, you may be pleasantly surprised at an unexpected moment when your brain runs a familiar pattern and suddenly shifts out of it. I encourage you to be curious.

Metta Helps Us Stand Next to What Is Difficult

We can also bring the spirit of Metta to our aid whenever we find ourselves on the verge of fleeing a painful experience. One of the most difficult and yet key aspects of mindfulness is staying present and steady when the going gets rough. We know that by learning to stay, while being curious and accepting of the pain or difficult emotion, we discover our way through it. The obstacle is the path. The way out is through. Pairing one or two Metta phrases to the difficult state can help us keep our stable ground: "May I be *peaceful in the midst of this anxiety* (pain, doubt, grief, jealousy)." "May I have *ease in the midst of this sadness* (worry, guilt)." "May I be *safe and protected in the midst of this confusion* (fear, anger)." Using the phrases this way reminds us to remain steady, and on our own side with our hearts open, rather than abandon or turn against ourselves.

Such staying power allows us to witness the natural movement of impermanence — we see how the experience shifts and changes. By

The more Metta
the betta.

staying, we are likely to learn more about the workings of our mind and what this upset is really about. Equally significant, learning we can stay steady with ourselves through the storm builds our unshakeable confidence.

The Loving Kindness practice is an incredibly useful and transformative practice. It's so very flexible because we can apply it to ourselves and others in so many ways. I invite you to experiment with it and see how it can be helpful to you. Remember, we can't over dose on it. The more Metta the betta.

Ownwork Suggestions

Formal Sitting Practice:
Choiceless Awareness and Loving Kindness for Yourself

Now you're paying mindful attention to whatever arises that is predominant. This is called "choiceless awareness".

Decide how long your sit will be and arrange your body in a comfortable posture with spine aligned.... Invite your body, mind, and heart to relax.... Slowly sweep attention through your body to directly invite relaxing and easing.... Now drop down into your body to connect with the sensations of the breath.... Expand the field of your awareness.... Stay with the breath until some other experience becomes predominant: noting "thinking" when attention is drawn into a thought.... or name the sensation, "Pressure. Itching. Tingling," when a sensation is predominant. Investigate the sensation letting it be until it fades away.... When an emotion arises turn mindfully towards it, noting it, "Sadness. Frustration. Shame." See the story behind it and drop into the body to the sensation it creates, cradling it gently and spaciously...always coming back to the breath when nothing else is predominant.... Practice this way until you feel settled....

Now shift to the Loving Kindness meditation by moving attention to the heart center and invite yourself to be filled and surrounded with the energy of kindness and love, any way you can imagine it right now.... With the sense of cradling yourself in your heart center, begin offering yourself your phrases, one at a time, with as much sincerity and kindness as you can: "May I be safe and protected. May I be peaceful. May I trust and accept myself. May I live with ease and with kindness." Concentrate on each phrase...and when you realize your attention has wandered away, gently and kindly shift it back to the next phrase, beginning again.... Continue offering yourself Metta for a good amount of time....

Now let the phrases go and shift back to concentrating on the sensations of breathing and take the last few minutes of your sit to again practice choiceless awareness, the regular insight meditation practice....

Notice the effect of this practice.

Informal Practice

• Be mindful of the habitual ways you negate yourself: criticize, bully, hold yourself back, compare, doubt, and so on. As soon as you spot one of these habits, Drop In and breathe at least three full breaths, be glad you're seeing it, and note it with kindness, curiosity, understanding, and compassion: "Here's the habit of hating myself." Then apply your phrases of Loving Kindness with as much warmth as you can. Notice the effect.

• Find ways to offer yourself the phrases of Metta as much as you can throughout the day: whenever you're stopped at a traffic light, waiting for someone, or while you're washing your hands. Notice the effect.

• Whenever you realize you're worrying about another, offer them Metta. Notice the effect.

• Whenever you feel disturbed or stressed, Drop In, mindfully breathe, and ask, "What's going on with me right now? What am I thinking? Feeling? Resisting? Wanting?" Offer Metta and hold it all with kindness and acceptance. Notice the effect.

• Practice offering yourself your Loving Kindness phrases before you fall asleep at night, and then again as soon as you wake up in the morning. Notice the effect.

17

The Alchemy of Befriending Our Difficult Emotions

Don't turn away.
Keep your eye on
the bandaged place.
That's where the light
enters you.

Rumi

Making Friends With Our Emotions

Now that you've been practicing both mindfulness and Metta, recognize the habit of resisting the unpleasant, and understand the necessity of acceptance, you've laid the foundation for working with difficult emotions more deeply. This is an area where the benefits of mindfulness can be remarkably healing and transformative. After you learn how to work with your emotions in this deep explorative way, you'll have the basics for being your own psychotherapist, to a large degree. This may sound bold, but my conviction comes from using this approach with people every day in my psychotherapy practice. When we learn how to create the *right inner conditions*, our wise trustworthy body-mind-heart system opens naturally, and transformation happens spontaneously. This empowering way to work with emotions builds faith in ourselves. We discover we are truly wise, can handle what arises, and have the resources and stability to stay with ourselves through thick and thin. This leads directly to living with unshakeable confidence.

As we learn to befriend difficult emotions, we need to remember this approach is diametrically opposed to our conditioning. We *strongly* prefer the pleasant over the unpleasant. We fear unpleasant and painful sensations and emotions. Conditioning has taught us to disconnect from them through suppression, denial, avoidance, and projection. However, these reactions leave us generally cut off from ourselves, feeling numb, anxious, or depressed. As one woman said, observing her habitual emotional palette, "Most of the time I just feel kind of nervous, dull, and gray."

To summon the courage to face our painful emotions, it helps to remember they offer significant information for us. They point to

> When we learn how to create the right inner conditions, our wise trustworthy body-mind-heart system opens naturally, and transformation happens spontaneously.

Checking in

• Have you been able to spot old habits of self-hatred? Criticizing yourself, second guessing, minimizing your experience as compared to others', assuming you're limited in some way, feeling ashamed of yourself? Please recognize these patterns with kindness and compassion, and give yourself a good dose of Metta right on the spot.

• How do you like the formal practice of Loving Kindness? Many find it easier to concentrate on the phrases than on the sensations of breathing in the mindfulness practice.

• What about doing the Loving Kindness on the spot? Have you noticed if it's helpful in moving your mind to a calmer place? Please keep working with it.

• What's it like giving these loving wishes to yourself? Many women find it uncomfortable at first. Even so, or perhaps all the more so, please keep practicing giving yourself doses of Metta as often as you can. Most of us really need it.

• Feel free to experiment with the practice. Some find it helpful to begin the sitting meditation with some minutes of Metta. It can help us settle in more deeply and help the heart open more kindly towards ourselves. I like ending the sitting practice with offering some Metta to myself, to those I'm worrying about, and then to all beings everywhere.

where we have wounds that need healing. They show us where we may be clinging to something we want that isn't happening right now, and where we need to let go. They remind us to bring compassion, kindness, and love to ourselves when we are hurting. Difficult emotions ask us to bring discerning wisdom to see through and update our false conditioned beliefs.

> Difficult emotions ask us to bring discerning wisdom to see through and update our false conditioned beliefs.

Creating the Right Internal Conditions

To make friends with our emotions requires cultivating a conducive inner environment. A number of attitudes, understandings, and skills need to be operating. First is a *sincere motivation* to want to learn from our emotions. When we realize that anger, fear, shame, or guilt has something useful to teach us, then we can form a *clear intention* to open to it. This can make experiencing the discomfort worthwhile. We also need a sense of *faith* in ourselves and in the practice, that working with the emotion will be beneficial. We need to trust that we are wise and really do have the answers we're seeking within ourselves, and that this ancient practice which has helped so many can also help us. Clearly though, this kind of trust and faith grows out of our direct experience, which only comes through practice.

Mindfulness is built upon awareness, personal inquiry and trusting one's authentic, embodied experience. The Buddha said to his students, "Don't take my word for it. Find out for yourself if these methods are helpful. Only through your own experience will you discover what is true." Instead of blind faith, we are asked to rely on our own data. Because we've been living with ourselves every moment of our lives, we have all the information we need about ourselves. Everything that has happened to us, everything that is known to us, everything that has shaped us and brought us to where we are in this moment, is accessible within our own body, mind and heart. Not that we all don't have our blind spots, but we are the experts on ourselves. Respecting our own experience, knowing it is valid and worthy of our attention, helps us feel safe enough to open to the difficult.

> Respecting our own experience, knowing it is valid and worthy of our attention, helps us feel safe enough to open to the difficult.

The willingness to *suspend judgment* and be *curious, receptive,* and *accepting* of our direct experience is also necessary. This willingness applies to everything we notice. We don't choose what we notice, preferring the more comfortable experiences. Rather, we open to it all that's here, no matter what. We practice Beginner's Mind, fresh attention, and dropping all our preferences, assumptions, predictions, and conclusions. We refrain from judging anything that arises. This approach is, as I'm sure you've been discovering, radical and transformative.

Still another essential requirement is being able to *sustain attention* and *stay* with all that's unfolding as it unfolds. Staying with our experience, while maintaining concentration and receptivity, allows the space for our truth and wisdom to emerge. *By staying steady and spacious,* the difficult emotion can shift and change naturally on its own, and we can discover what it is really about, along with the wisest and kindest way to respond. As the wise Sufi poet Rumi advised, "Don't turn away. Keep your eye on the bandaged place; that's where the light enters you." With these inner conditions, the alchemical transformation of the emotion often happens spontaneously.

> Becoming friends with our emotions takes courage. We are developing our spiritual warriorship.

Becoming friends with our emotions takes *courage.* Every time we practice being curious, open, and accepting of what's here, we're going into the unknown, not knowing what it will be like or what we'll discover. We are developing our spiritual warriorship. We are learning to be present and steady, no matter what shows up. So as you venture into mindfully exploring a painful emotion please appreciate the courage you are exercising. With each foray into your inner landscape, you're getting to know yourself more intimately and deepening your relationship with yourself. You're building your friendship and loyalty, along with your confidence in being able to handle whatever you experience.

Using Our BRAINS♥

What follows is a step-by-step guide for working skillfully with challenging feelings. This method is especially useful for emotions that are frequent visitors, or that tend to hang around longer. These are the feelings that don't naturally dissipate and "go out the other door" of the mind when you softly note them. You know the ones — persistent anxieties and fears, old feelings of guilt or shame, self-doubt, sadness — those familiar othering companions you wish would go away for good.

I'm sure you've now noticed many emotions arise and pass away quickly when we stop resisting them and can turn towards them mindfully. When a feeling sticks around, it's a message something deeper is affecting us, and it's an opportunity for further exploration and understanding. It's likely this emotion is rooted in deeply conditioned beliefs. If you can access these beliefs and work with them through this method, you may be able to transform and heal old patterns.

I call this process using your BRAINS♥. It builds on to the basic steps we discussed in Chapter 14 for working with emotions, but explores the experience more deeply to discover the root belief behind the emotion, the conditions that birthed the belief, as well as accessing our healing wisdom about what we really need. This deeper exploration is best done in sitting meditation when you have the time and space to create those necessary inner conditions for paying sustained mindful attention.

Transforming Our Difficult Emotions: Use Your BRAINS ♥

+ Step 1 **B**reathing: mindfully breathe and pause.
+ Step 2 **R**ecognizing that you're feeling an emotion: softly note it.
+ Step 3 **A**ccepting: turn towards your experience with acceptance and openness.
+ Step 4 **I**nvestigating with curiosity: what's the story? What's the sensation, felt sense?
+ Step 5 **N**ot identifying: refrain from taking this personally.
+ Step 6 **S**earching: inquire more deeply into the sensation.
+ Step 7 **♥**: What's the wisest and kindest way to respond?

Step One: **Breathing:** mindfully breathe and pause. The moment you realize a difficult emotion is here — whether it's at the slightest whiff of feeling upset or a sudden tidal wave that sweeps through you — *choose* to intentionally Drop In, and take one to three mindful breaths. Connecting with the breath instantly grounds you in the present and in your body, centers your energy and attention, and gathers your wits so you can step out of the storm. Breathing also helps bring spaciousness and calm, creating inner stability. This first step is powerfully useful. You now have yourself, you're connected, and are awake to what's here.

Step Two: **Recognizing** that you're feeling an emotion: softly note it. "Here's sadness," or "Anger is here." You're making the observation that an experience called sadness or anger is predominant right now. Pay attention to the tone of your softly noting; it needs to be neutral and calm. It's not helpful to note anger by saying, "ANGER!!#!X!!" Instead simply, softly, neutrally note, "Ah, anger is here."

This step begins the transformation as you turn and face the feeling. Because we're accustomed to being on the run from our emotions, turning around and squarely facing it can be a 180-degree shift. Usually we're automatically swept up in the emotional storm, and without any separation from it, we're at its mercy. The emotion is our master and we're its slave. However, *consciously recognizing* we're feeling mad or scared is empowering and clarifying. Squaring up to it by naming it creates a separation from it that's stabilizing and freeing.

Sometimes in the heat of being upset it's hard to identify the exact emotion you're feeling. It really doesn't matter if the name of the emotion eludes you. The terms we use for emotions are just labels we've learned for a certain body sensation that's paired with a particular story. For example, when we feel butterflies in the stomach and imagine we will fail in front of important people, we call that anxiety. If all you know is you're upset right now, then softly note, "Here's feeling upset." We're more interested in the details of our experience as it's unfolding than having the correct term for the emotion.

Step Three: **Accepting:** turn towards your experience with acceptance and openness. Contrary to our conditioning, we are training ourselves to view feeling upset as a beneficial event. It's "good news" because of the potential for healing and growing. Remembering that the obstacle is actually the path is helpful. So instead of judging, turning against yourself, and resisting the experience, you practice accepting what's happening right now, and invite yourself to become really interested in exactly how you are experiencing the emotion. Even if it's something you've felt many times before, right now you approach it with an open mind and heart. Remember Joseph Goldstein's wise advice: "Whatever it is, it's okay. Just let me feel it." Even though you may wish you weren't feeling this emotion right now, undeniably you are, so it's wise to accept and open to it. It's also deeply helpful to remember *impermanence* — this disturbance is a temporary storm. You won't be feeling this way for the rest of your life.

Step Four: **Investigating** with curiosity: exactly how am I experiencing this emotion? What's the story? What's the sensation or felt-sense of it in the body? Because emotions are created by our thoughts, we want to discover what we were thinking, imagining, or telling ourselves that produced it. Ask with sincere curiosity and interest: "What was I just thinking? What was I just imagining? What was I just telling myself that created this feeling? Is there something I'm wanting or attached to

293

that isn't happening right now?" Sometimes when we're upset thoughts zip by so fast it can be hard to track the story. In this case, be patient and encourage yourself to ask again. I find that when I can spot the actual story, it's blatantly obvious why I'm upset. My reaction is logical, given my mind's story. When you discover the story, remember that *it is just a story*. It is made up and not real, and probably not the complete truth.

After discovering the story, we don't want to remain in "thought land" because if we do, we're likely to increase our suffering. Although it's an old habit to try to "think" our way out of our misery, thinking mostly traps us there. Either we start trying to talk ourselves out of our feelings, arguing they aren't rational, and turn on ourselves with the charge, "I shouldn't feel that." Or, we create add-ons and second arrows. We may recall memories where we felt the emotion before, or imagine future situations where we'd feel it — both of which amp up our discomfort and create more painful stories, making us more stuck. If you aren't able to perceive the story clearly, though, please don't fret. With practice, as you keep inquiring about what you're thinking, it will become more accessible. Regardless of what you can discern, the next step is to leave the thought realm and move your attention under the storyline into the felt sense of it your body. This is key.

> Leave the thought realm and move your attention under the storyline into the felt sense of it your body. This is key.

Because emotions are the body's reaction to the mind, we feel them as sensations in the body. So we shift attention from the story into the body by asking, "Where do I feel this emotion in my body right now? What is its actual sensation or felt sense?" Many of us aren't aware of what's happening in our bodies when we're upset because we're so caught up in the story. Encourage your curiosity and interest in detecting the sensation. For example, perhaps you'll notice a heavy feeling in your chest when you feel sad, or tension in your shoulders or belly when you feel anxious, or an aching in your heart center when you feel lonely. With practice you'll discover the liveliness of emotions in the physical body.

When you discern the felt sense of the emotion, no matter how subtle or blatant it is, you explore it the same way as with other bodily sensations. Mustering up as much curiosity as possible, ask: what's this sensation actually like right now? What's it's feeling tone? Unpleasant, neutral, or possibly pleasant? What is its size, shape, weight, texture, and temperature? Does it have a center? An edge? Is it still or moving? Is it changing or remaining the same as I stay with it? By becoming sincerely interested in the exact qualities of the sensation you're moving attention away from the dramatic and compelling story into the direct sensate experience. This helps to bring you into a receptive, grounded place as you investigate more deeply.

Next, cradle the sensation spaciously in your awareness, letting it be just as it is. Remember the principle of spaciousness and the metaphor of our consciousness being like a changeable room with an "In" door and "Out" door? We want the field of our awareness, the room of our mind, to be greater, larger than the predominant object we're focusing on. Creating inner space makes it possible to remain steady and stable as we explore and learn more about the emotion. To encourage expansion, ask, "Can I hold this emotion spaciously right now? Can I give this a little more room? Can I relax and soften around it?" If the sensation grows larger as you give it more space, simply continue to expand around it. You might recall the vastness of the sky and imagine cradling it with blue sky all around it. There's no limit to the amount of internal spaciousness we can create. It's even possible, to gently hold the sensation of the emotion in the vastness of the entire universe.

Step Five: **Not identifying:** refrain from taking the emotion personally. Identifying creates instant attachment and fixes us to the emotion in the first place. From the onset of opening mindfully to the emotion, you softly note, "Ah, here's anxiety." "Here's shame." Instead of "*I'm* really anxious," or "*I* feel ashamed." Omitting the "I" creates separation and spaciousness and releases our grip on it. This creates the freedom to open to the experience just as it is, instead of being pulled back into the storyline, or adding on to our misery by thinking, "Why does this always happen to me? I'm such a dolt! I'm always going to feel this way. There's something wrong with me."

Not identifying also serves to keep our mind and heart open as the experience unfolds moment by moment. We practice softly noting every experience, as we become aware of it, throughout this entire exploration. This maintains the spaciousness that allows our wisdom to come through the inner storm clouds, and for impermanence to naturally have its way. Precisely because you've been recognizing, accepting, inquiring, and not identifying — creating the most ideal conditions for nature to prevail — you may witness the emotional storm naturally shifting, dissolving, and moving out the exit door of your mind on its own.

> Not identifying also serves to keep our mind and heart open as the experience unfolds moment by moment.

Step Six: **Searching:** inquire more deeply into the sensation. If though, the emotion continues to be predominant then more discovery is possible. As you stay steady and spacious, cradling the sensation, you can ask several key questions to deepen your understanding. First ask, "What other emotions are here?" Because emotions often group together, other feelings may reside with the predominant one. Open and accept whatever spontaneously emerges in your awareness — anger, hurt, sadness, or guilt, for example.

Then, continuing to hold the sensation, ask, "When have I felt this feeling before?" Or, "When was the very first time I ever felt this?" Or, "How old do I feel right now as I feel this?" Remain open and receptive to whatever occurs to you in response. Snippets of memories may come to you, reminding you of previous experiences with it, or what was happening for you when you first felt the emotion. You aren't "trying to figure out" the feeling, so watch out for the tendency to slip into discursive and analytical thinking. Rather, by staying with the actual sensation, just as it is, accepting whatever you notice or occurs to you, you're creating the internal conditions for your wise body-heart-mind to reveal what is important to discover right now. This is a practice in trusting yourself, inviting access to your deeper understanding, and allowing your inner knowing and intuition to emerge.

Finally, cradling all you've been discovering in your awareness, ask, "What is this emotion trying to let me know? What is it *really* about for me?" Meaning, what is at the root of the emotion? Again, open to whatever pops into your awareness with acceptance and curiosity. The final question — what is this really about for me? — is aimed at discovering the deeply conditioned beliefs that drive the emotion and link the various memories you've recalled. Stay receptive as this root belief is revealed and simply hold it gently in your awareness. Most often these are beliefs we unconsciously formed from experiences in our childhood. They often reflect our conditioning to other, such as "I'm not smart, attractive, kind, or loveable enough. Whatever I say isn't good enough. I'll never belong. I don't matter."

Searching more deeply into our experience creates the conditions where our system can open naturally into deeper layers of what

> What's the wisest and kindest way to respond?

is really going on. It allows the shields and coverings we've built over our wounds and sore spots to gently fall open. The more you can remain inquisitive and receptive to all you notice, trusting that whatever arises is valid, the better.

Step Seven: ♥: **What's the wisest and kindest way to respond?** Lastly, you listen to your wise, kind, loving self, your heart. When you've come to the root of your upset and have discovered what it's really about, you can tap into the wisdom, intelligence, and kindness of your true compassionate self. Stay with the felt sense of your experience, hold all that you've noticed spaciously in your awareness, and directly ask: "Well, given this upsetting feeling is really about _____ (the conditioned belief), what's the wisest and kindest way to respond to myself right now?" Or, "What do I really need?" Pause, listen, and open to whatever spontaneously enters your awareness.

We aren't searching for an elaborate or clever strategy to fix a problem or to guarantee you'll never feel the emotion again, but to find what might be useful to help you move forward into the next moment, rather than be caught again. You're listening to your intuition, your spirit, your wise all-knowing true self, your blue sky heart-mind. In my experience, the messages I receive are usually simple, wise, and affirming, such as, "To feel myself breathing right now." Or, "To remember I am enough."

When you receive your own wisdom, please follow your advice, and then notice the effect. This is how we learn to trust ourselves. We discover our advice is solid. We are wise. We are kind. We can discern what we truly need. Don't fret if nothing occurs to you when you first ask what you need. You are building a new skill set for accessing yourself that takes practice and patience. Trust is developed by observing the effect of relating to the emotion this way. You've learned something new about yourself, done some healing, and created more freedom for yourself. Chances are you now won't be as caught in this emotion because this deeper exploration shifts your relationship to it.

Remember Your Breath and to Offer Loving Kindness

If using BRAINS♥ seems complicated or daunting, take it one step at a time, and only go as far as you want to go in the moment. Be kind and gentle as you practice, respecting the power of past conditioning to make us fearful of our emotions. Even putting your toe in the direct experience of these emotional waters for a few moments helps — softly note it, get curious about the story, and wonder about the sensation. Little by little, you'll be brave enough to open to it more each time the feeling shows up.

Whenever you become confused, feel lost, or realize you are caught in the story that's feeding the emotion, simply shift your attention to the sensations of breathing again. Awareness of breath is our home base, our stabilizing place, our centering place. Connecting with these sensations creates a safe neutral ground. From here we can gather our attention and intention to explore the emotion again.

If you encounter moments when the discomfort, or the fear of feeling overwhelmed by it is too great, your instinct may be to shut down. Please combat the fear by offering yourself Metta right on the spot: "May I be safe and protected. May I be peaceful and calm. May I trust that I can handle it. May I be free from suffering." Or the short cut version, "May I be peaceful in the midst of this difficult emotion." The Loving Kindness meditation is calming and stabilizing, so use it whenever your wisdom prompts you to. The breath and the attitude of kindness are our steady anchors and allies in this courageous exploration.

> The breath and the attitude of kindness are our steady anchors and allies in this courageous exploration.

Remember Impermanence

We often fear painful feelings will last forever, which keeps us on the run and trying to avoid direct contact. Remembering that emotions, like everything else, are temporary can help us find the courage to turn towards it and sustain our attention with it. As you choose to be brave and stay with it, at any moment the emotion can shift, transform, or dissolve. When it does, you don't need to try to get it back. Instead, simply return your attention to the breath, and enjoy the openness of this moment. Just as we don't try to get rid of the emotion, we also don't want to make it stay when our system is naturally releasing it. If you need to learn more from the emotion, you can trust it will return, and when it does, you'll have another opportunity to companion it.

Applying the Practice: Healing an Old Belief

Carol, a client and mindfulness student, came in to do some sessions recently because she was feeling anxious and angry about an upcoming event at work. A teacher in the public school system for almost twenty-five years, she learned she was going to be observed by the new principal the following week. She'd been fretting about the observation, creating stories about the negative things he might say, and then worrying what might happen because of that. On top of it all, she was mad at herself for being so nervous. "For Pete's sake," she said. "I've been doing this work for a long time, and I've been doing it really well, too. I shouldn't be worried. What's the matter with me anyway?" On top of the anxiety, she was criticizing herself for being upset. She believed she *should* feel completely confident in her ability to do her job, and was inflicting second arrows of suffering on herself.

She wanted to explore her reaction mindfully and find relief. I guided her into a more meditative inner place, asking her to feel her body sitting in the chair, connect with the sensations of breathing, and open to herself, just as she was, with gentleness and interest. After a few minutes I asked her to begin thinking about her boss's upcoming visit, allowing the familiar thoughts and reactions to arise until she began to feel the familiar anxiety. After a few moments of imagining the drama, the uncomfortable feelings arose. Having the clarity that these were the stories her mind was making, I asked her next to move her attention away from the thoughts, going under the storyline to discover the felt sensations they created in her body. I encouraged her to bring plenty of curiosity to where she felt the anxiety and what she noticed.

She described an unpleasant churning, heavy, sinking feeling in the core of her belly. The feeling was warm, about the size and shape of a volleyball and had a rotating center, like a vortex of energy moving inward. I asked her to simply hold these sensations very gently in her awareness, as if she could cradle them, giving them a lot of room and space to be just as they were. Next, I asked her to notice if these sensations contained other emotions. Immediately she said there was fear of judgment and disapproval, disappointment, and shame. Inviting her to remain open and curious, staying with these sensations, cradling them spaciously, I asked her to recall the first time she'd ever felt this sensation. After a few moments, she said she first felt it when she was five or six years old when she showed her dad some schoolwork she had brought home. She remembered feeling proud of her work, but he didn't seem interested. Instead he told her how she should have done it differently and better. As she stayed with this memory, other memories came to her where he responded similarly, always aloof and corrective. Even though she kept trying to win his approval, she never quite got it.

While encouraging her to stay steady and open to all she was noticing, I suggested she ask the sensation directly what it was trying to let her know. What was its message? What was this feeling really about? After a few moments she said, "Oh, this is about believing that no matter what I do I'm never good enough." With that realization, tears began to roll down her cheeks. I encouraged her to cradle the sense of her younger self who had formed the painful belief long ago, opening her heart to her with understanding, compassion, and kindness. I invited her to tell her little self that she was so sorry this had happened to her.

As Carol sat with this, gently and spaciously holding all that she was experiencing — the sensations, the memories, the conditioned belief that arose from the experiences with her dad, the sense of her scared little hurt self — bringing kindness and compassion to all of this, I suggested she ask, "Given that this is about the belief that I'm never good enough, what's the wisest and kindest way to respond to myself right now?" I encouraged her to open to whatever popped into her awareness. After a few moments she said, "To trust myself, and to remember to breathe and remind myself that I am good enough just as I am."

We ended our session with her commitment to remind herself of the truth that *she is good enough* each time she thought about the upcoming observation, and to bring a sense of gentleness and compassion to her scared little self who had learned the opposite. When she returned two weeks later, she reported that the principal's visit had been a breeze. She had felt calm and confident and actually enjoyed his presence and observations, which, not surprisingly, were all positive.

By mindfully exploring her experience as we did, rather than simply talking about it and staying purely cognitive, Carol was able to have a deep, transformative experience involving her body, heart, and mind. This created a new embodied experience and new memory — a fresh neural groove — that she can now resource when future situations trigger the old belief that she's not good enough. Now, the more she can be mindful when the old reaction is evoked and choose to respond to it by pausing to breathe, acknowledge the old incorrect belief and the anxious sensations it creates, and then shift to reminding herself that she is enough, this new neural groove will deepen. As she continues to practice, she will become increasingly free of the old reaction and more able to trust and accept herself just as she is.

Trusting in the Method

As mentioned in the beginning of this chapter, part of creating the right conditions for transforming painful emotions involves having faith in this ancient method, something that is only cultivated through practice. Recently, a woman with a daily meditation practice who has taken a number of classes with me, and whom I've worked with in psychotherapy sessions, described guiding herself mindfully through very intense suicidal feelings.

Julie spent many years in therapy working hard to recover from childhood incest. Although she still experiences some depression and anxiety, it's been many years since she's been stuck in panic attacks or felt suicidal. She discovered mindfulness six years ago and has found the practice stabilizing and very helpful in learning to relate skillfully to her emotions. In our individual sessions she's practiced opening to sadness, fear, shame, self-hatred, or anger in the ways I've described. She has seen how these emotions arise from her mind's stories, opened to the sensations in her body, inquired into their history, asked for their messages, discovered wise and kind responses, and witnessed their impermanence and transformation. Through practice, she's learned to be less afraid of her feelings and has developed more confidence and trust in the method.

On a recent necessary visit to the perpetrator, a family member, she practiced staying mindfully vigilant to protect herself from getting pulled into old painful neural grooves created by the abuse. But just as as they were saying goodbye, he made a disapproving comment about her appearance, and as she drove away she could feel herself falling into the old habits of self-loathing and disgust. His comment touched old wounds from the abuse and on the two-hour drive home she felt as if she were drowning in shame. By the time she arrived home she felt severely suicidal.

Fortunately, she was aware of what was happening. She bravely chose to sit with herself and open mindfully to all of her feelings and thoughts. She noted the terrible self-hating stories and remembered they were stories, not the truth. She opened to the sensations created by the stories and kept reminding herself to give them more and more space. She noted all other emotions that were there — fear, sadness, anger, resentment, and hatred — and she let them all be there. She said the pain became enormous, and as it grew she continued to expand around it and give it more and more space. She recognized the false beliefs that her innocent younger self had learned — that she was bad, dirty, and despicable — and she reminded herself they were not true. She stayed steady and tendered herself with gentleness and compassion. She offered Loving Kindness to herself over and over, and she returned to her breath many times to find stability each time she was pulled back into the painful stories. Little by little, the pain began to soften and subside, fading gradually until finally it was gone. She felt tired and spent, but also tremendously open, free, joyful, and grateful.

When she told me of this experience, I bowed to her. I had never before known of anyone bringing mindfulness to suicidal feelings. I had never heard of anyone being so courageous, all by themselves. I found her commitment to accept and love herself profoundly inspiring. Julie

303

had stayed and faced the "monster" — all the old stories, beliefs and feelings — all of it scary and hard, and the monster dissolved before her eyes. She is now confident, having directly witnessed the alchemy of mindfulness, that if suicidal feelings should ever emerge again, they won't hold the power to abduct and sink her as they once did.

We Need Courage to Be Vulnerable

To open to our pain, no matter what size, we need courage. Even though painful emotions lead to understanding and healing, it's hard to honestly see them as "good news." Exposing ourselves to fear, sadness, shame, anger, guilt, self-hatred, disappointment, despair, or grief makes us feel vulnerable, and that shaky, unprotected feeling usually frightens us. Yet it is precisely the openness of vulnerability, the groundlessness, being present without our shields up, that creates the inner spaciousness that allows transformation to happen. This is what generates enough internal roominess for our true nature's wisdom and intelligence to shine through, and the scaffolds holding up the old beliefs and patterns inherently fall away.

> The openness of vulnerability creates the inner spaciousness that allows transformation to happen.

Courage is about greatness of heart and is cultivated in the face of fear, not in its absence. It's about inviting our heart to expand and remain spacious even when what's here is scary and we feel vulnerable. When you realize you're afraid to open to an emotion, that's okay. It's normal to experience fear when we feel threatened. Feeling fear need not stop us. We don't have to bow down to it and keep ourselves diminished. When fear arises as we face a difficult emotion, the practice asks us to stay and open rather than bolt or collapse. This is how we develop our courage. We stay and learn, little by little, that it's okay to stay. We learn that in staying, nothing horrible or unbearable happens. By sustaining our attention on what's difficult, we make new discoveries that heal and free us, deepening our understanding of how things really are. Through the courage found in our open heart we experience the alchemy of fear changing into confidence. Gradually, as we develop the faith that we really can depend on ourselves, our need for validation and approval from others diminishes.

Gradually, as we develop
the faith that we really can
depend on ourselves, our need
for validation and approval
from others diminishes.

Ownwork Suggestions

Formal Sitting Practice: Choiceless Awareness and Applying BRAINS♥ to an Emotion

Arrange your body in a comfortable, stable posture, spine aligned.... Feel your whole being sitting here.... Open to yourself just as you are in this moment with kindness, curiosity, and acceptance.... Drop attention into your body to concentrate on the sensations of breathing.... Expand the field of awareness to allow plenty of room to relax around these sensations, dropping into open choiceless awareness, staying with the breath until some other experience is more predominant....

When a thought or story is predominant, softly note "Thinking", or name the kind of thought, without resistance or adding on to it, and shift to the sensations of the breath....

When another sensation is prominent, softly note it: "Tightness, tingling, aching." Note the feeling tone: pleasant, neutral, or unpleasant? Scope out all the actual properties of it just as it is right now.... Relaxing around it, staying with it until it's no longer predominant....

When an emotion becomes predominant, practice the BRAINS♥ method: shifting to **B**reathing several breaths first...then **R**ecognizing; softly note it, "Sadness, anger, fear, disappointment." **A**ccept that it's here.... Next, **I**nquiring into it, ask: what was I just thinking, imagining, telling myself? Then shift your attention under the storyline to the feeling (felt sense) in the body.... **N**otice the exact qualities of this sensation, opening to it just as it is.... **N**ot identifying and relaxing around it, giving it plenty of space.... Ask: what other emotions are here? If the emotions is still predominant, then **S**earch more deeply into it, ask: When have I felt this before? When was the first time I ever felt this? What is this trying to let me know? What is this really about for me? Opening to whatever occurs to you.... Finally, ♥, *access your heart and your wise, kind self*, ask, "Given all of this, what's the wisest and kindest way to respond to myself right now? Open to what arises.... Always returning to the sensations of breathing.... Staying present, steady, receptive.

Notice the effect of this practice.

Informal Practice

Notice when you're upset and softly note it: "Oh, here's irritation. Here's anxiety. Here's sadness. Oh, shame is here. Here's disappointment," and so on. Then:

- Mindfully breathe for one to three breaths.

- See if you can spot the story that created this upset. Ask, "What was I just thinking, imagining, or telling myself?" Remember that these are just thoughts and you can choose to believe them or not.

- Ask yourself, "What am I attached to here? What am I wanting that isn't happening?"

- Finally ask, "Okay, given that this is what's happening, what's the wisest and kindest way to respond to myself right now?" Notice whatever pops into your awareness.

When you feel caught in a painful emotion, especially if it keeps showing up over and over, see if you can carve out some time to sit down and explore it mindfully using the BRAINS♥ method. Be sure to notice the effect.

18

Compassion:
I'm So Sorry
For This Pain

*She who hears the
cries of the world.*

Kuan Yin,
the Bodhisattva of Compassion

Compassion Is Powerful Medicine

Along with Loving Kindness, compassion is a spiritual medicine that helps us directly address the pain within ourselves, in others, and the world, with wisdom. Compassion, *karuna* in Sanskrit, is traditionally described as the natural trembling and quivering of the open heart in response to pain and the desire to alleviate that pain. It's embodied in Kuan Yin, the Buddhist goddess of compassion. One of the few female-gendered deities, she is called, "She who hears the cries of the world." Kuan Yin symbolizes unconditional love and compassion for all beings, equal in intensity to a mother's love for her child.

Compassion brings heartfelt sympathy to the experience of pain, and expresses sincere sorrow for one's suffering. Considered one of the Brahma-viharas, or highest abodes of the heart, it is a natural state of the awakened mind, our true nature. Compassion enables us to be stable, open, gentle, and accepting of pain, rather than resisting or being consumed by it. It reminds us that when conditions are right, we all experience suffering. We are all truly in the same boat. Out of this deep understanding, compassion is the heartfelt wish for all beings, without exception, to be happy and free from suffering.

> Cradling the pain in our open tender heart instead of shutting down and turning away is healing.

As we bring mindfulness to our painful experiences, both emotional and physical, we need the power of compassion to truly heal. In fact, in my experience, it is the element of compassion that allows the most profound transformation of our wounds and their conditioned patterns. With compassion, we companion the painful feeling in the vastness of our loving open heart, enabling us to open to the difficult experience with sympathy and tenderness. Cradling the pain in our open tender heart instead of shutting down and turning away is healing. Clearly, to be stable and spacious in the midst of pain and suffering requires great courage.

Checking in

• I hope you're feeling more stable and confident in your formal sitting practice now. Please make some time to sit every day, and remember to be kind to yourself when you don't. Just renew your intention to meditate and see what's possible today.

• Keep gently encouraging yourself to work with difficult emotions as much as you can. Remember that through practice we build our mindfulness muscles and our trust in our authentic experience, so any amount of practice with them counts.

• Remember impermanence, too. Whatever is difficult now will not last forever, so encourage yourself to be brave and experiment with using your BRAINS♥ — see what you can discover.

• Please keep tracking disempowering othering habits. They are deeply embedded in our habits of thinking and reacting. The more you can spot them, the more freedom you'll cultivate. Appreciate yourself for every effort and new awareness you have.

• Don't forget your daily doses of Metta. Think of this practice as a nutritional supplement for your mind and heart.

In a retreat with Pema Chödrön, someone asked her what was needed to end the many wars on the planet. She was quiet for a long time before answering, and then finally, with a somber look on her face, she said, "Compassion is our only hope." Only compassion can truly transform suffering and create peace within ourselves, each other, and the planet.

Warp of Conditioning

As women, we're taught that we're supposed to feel compassion for the other's pain and misery. When it comes to our own pain, that's another story. For ourselves, our hearts are frequently closed, if not hermetically sealed, when pain arises. Our habit is to be tough and impatient with ourselves, often demanding that we stop hurting or feeling the pain rather than opening our heart in kindness and sympathy to ourselves. We've learned to close down to our pain, attempting to shield our heart from feeling it through habits of disconnection. We operate under the illusion that if we don't let ourselves feel the pain, we won't be hurt by it, so we reject and abandon those parts of ourselves that feel it. In reality, our conditioned habits only serve to solidify pain and further alienate us from ourselves and others, thereby adding to our isolation and suffering.

In addition to denying our own suffering, our striving to be perfect inclines us to *act* as if we are there for others when they're hurting. I say "acting" because if we don't know how to be truly compassionate towards ourselves, to stand steady and open with our own pain, we are limited in how much we can authentically open to another's pain. Othering prompts us to pretend, and often that pretense makes us feel worse because we know in our heart of hearts that to some extent we're faking it. We want to be there for the other, but their pain can be frightening. Because conditioning teaches us to be afraid of our own pain, there's a limit to how much we can open our hearts to another's pain.

When we aim to be perfect, suffering presents a problem. It's not okay. Embedded in our emotion-phobic culture is the cockeyed view that suffering is wrong and weak. If we're strong, smart, and doing things right, then we shouldn't suffer. We have little tolerance for appearing to be distressed, so we've learned to hide and resist our own suffering. Of course, this conditioned view only serves to create more suffering. Resisting requires disconnecting from our authentic experience, and sets in place strong habits of comparing self to other, along with abandoning and turning against ourselves through harsh judgments, condemnations, and self-hatred. In fact, we often think that it's self-indulgent to feel sympathy and compassion for ourselves. Often I hear, "I shouldn't be feeling bad about this. Look at how awful people have it in Syria/Haiti/Iraq." To which I say, "Yes, they do have terrible suffering there. But this is the suffering that you have right now. You matter, too, and so you are worthy of giving your wise and loving attention to the pain you feel."

> Only compassion can truly transform suffering and create peace within ourselves, each other, and the planet.

Contrary to the prevailing societal view, being able to relate to pain with an open heart takes great inner strength. Being able to stay steady, spacious, and accepting with it, even though doing so makes us feels vulnerable, takes tremendous courage. Naturally, the more we can feel compassion for ourselves when we are suffering, the more we can authentically feel it for others. When we can truly be there for ourselves with our pain, we have the capacity to truly be there for others in their pain.

Once while I was attending teachings at Deer Park, the Tibetan Buddhist Center near my home, I heard a wonderful message about our open hearts. The teacher was discussing the concept of guru devotion. He said being devoted to a teacher, such as the Buddha, is very helpful because the teacher serves as a model for the student. As you study the teacher, you aspire to embody their same qualities. He went on to use the metaphor of making *satsas*, which are small gold-painted clay images of Buddha. Here the guru or teacher is the mold, he said, and the student is the clay, pressed in to take the shape of the guru. Upon hearing this, a student burst into sobs, loud, weeping sobs. The teacher began weeping too, tears flowing down his face. The reaction quickly spread to the whole group, all of us feeling touched, and many also began crying. This crying, weeping, and sniffling went on gently for almost 10 minutes. No one said a word, we were all just there with our raw and tender feelings. At last, when this response had moved through all of us, the teacher said gently, "Often when someone cries, it causes others to cry too. It touches our heart. People think it's weak for a big person to cry — but this is not so. It's very strong to cry — it means your heart is open and big." I was deeply affected by the truth of this experience, which is quite the opposite of our conditioning.

You Will Get Hurt

We get hurt in life and experience suffering in many ways. Likewise, our loved ones also can get hurt in many ways, and no matter how much control we try to exert, we can't totally protect them from getting hurt. If we haven't learned how to accept that suffering is unavoidable, then it's only natural that we try to shield ourselves from pain by armoring and closing our hearts. We sometimes fear that if we feel it all, we'll be overwhelmed. It will be too much to bear.

One of my early teachers, Dawna Markova, an author and co-founder of Professional Thinking Partners, gave a teaching in our year-long study group that I will never forget. Jane, a woman in the group, had been in a long-term relationship that ended painfully. After several years of being single, she was now feeling attracted to someone and thought she was ready to begin a new relationship. However, she said she was afraid because she didn't want to get hurt again. Hearing that statement, Dawna commanded all of us to stand up and form a circle. When we were all standing in a circle, facing in towards each other, she stood squarely in front of Jane, and firmly said, "Jane, you are a human being. You will get hurt!" Then she stood in front of the next person and said, "Lonnie, you are a human being. You will get hurt!" Moving to the next person, she said, "Michael, you are a human being. You will get hurt!" Around the circle she went, standing in front of each person, and telling each one they will get hurt. "Mare, you are a human being. You will get hurt!"

This greatly impressed me, and was an early motivator for wanting to learn how to skillfully work with pain. It is undeniably true. We all have been hurt. We all will get hurt. As long as we are alive, we will experience pain– it's not possible to avoid it. With mindfulness, though, it is possible to experience pain without suffering. Pain is not avoidable, but suffering is. When we can bring compassion to our pain it's not only possible to bear it with more ease, but the power of opening our tender wise heart to it can generate a deeper level of healing and freedom.

Compassion Is Healing

During another retreat with Pema Chödrön, she reported on a remarkable study of Tibetan monks and nuns imprisoned by the Chinese in Tibet. While in prison, these people were beaten and tortured. Remarkably, after their release, they showed no signs of post-traumatic stress disorder, a response completely expected under such brutal conditions. Inquiring into how they avoided permanent psychological harm, the researchers learned that the entire time the nuns and monks were imprisoned, they practiced compassion, for both themselves and their perpetrators. The more they were abused, the more intense their compassion practices became. The researchers concluded that these practices allowed them to keep their hearts open in love and sympathy rather than contracting in fear and hatred, which protected their minds and hearts from the horrific stress of their situation.

Author Kristen Neff, a researcher and associate professor at the University of Texas, has been studying the impact of gender, culture and power on self. She was the first to conduct research on self-compassion.[45] Her research consistently shows that cultivating compassion for ourselves when we're hurting, when we've made a mistake, when we charge ourselves with some failure, is more helpful than any other response we can make. It helps us recover quickly from the pain. Self-compassion builds resilience. Her work shows that practicing compassion towards ourselves is more beneficial than trying to boost confidence by raising self-esteem. In fact, she has found that when we don't know how to give ourselves compassion and we make a mistake or suffer in some way, our self-esteem plummets. On the contrary, when we offer compassion to ourselves we recover quickly and learn from the experience. Her work also shows that self-compassion develops resilient self-esteem. When we learn how to be consistently kind and compas-

> Self-compassion builds resilience.

sionate towards ourselves no matter what, our self-respect and confidence remain stable even when we've failed miserably, or we're having a hard time.

Self-compassion is a vital remedy for us as women because we get so caught up in trying to be perfect, which leaves no room for mistakes. Perfection addiction, part of the foundation of othering, is ruthless and causes us incredible pain. To free ourselves, we must understand that we can never be perfect and making mistakes is part of being alive. Ned Twing, a former colleague and very wise man once said to me, "We can never make mistakes, only discoveries." We learn the most from our mistakes. In practicing self-compassion, we understand that making mistakes and feeling pain are part of the human experience. They are normal. When we make a mistake, we recognize it, remind ourselves this is a moment of suffering, and remember that everyone experiences suffering at times. We turn towards the suffering mindfully, offering sympathy to ourselves because the experience is painful, and discover a wise and kind way to respond to ourselves.

Bringing Compassion to Physical Pain

The basketball injury I recounted in Chapter 10 prompted my first intentional experience with the power of compassion. Raised in the "Fine" family, I was loathe to reveal physical discomforts to my parents because their reactions were judgmental and dismissive. The attitude of "keep a stiff upper lip" was part of our family ethos. I dealt with physical injuries by minimizing and denying them as much as I could. This time, I couldn't hide my injury — I was on crutches and wearing a big immobilizing brace. I decided the injury was an opportunity for healing more than my knee alone. I made a holistic treatment plan for myself that included paying attention to some of the more prominent psychological patterns I suspected might block complete healing. One of these patterns was the habit of having no sympathy for myself. I had the hunch that feeling sympathy might be part of my healing process.

When I could straighten my leg out enough to get into the bathtub, I held my first treatment session. At this point in my life, I was using a lot of interactive imagery in my work with clients. Imagery is a wonderful way to work with our creative mind to access our inner wisdom for physical, emotional, and spiritual healing. Once I settled into the warm bath, I dropped my awareness into my knee, and asked for an imagining of what was going on and what was needed. To my surprise, I felt, saw, and heard nothing. It was as though the door of inner connection to my knee was slammed shut. Intuitively I knew I needed to express sympathy. I needed to feel sorrow for my knee's injury. Having really no experience with self-compassion, not at all sure about how to express it, I gently cupped my hands around my hurt and swollen knee, and with as much kindness and tenderness as I could marshal, I said, "I'm so sorry you are hurt. I am so, so sorry you are so hurt. I am so sorry that I am so hurt." Surprisingly, within a few moments I began to cry a little. I couldn't remember the last time I had cried about myself.

After a few more moments of gentle tears and truly accepting that my poor knee was indeed seriously hurt, I tried taking my awareness into my knee again to see if I could get an image and message. To my amazement, the door was now open. I could easily "see" the torn ligament with lots of hot redness around it. I asked the image what my knee needed and I heard the words "Oil. Castor oil." I had the sense I should warm my knee and wrap it in a cloth soaked with castor oil. Knowing nothing about castor oil, the next day as I was crutching around my office, I recounted this tale to a colleague. She said castor oil soaks were an old home remedy often used for such injuries. Amazing.

The most remarkable part to me was witnessing the power of compassion, of heartfelt sympathy. Before this session with myself, I hadn't realized I was still deeply resisting the injury. My heart was closed to it. I didn't want the injury, didn't want anyone to see that I was injured, and I was emotionally blocked to it. By sincerely feeling and expressing sympathy for both my knee and myself, my heart, body, and mind opened, and I could then uncover my own healing wisdom.

This learning has served me well since then in companioning my body's physical challenges, and I encourage you to apply it this way, too. Our bodies are innocent; they are always doing the best they can for us. We need to bring our kind and sympathetic heart to their inevitable aches, pains, diseases, and injuries.

Bringing Compassion to Shyness

I learned much more about the power of compassion when I attended my second retreat at the Insight Meditation Society in Barre, Massachusetts. This was a seven-day silent retreat with Christina Feldman and Narayan Liebenson, and I was eagerly anticipating it because my first retreat had been so amazing. One of the aspects I had loved the most was observing Noble Silence. No talking, no communicating with others except in two group meetings with the teachers where we could talk about our experience, and receive support if needed.

Silence was a respite for me because I think of myself as shy. To not have to talk to anyone, especially people I don't know, was a huge relief. I drag along a lifelong history of anxious experiences where I was expected to talk but always felt tongue-tied, self-conscious, and awkward. On the first retreat, I luckily managed to escape having to say anything in the interview groups. On the last night of the retreat, we formed a large circle of all the retreatants in the meditation hall, and silence was broken for an hour. The teachers invited anyone who wanted to share something of their retreat experience to do so. I completely surprised myself when I decided to speak. Feeling inspired, I overcame my "I am shy" identity and expressed great appreciation for the teachers and the experience. Afterward, I patted myself on the back for having the courage to speak, recognizing that a week of meditating helped me become more connected to my authentic self and slip past the prison of this deep neural groove.

Now, as I traveled to the retreat center again, I remembered the ritual of the retreat's last night and thought, "Oh no! What am I going to say?" A wave of anxiety passed through my body. My excitement for the retreat was now contaminated with fear. From that point on, although I tried to push it away as much as I could, I obsessed about what I was going to say on that last night. Every sitting meditation, every walking meditation became burdened by my mind's entanglement with the worry, "What am I going to say?" accompanied with the unpleasant sensations of anxiety and fear.

I practiced working mindfully with it as best I could. But I was drawn into reviewing every theory I had about why I was shy, every painful situation where shyness was excruciating, where it stopped me from connecting with others, the self-doubt it watered, the embarrassed reactions my mother had to my shy behavior as a child, and all the tools I've ever learned to overcome it and get rid of it. Of course, I realized my shyness was all about othering, fearing the judgments others would make listening to what I said. In some moments I could laugh at myself, at other moments, I was deeply caught. My inner incantation seemed to be, "Why was I like this? Why can't I change? Why aren't I like those other people who can talk so freely and easily? What is the matter with me?" I was trapped in my own personal hell, and suffering terribly.

During an interview group, a woman asked Christina about what to do when the same thought kept coming up repeatedly, even though she had a lot of insight about it. I listened eagerly because this repetition was exactly what was happening for me. Christina suggested that as soon as you notice the thought, quickly move your attention back to the breath and refrain from dwelling on the thought. Relieved to have a new method, this became my practice. As soon as I'd think "What am I going to say?" I'd scoot my attention back to the breath. I practiced this diligently every time the fear arose. After a while I began to realize than even though the thought was arising with about the same frequency, the sensations of anxiety that accompanied it were beginning to die down. I was experiencing some relief from the discomfort. The lessening of the unpleasant sensations allowed me to relax with the persistent thought. I began to feel less aversion to it.

In a subsequent sitting meditation two days later, I had an amazing experience. I was once again noticing, "What am I going to say?" when I suddenly had a sense of a little me, maybe four years old. That younger me looked really sad, scared, lonely, and very innocent and vulnerable. For a few brief moments, I actually felt the pain of being four years old, feeling terribly alone and terrified to speak. In a flash, I realized that for my whole life I'd been terrified to speak, but now I actually *felt the pain of this fear* clearly for the very first time. Then something astonishing happened: spontaneously, my heart opened to my little four-year-old self and all the subsequent me's who have struggled with shyness for a lifetime, right up to this very moment. I was filled with compassion for myself. I sensed enormous tenderness and sympathy for myself. I began to weep for all those scared lonely younger me's who had felt so much pain. I realized that for all those years, I'd been hating myself for being shy. I had been blaming myself and demanding that I be different than I was. I'd been demanding that I stop being shy and be how I'm supposed to be instead –comfortable talking in every situation — a version of perfection, of course. Rather than feeling the actual pain of shyness — the fear and shame — I had been avoiding it. Instead I had been fixated on being angry at myself for being like this. I had been avoiding feeling the actual pain of shyness by hating myself instead.

In those brief moments of actually *feeling* the pain of shyness and the spontaneous compassion that followed, I opened my heart to the part of me I had hated, rejected and abandoned my entire life, or more accurately, tried to abandon. In truth, the shy me was a big part of my everyday experience. Even though I hated this part of me, I carried her with me everywhere — this is the fixation and solidity that resistance constructs. Now I felt so much sympathy and sorrow, so much tenderness and love for this scared little self. I no longer rejected her.

From that moment on, my relationship to feeling shy changed. It was truly alchemical. The moment when I felt compassion for my pain — opened my heart to the pain, with acceptance instead of judgment — was transformational. The self-hatred I'd been so stuck in changed to acceptance and love. My judgment of it being wrong to be shy was gone; my judgment of me being wrong for feeling shy was gone. I relaxed with myself in an entirely new way. I knew that my practice would now be to notice the feeling of shyness when it emerged, open to it with curiosity, acceptance, and compassion, and stay steady with myself as I inquired about the wisest and kindest way to respond to myself right now.

As the retreat continued on, the thought of "What am I going to say?" still arose, but a new feeling accompanied it. Now I was curious rather than afraid when the thought appeared. When the last evening arrived and we spread into our big circle and broke silence for that hour, I was still wondering what I would say, but did not feel anxious. I reminded myself that I really didn't have to say anything, and immediately thought, "Oh yes I do. I've been aiming towards this moment the entire retreat." When my moment came and I spoke, I spoke in a way I had never experienced before. For the very first time, speaking to a group of people I didn't personally know, *I felt absolutely no self-consciousness*. I was simply present, connected, authentic. I spoke about the whole remarkable experience I'd gone through, the transformative power of compassion, and how it had powerfully deepened my faith in this practice. When I finished speaking, I was simply in the next moment. I felt relaxed, free to be authentically me in this new moment.

The Practice of Compassion

While compassion is a quality of our true nature that arises spontaneously when we truly open our heart to pain, the habits of conditioning commonly thwart our natural access to it. Fortunately, compassion is an attitude and a skill set we can develop and learn to bring to our painful experiences. Like Metta, compassion can be practiced formally and informally. We can be flexible and experimental in applying it in all kinds of situations and conditions.

To practice compassion formally, we begin by offering phrases of compassion first to ourselves, and then gradually we spread out the offering, following the same order as with Metta: to our benefactor, our loved one or friend, a neutral person, a difficult person, and eventually to all beings everywhere. The phrases are of our own making, but can be something like: "I'm so sorry for my pain. May I care for this pain. May I have ease with this pain. May I be free from suffering." Like Metta, because this practice is aimed towards comforting the wounded self, we use the personal pronouns in the phrases. Informally, in those moments when you realize you or someone else is experiencing pain, you can offer compassion on the spot to invite your heart to open to what's difficult. "I'm so sorry this is hard for me right now," or "May you find ease with your pain."

> Compassion is a quality of our true nature that arises spontaneously when we truly open our heart to pain.

Like my initial experiences with Metta, when I was first taught this practice, I found these phrases one-dimensional and flat. Out of context, not connected to a painful experience, saying them didn't seem particularly potent. My initial reaction to the instruction that we say, "I'm so sorry for my pain," was to sarcastically think, "Oh sure. That's going to help a lot. I doubt it!" However, while on another retreat, I had an experience that radically changed my view on the benefit of these phrases.

Several days into the retreat, I found my attention pulled into feeling pain around my relationship with my mother, which had been disappointing to me. I had always longed for more closeness with her, but she never seemed especially interested in me, or capable of being very present. In one meditation, drawn deeply into memories and the raw pain of feeling rejected and hurt, I somehow remembered the instruction to say, "I am so sorry for my pain. May I care for my pain." I offered the phrases to myself with as much warmth and earnestness as I could, repeating them several times. To my surprise, I began to weep and feel tremendous sadness. I felt sad for myself and sad for my mom. I felt so sad that we couldn't connect with each other, that we had missed so much of each other as we grew older. As I stayed with the sadness, still offering "I'm so sorry for this pain," the dark heavy sadness slowly lifted and became lighter, as if the sun gradually came out from behind a cloud. I realized that all along, we had both been doing the best we could, given our conditioning. I accepted both of us. I forgave her and forgave myself.

This experience changed my relationship with my mother. The moments of offering myself heartfelt compassion allowed my heart to soften and open, and I could naturally release my attachment to what I'd been clinging to for years: wanting her to be the kind of mother I'd always wanted. Now I could open to and feel the pain of what had been, accept what actually is, and forgive us both. The pain lightened and shifted from feeling disappointed in our connection, to being able to see her more clearly as a separate person and simply different from me. At the same time, I cradled my feelings of wanting more with acceptance and compassion. This made the remaining years of our time together much sweeter, and I could be authentically compassionate with the pain she experienced as her body gradually came to the end of its life.

Holding a Wise View

Cultivating a wise understanding of how things really are is integral to developing compassion. We have to truly understand that we cannot encounter life without discomfort. As much as we all want to be free from suffering, we all do experience it at times. With mindfulness we recognize when we're experiencing pain and turns towards it, without aversion and resistance. "Yes. This is a moment of suffering." This fundamental recognition allows us the opportunity to choose a wise and compassionate response.

We can also take a big, wide, and deep view to recognize the numerous causes and conditions that have come together to create a moment of suffering. By understanding that our painful reactions are deeply conditioned and out of our conscious control, we can release blame and accept what is without taking it personally. For example, when I could clearly see not only the conditions that taught me to fear and hate my shyness, but also the conditions that shaped my mother and her reactions to it — the imprint of her parents, her embarrassment in having a daughter who was shy, her othering habits — helped me release all blame. My heart could open compassionately to both of us.

> We have to truly understand that we cannot encounter life without discomfort.

Compassion Practice in Sitting Meditation

To bring compassion to ourselves, we need to understand how to relate skillfully to both physical and emotional pain. In using the BRAINS♥ method (Chapter 17) to work with painful emotions, we simply add compassionate phrases when whatever is here is difficult to bear.

After breathing mindfully and recognizing the discomfort by softly noting it, "Here's fear/anger/worry, etc.," we accept that this difficult feeling is indeed here. Then we investigate the actual direct experience of the feeling, discovering the story, remembering it is a story, and then moving under the storyline to the felt sense of it in the body, discerning the actual qualities and properties of it. We ask questions of the sensation, "What else is here? When have I felt this before? What's it trying to let me know? What is this really about?" All the while, we're holding all we notice with tons of spaciousness and without identifying with it. When we feel the intensity of the pain or realize that, "Wow, this really is painful!" we offer *compassionate sympathy* to ourselves. "I'm so sorry this is so painful. I'm sorry this is so hard. May I care for this pain." Be sure to offer this sympathy with warmth, tenderness, and as much sincerity as possible. You may want to say these phrases over and over to help stay with your experience and to remain open. We can give sympathy to ourselves at any point in the process — even at the beginning when you may already know something is painful and you sense your aversion to it. Be flexible and trust your intuition. Only you will know when the timing is right.

> "I'm so sorry this is so painful.
> I'm sorry this is so hard.
> May I care for this pain."

Throughout this practice, continue to open to all that's unfolding, being sensitive and receptive, following what you notice. After you discover what's at the root of the pain, ask your wise and open-hearted self, "What's the *wisest and kindest* way to respond to myself?" Because the experience was painful, give comfort to yourself. Comfort may simply be remembering to breathe and feel your aliveness in this moment. Perhaps you need to take a walk outside or to call a friend to tell her of your experience. It might be comforting to make a commitment to be kind to yourself no matter what. Only you will know what you really need right now.

In case you are afraid you'll get lost in offering compassionate sympathy to yourself, worried that you'll wallow in misery, understand that we are offering compassion to our present moment experience of pain and discomfort — to the reality that, *in this moment*, something hurts. Watch the mind's stories. If, in being with this particular pain, your mind wanders into old memories, recalling how this always happens to "poor *me* or pathetic *me* or wounded *me*," wake up and realize you're running these stories. The "poor me" storytelling can also involve imagining future scenarios where you fear you'll feel this pain. Primarily, we're intending to stay with the present moment experience that's painful, so if you realize you've moved away from that and have lost your connection to the present, come back emphatically to the sensations of your breath in this moment and to what's actually here now.

Informal Compassion Practice

Like all of the practices, we can practice compassion anywhere in any situation, on the spot. The more we practice, the better. Remember, whatever we practice grows stronger in the brain. When you are caught up in painful othering, a difficult physical sensation, or chastising yourself for making a mistake, follow these steps to weather the event with your open heart and inner stability.

I encourage you to play with the compassion phrases informally. I have found it helpful to offer these phrases to myself even in situations where I'm not that upset, such as feeling impatient stuck in traffic, or waking up with a headache, or feeling a twinge of anxiety when I'm boarding an airplane. Offer compassion instead of blame whenever you realize you're caught in an othering jag again. Compassion helps our hearts stay open and our minds remain more relaxed. It's in that openness, that blue sky of our minds, that our wisdom and knowing can shine through the clouds.

Bringing Compassion to Ourselves Informally

1. Recognize I'm suffering: this is a moment of suffering. It's part of being alive. Everyone experiences suffering at times. This is my moment of it.

2. Apply mindfulness: with acceptance and curiosity, inquire into the story, sensations, messages. Stay spacious, stable, and receptive. Understand the conditions that created this.

3. Express compassionate sympathy: "I'm so sorry for this pain. I'm so sorry this is so hard right now. May I care for this pain. May I be free from suffering."

4. Ask: "What's the wisest and kindest response I can make to myself? What do I really need right now?" Give comfort to yourself.

Offering Compassion to Others

When someone is suffering, the over-responsibility habit propels us to want to jump in and fix it for them. Compassion is an excellent antidote to over-responsibility. It keeps us correctly in our lane. By sympathetically offering, "I'm so sorry you're in pain right now. I'm so sorry this is being so difficult," we create space for their suffering without being intrusive, and without losing our boundaries. We are acknowledging that suffering is happening, versus trying to avoid or pretend we don't notice, or worse trying to solve it for them. We're squaring up to their suffering, accepting it and letting it be here. We are standing steady with their pain instead of feeling aversion for it. Expressing our compassion without trying to immediately make it better also generates authentic connection between us. Compassion is often what we need the most. Our acceptance and expression of sympathy can then build enough room for that person to accept their experience and find their wisdom. Allowing someone to find their own wisdom is profoundly helpful and kind. We don't need to do anything else. The next time a friend needs support, I encourage you to respond with compassion, kindly acknowledge their suffering, and notice what happens for you and for them.

As a therapist, being able to offer compassion to my clients when they're suffering, and helping them learn to give it to themselves, is obviously essential. Compassion also keeps my own heart open so I can stay steady and connected with them, and it maintains access to my intuition, knowledge and skills as I work with them. I'll never forget, though, the profound experience I had in a session with a very dear woman where I did the exact opposite.

Compassion is an excellent antidote to over-responsibility. It keeps us correctly in our lane.

Pat suffered from a long history of self-hatred, anxiety, and serious depression. When I first began working with her, she described herself as severely damaged goods. Over time, through the principles and tools of mindfulness, she began to gradually shift this view of herself, seeing it as conditioned and not the truth. She began to feel better about herself, less anxious, more stable, and able to cope with the stresses of her work as a middle school teacher. Although she had periods of feeling bad and getting caught in the old beliefs, on the whole she was making progress. In this particular session, however, she came in feeling enormous self-loathing again. Upon hearing her sad and painful state, I began correcting her, reminding her that her thoughts were just painful stories that she didn't have to believe. I said her ideas were old views that she could choose to let go. Her response, though, was to feel even worse because on top of her distress, she believed she was disappointing me and being a bad client. I tried to reassure her this wasn't so, but she reacted by feeling more angry at herself for forgetting what she knew to be true — that thoughts are just thoughts. This miserable trajectory continued until she felt so bad that she got up abruptly and ended the session early. I sat in my chair feeling miserable, dumbfounded, and tense.

After Dropping In and taking several full breaths, I asked myself what was really going on for me. I realized that I had totally resisted her mind-state. I didn't want her to be depressed and self-hating again. I wanted her to continue on her trajectory of healthy self-growth. I didn't want her to be in pain, and I didn't want to open to her pain. I had reacted with corrective instructions that caused her to shut down against herself and me. I also realized I was tired, and most importantly that I hadn't responded with compassion. My heart had been closed to her state. I had not said, "Wow. I'm so sorry you're feeling so awful." I hadn't companioned her in her pain at all. Suddenly I felt great compassion for both of us — we were both trying to do our best, but we were seriously stuck in our patterns. With that insight, I immediately made a phone call to her and I apologized for my lack of awareness and compassion. She responded by saying, "You're human, Mare. You make mistakes, too. It's okay." With that, we both found our way to forgiveness and our open hearts again.

Over time and through practice, by bringing compassion to our pain, we realize we can be steady with it and we witness compassion's tremendous healing power. Gradually, we lose our fear of pain. Our confidence grows in being able to handle all that happens in life.

Ownwork Suggestions

Formal Sitting Practice: Bringing Compassion to Your Pain

Settle into your meditative space, inviting relaxing and softening, and connect with the sensations of the body breathing.... Stay with the breath until you feel present, calmer, more collected, and settled....

With the intention of practicing compassion, invite a pain, fear, or distress into your awareness — something you're struggling with.... Let the story roll and remember it in the familiar ways — what happened, your reactive thoughts and imaginings — let the drama play out until you begin to feel the painful reaction.... Now, *softly note*...and *accept it*, realizing that this is suffering, we all experience suffering, and want to be free from suffering. You might even say, "Yes. This is an experience of suffering." Now move attention under the storyline to the *sensation* of it, the feeling of it in your body.... Open to these sensations with lots of curiosity and hold them spaciously.... Feel the hurt of it.... Let the painful sensations float in the spaciousness of your heart, allowing your heart to open to this pain.... *Express compassion*: "I'm so sorry for this pain.... May I care for this pain.... May I have ease with this pain." Stay present, open, steady...then, if you like, investigate more deeply into the causes and conditions by asking: when did I first feel this? What is this really about for me? Open to all that unfolds in your awareness, accepting all you notice.... When you feel you understand what this is about, or have gone as far as you'd like to go, hold all that you're noticing in your spacious open heart, and ask, "Well, given this, what's the wisest and kindest way to respond to myself right now?" Or, "What do I really need right now?" Open to and accept whatever you notice....

Return awareness to the sensations of your body breathing....

Take a few moments to pause and notice the effect.

Informal Practice

• Continue the Dropping In practice, paying special attention to those moments when you're feeling discomfort — the pain of judging, comparing, self-hatred — and practice giving yourself compassion: "I'm so sorry for this pain. I'm so sorry this is hard for me."

• In moments when you realize you're swept away and caught in suffering — sucked into an othering groove, feeling physical pain/discomfort in your body, reacting angrily to your kid's or loved one's mood — pause and go through these four steps:

1. Recognize: This is a moment of suffering. Everyone suffers — it's human and part of being alive.

2. Mindfully care for your experience: softly note it (disidentify), accept it, bring curiosity to it, cradle the sensations, and investigate more deeply.

3. Offer sympathy: "I'm so sorry for this pain. I'm so sorry this is hard. May I care for this pain. May I be free from this suffering."

4. Ask: "What's the wisest and kindest way to respond to myself right now? What do I really need?" Offer comfort to yourself.

• Experiment with offering these compassionate phrases to others when they are suffering instead of jumping in to try and take away their pain (the old othering habit of over-responsibility). "I'm so sorry this is so painful right now." Notice the effect on you and them.

19

From Somebody to Nobody: The Freedom of No Self

To know yourself is to
forget yourself.
To forget yourself is to
become enlightened
by all things.

Dogen Zen-ji

A Clearer Understanding of Self

Now that we've explored the fundamentals of how to use mindfulness to gain freedom from our mind's conditioned habits, especially othering, let's look again at the idea of self and what is often called no-self. Buddhist teachings say our happiness and freedom are born from discovering, understanding, and being able to dwell in *selflessness*. They posit that liberation from suffering is rooted in releasing attachment to the self. In fact, learning to rest in selflessness is said to be fundamental to our true nature. Though the habit of othering has the appearance of being selfless because we're so focused on others, in truth it is far from selfless. When we investigate our experience more deeply we realize othering is actually firmly rooted in attachment to self. It's attached to a sense of self that is flawed. Let's discover how we can move from being so attached to self to experiencing the freedom of no-self.

> Liberation from suffering is rooted in releasing attachment to the self.

Forming Attachment to a Solid Self

Our sense of self, or what we call ego, self-identity, or self-image, is shaped and sculpted by a myriad of influences and experiences with messages about how we're supposed to be. We internalize these how-to-be instructions into beliefs that become hard-wired in our brains. As we've been discussing, for most of us, gender is our root identity. Some gender beliefs creep in silently, inclining us to assume that a "good woman" is always giving, puts herself last, and never complains about it. Other directives are more blatant, such as, "It's selfish to think of yourself first." These form the basic view and mantra of the subordinate position: make sure the other is happy, and then your life will be secure and better. These "shoulds" become our standard criteria of acceptability. "I should be loving, kind, and generous. I should be patient, accepting and compas-

Checking in

- When you recognize you're caught in suffering, are you finding it beneficial to gently offer a compassionate phrase to yourself such as, "I'm so sorry this is so difficult right now"? Please be generous in giving this to yourself as it is wise and kind. It softens your heart and helps you stay present and connected with your authentic experience.

- If you haven't yet offered compassion to others when they are having a hard time, please experiment with doing so. When these words come from your open compassionate heart, it can make a world of difference for both of you.

- Please keep meditating every day. Remember, formal practice is the intensive workout period, the gym, for developing critical mental muscles. The more you practice, the more you benefit. Always encourage yourself kindly rather than with criticism or impatience.

sionate. I should be smart, funny and helpful. I should be attractive, fit, and healthy. Above all, I should always be selfless and never selfish."

Fundamentally, of course, the self we believe we should be, is *perfect*. The judging and comparing mind keeps the image of perfection alive by pushing away parts of the self it deems unacceptable, chiding us to embody only our "desirable" parts. The judging mind selects those thoughts, memories, and emotional states it unconsciously decides are "me," and ignores the ones that don't fit. We form imaginings of the *ideal perfect self* and the *imperfect* or *bad* self.

Through this self-selecting process we develop rigid and fixed ideas of ourselves that we mistakenly believe are real and unchanging. We say to ourselves, "*This* is how I am. *This* is how I've always been. *This* is how I'll always be." The more we try to be the ideal, perfect self we think we are supposed to be, and reject the parts we deem unacceptable, the more fragmented and insecure we feel. We become enslaved to a constructed self-image. The ego, with its endless efforts to control and dominate our experience, becomes our master. Othering is based on the construction of a fixed self that we believe is inadequate. As long as we hold to the illusion that we are not enough and our happiness and security depend on others, we are moored to insecurity and destined to a lifetime of suffering.

> Othering is based on the construction of a fixed self that we believe is inadequate.

A New Understanding of Selfless

After many years of studying the dharma, I now realize that the instruction to be selfless doesn't mean overriding our authentic experience to attend to others. The point isn't to reject or ignore ourselves for the sake of loving and caring for others. We aren't annihilating a sense of self. On the contrary, we need a healthy, confident sense of self to care for our own well-being and to sustainably love and care for others. Being selfless simply means releasing attachment to the mind's fixed *ideas* of a me. It's being free from the ego-mind's stories about "What will happen to *me*? What are others thinking about *me*?" It's letting go of the judgments and comparisons that keep us trapped in "shoulds" about how we're supposed to be. By releasing attachment to these ideas of self, our minds are freed from the worries and endless analyses that automatically accompany a "me."

Through mindful investigation, we can observe how the mind's stories create "me" over and over, and choose to release our attachment to those stories. One morning on a recent retreat, as I began my yogi job of cleaning the hallway floors, I observed my mind saying, "Well, how are *my* floors this morning? Has anyone noticed what a fantastic job *I'm* doing making them so shiny?" I was amazed at how automatically my mind attached ownership and pride to something that wasn't mine at all. Seeing this clearly made it easy to drop the attachment with a chuckle.

> Being selfless
> simply means
> releasing attachment to the
> mind's fixed ideas of a me.

Other times we may be trapped in a more severe mind-created me misery. "*I* shouldn't have sent that email to Jane yesterday. She is going to misinterpret it and be furious with *me*. *I* always screw things up." It's stunning to realize every moment of stress and suffering is rooted in an idea of *me*. Think of it: our painful memories are fixed in recalling a younger self who no longer actually exists. Embedded in every fear is an imagined painful impact on a future *me* who doesn't actually exist.

> Every moment of stress
> and suffering
> is rooted in an idea of me.

The Buddha's Core Teaching: Anatta

To understand the Buddha's teaching that all suffering is rooted in attachment to a sense of self, we must understand that a permanent "me" does not exist. The self is not ultimately real. It is a mental formation,

335

purely created by the mind. *Anatta*, the Sanskrit word for no-self, means there is no *permanently* abiding self, and despite appearances, we human beings are ultimately without a true separate existence. No "me" lives independently from everything else. Rather, we exist interdependently, entirely contingent upon and connected to everyone and everything. We are composed of a vast array of elements and conditions coming together, moment by moment, which are all changing and in process. As the author David Richo suggests, "We are more like kaleidoscopes, where the glass beads represent the basic aspects of the body-mind that endure over our lifetime, but who we are in the moment, the current arrangement of the beads, keeps changing with each turn, with each new moment's set of conditions. There is no original arrangement to return to, no reset button. In fact, if we tried to locate a core permanent self we would eventually get the message that can pop up in an internet search: site not found."[46]

> The self is not ultimately real. It is a mental formation, purely created by the mind.

We are each part of the web of life, interdependent and united with all other beings that exist. We change in response to the continuously changing conditions. We are only the experience of me-in-this-situation or me-feeling-this-in-this-moment. We are never one fixed permanent self, but many selves, with unlimited facets, continuously rearranging.

Yet on the physical and functional levels of life, we are obviously separate. We each live in our own unique bodies, have our own histories and personality characteristics, live in our own homes, and have our own bills to pay. We must learn to function effectively within this conventional level of reality. When we're caught in our conditioned ideas of self, we tend to forget our interdependence, believing instead in the illusion of a separate and independent existence. This mistaken perception propels us into a defensive stance. We suffer the chronic stress of trying to protect ourselves, and all that we think is ours, from every imagined threat.

Here's the hopeful and exciting possibility: when we pay mindful attention to what is actually going on when we're suffering, we'll realize it's attachment to self that is running the show and creating our misery. The constructed "I" is the governing force behind all our desires, emotions, arguments, worries, and struggles. When we wake

No "me" lives independently from everything else. Rather, we exist interdependently.

up to this, we have the opportunity to see through the mirage of the ego's stories, release our attachment to these selfies, and rest in the freedom of present moment awareness.

Conceit Is Attachment to Self

The Buddha defined attachment to self as *conceit*, calling it the habit of the mind to compare one's self to the other by feeling either superior, the same as, or inferior to the other. We're all familiar with conceit as the temporary exalted feeling of being better than someone. We also know the inevitable swing to the bottom when our comparing mind decides someone else is better. In my conditioning, this position has a better rap, something closer to humility. "Don't get a big head," my mother would say. Yet, both of these comparisons are the action of the ego creating the illusion of separateness.

The reassuring judgment that someone is the same as me is also born from clinging to an idea of self. I remember a moment on retreat when I saw one of the teachers fumble around and drop her silverware on the floor in the lunch line buffet. I thought, "Oh too bad. Gee, she does clumsy things, too, just like me. She's probably feeling hurried right now." I instantly felt a camaraderie with her, a comforting sense that we were on the same level. For a moment, this sameness was a relief. All of these judgments and comparisons arise from being attached to a self-image and cause us suffering sooner or later.

What Is Freedom From Attachment to Self Like?

It can be hard to fathom existing without attachment to a self. In fact, until we really understand this experientially, the notion can seem bizarre. Being free from clinging to self doesn't mean we dissolve on the spot or vanish into thin air. It doesn't mean we become bland or limp. We don't lose connection with reality.

On the contrary, letting go of attachment to self enables truly accurate and fresh connection with reality. When we aren't absorbed in the mind's stories about what did or might happen to me, we are fully alive. We are completely here, resting in simple awareness of our authentic experience, mindfully observing the moment-to-moment flow of experience. We're freed from the restlessness of the ego and from assigning any meaning about ourselves to the experience of the moment. We are aware of all that's authentically happening without a story in the mind about "me."

When we release attachment to self, we are totally awake.

Letting go of the self is like this: "Right now hearing the sound of the waves; now hearing the ticking of the clock; seeing a planning thought arising; feeling the sensations of this exhale; hearing a dog barking." When we are free from attaching to ideas of a "me," we naturally rest in the spacious awareness of our true nature. In fact, when we release attachment to self, we are totally awake.

Rodney Smith, in his insightful book, *Stepping Out of Self-Deception*, says, "Although the thought of annata may be frightening, its realization is liberating. Once freed of the constricting bonds of a self-image, the heart is free to open and be fully affected. All the qualities we spend our spiritual life trying to cultivate — love, compassion, patience, integrity, and intrinsic joy — are inherent in the presence that remains when the self-image abates."[47] We are here, whole, and no longer fragmented. We are aware of exactly what's happening within ourselves as well as what's happening around us. We are one hundred percent authentic.

An Experience of Somebody and Nobody

On the fourth day of a seven-day retreat, with my mind-body-heart state feeling slowed down and more collected, the teacher gave the instruction to begin our meditation by simply observing our mind-state: for example, was it calm, restless, dull, agitated, spacious, or contracted? As I settled into the sit, I noticed my mind-state was restless and agitated. Curious, I inquired more deeply to discover exactly what was going on. My mind was creating stories where I was busy doing things: imagining being at work, writing this book, explaining these teachings to colleagues, and figuring out when I'd wash my underwear and do my yogi job of cleaning the bathrooms. I realized that "I" was very busy doing these projects. My mind was spontaneously constructing various imaginings of a "me." I was a definite *somebody* actively doing a lot of things. Observing how busy the imaginary "me" was, it was obvious why my mind-state felt restless and agitated.

Seeing my mind-state clearly, I shifted my attention from these stories to feeling the sensations of my body breathing and sitting on the zafu. The "me" stories instantly dissolved. Connecting with the actual sensations in my body, I felt a lovely a sense of spaciousness, calm, and rest. I realized *nobody* was here now. There were no ideas of a "me" busy doing something and being *somebody*. There were no stories at all. Instead, there was simply a sense of calm presence, openness, and stillness. Quite pleasant. My experience was empty of a constructed self. Even so, the compulsion to create a "me" was strong, because a moment later I observed that I was now imagining excitedly telling a friend "I" had just experienced no-self. My mind was again affirming the existence of a self. The sense of resting in spacious awareness was gone and "I" was back being *somebody*.

This realization was fascinating to me, so in the next sitting practice I wanted to return to the clarity of experiencing self and no-self again. I began the sit with the same question: what's my mind-state right now? I noticed more restlessness, agitation, and now some definite tension in my body. As I inquired into my mind's stories, I imagined myself in the upcoming group interview feeling anxious; then I worried about a future visit with my daughter-in-law's mother; and next I heard, "Who do you think you are to write a book? You don't really know anything." I mindfully noted *self-doubt* was now here. The self my mind imagined now was uncertain and anxious, and I felt a heavy tightness in my heart from the created stories.

Investigating this sensation, a flood of painful memories swept through my awareness: my mother washing my mouth out with soap for something I said; dreading that the teacher might call on me in school; a torrent of memories feeling painfully shy. As I opened to the memories, an insight emerged: "I'm supposed to know everything, say the right thing, and be perfect. But I'm not perfect and therefore I'm not how I'm supposed to me. I am not okay." I saw how my mind created the belief of an inadequate me many years ago, and how it continually reconstructs this image, keeping the belief in a wounded self alive. Further, I realized it's likely these stories arise whenever I'm othering and feel I must prove, protect, or defend "myself" because I'm afraid I'll be judged by the other.

When I chose to let the memories and my mind's created beliefs go, shifted my attention to the sensations of breathing, and made contact with the zafu again, the stories instantly dissolved, and my awareness was again simply resting in the moment. I felt calm, stable, spacious, and still. Really quite pleasant. My experience was now empty of ideas of self, absent of being somebody. Nobody here. Free.

Selfless: Centered and Abiding in Open Awareness

Rather than anchoring our awareness in the other, as we do in othering, or only being aware of ourselves, selfless is simply being centered. Our attention is whole and inclusive. Ayya Khema, a vipassana teacher and

Buddhist nun, said, "Being without attachment to self means that we act without self-display and without craving for results."[48] When we aren't trying to prove ourselves to anyone, we naturally experience inner peace. We can rest in our present moment experience just as it is, free from our ego thrashing around thinking something should be different, especially that "I" should be different. We naturally connect with the reality of our present moment and the truth of our experience, whatever it is: sadness, excitement, calmness, irritation, and their sensations of pleasant, unpleasant, or neutral. We are just as we are in the present. We have no pretense to be anything else. We may feel vulnerable in this openness, but also empowered and naturally confident because there's no judgment about ourselves — there's no self to judge. Completely accepting our present moment experience, free from clinging to a fixed idea of self, naturally gives rise to unshakeable confidence.

Selfless is simply being centered. Our attention is whole and inclusive.

In contrast, when we're "somebody," absorbed into the storylines about a "me," our attention is always in the future or the past, not here in this moment. Either we are recreating a memory of a past self or imagining a future self, neither of which exist in the now. The constructed idea of "me" is wobbly and we're easily knocked off center as we fall into worrying about the other or ourselves, and inevitably we're swept into insecurity and fear. When we can drop into "nobody" by releasing the storyline about self and bring attention to our senses, we are centered again in the present, able to respond skillfully to whatever is happening with the natural wisdom of our true nature.

Recently I've experienced increasing moments of being able to clearly see when the mind has "me" doing something. It's immediately liberating. For example, when I realize my mind is imagining a conversation with a friend, teaching a class, winning a bike race, having an argument with my spouse — stories where I'm being a somebody — and

I shift attention out of the story to feel the breath, the story instantly dissolves. I experience the feeling of ease and spaciousness in being with what is actually real in this moment, resting in open awareness, without a "me" story. Back to being nobody. It's peaceful, open, nourishing, and liberating. With practice, our appetite for presence will grow as we naturally transfer our identification with the conditioned mind's dramas to experience awareness as our true and safe home.

Completely accepting our present moment experience, free from a fixed idea of self, naturally gives rise to unshakeable confidence.

We Need a Healthy Self to Let Go of Self

Before we can *truly* loosen our grip on our attachment to self, however, we have to heal and transform those incorrect ideas about ourselves. We had no choice but to develop a damaged sense of self as we grew up. Given our position in the patriarchy, it's unavoidable. We've learned countless ways to criticize and turn against ourselves. Trapped in believing something is wrong with us, we replay a host of painful stories, deepening the neural grooves of self-hatred. These painful stories generate so much mental and emotional agitation it's difficult to see through them and establish enough inner stability to let them go. Like quicksand, the stories can keep pulling us back in and down.

To transform our wounded relationship with ourselves, we need to cultivate appreciation, compassion, and kindness for ourselves so we can become our own trustworthy refuge. Only when we've worked to understand the roots of our conditioning, recognize the conditioned beliefs as false, and accept all aspects of ourselves can we feel safe enough to let go of these painful self-concepts and relax with ourselves as we are. As long as we're striving to prove our worth, we will continue to be ruled by an inadequate and wounded ego. In other words, we need to believe we are a respectful "somebody" before we can be a free "nobody."

A profound benefit of mindfulness is that it transforms our relationship to ourselves. By repeatedly relating to what's here with curiosity, kindness, acceptance, and without identifying, we come to understand that we are not our mind's habits and that our true nature is wise, kind, and basically good. We gradually shift from taking our painful experiences and beliefs personally. We learn to drop our identification with fearful stories, condemning judgments, and harsh criticisms. As we experience our ideas of self as conditioned habits and not the truth of who we are, transformation happens organically. We learn to fully inhabit and stay with ourselves, especially when the going gets rough. Our view of ourselves naturally becomes more trusting, self-respecting, and healthy.

> We need to believe we are a respectful "somebody" before we can be a free "nobody."

Gradually through mindfulness practice, we grow into a reliable and trustworthy friend for ourselves, and our awareness becomes balanced between ourselves and others. Abiding in no-self or selflessness shifts us from assuming the subordinate pose to a position of mutuality and equality. As one woman said, "Now that I've been practicing mindfulness, I'm not automatically feeling like I don't matter and losing myself in others. I feel more of myself. It's like mindfulness is filling me out. I feel bigger from the inside. I know and understand myself better. I feel less self-doubt and I'm definitely more encouraging to myself." Free of the pain of self-consciousness, we naturally relate to others and whatever is here authentically, with our open hearts and minds.

> Selflessness shifts us from assuming the subordinate pose to a position of mutuality and equality.

Cultivating No-Self

The fundamental practice that frees us from clinging to self is to *not identify* with our experience. Identifying instantly glues us to whatever is happening. The good news is we've been practicing this all along, so you're already familiar with not identifying with your experience. We do this by purposefully deleting the all-powerful first-person pronouns "I, me, my, and mine" as we softly note what's here. We note, "Breathing in" versus "I'm breathing in," or "Planning" versus "I'm planning," or "Here's grumpiness" versus "I'm grumpy." This simple method helps us stay with our direct experience and refrain from stimulating the mind's selfies. Over and over, when we are drawn away from the reality of our physical senses into a story, we simply note it without a pronoun and shift attention to our senses again to naturally release the mind's grip on the story.

> The fundamental practice for freeing us from clinging to self is to not identify with our experience.

By practicing nonidentification, we see our habitual desires, fears, beliefs, addictions, and reactions for what they are: neural grooves of the conditioned mind and not self. Gradually we begin to understand the emptiness and impermanence of our unskillful habits and find we can naturally abandon them. In fact, when we're no longer pulled into our neural grooves, they gradually shrivel away. Our no-self, or blue-sky mind of open awareness, which is always present, is then revealed, and we experience inner calm, spaciousness, and the wisdom and compassion of our true nature.

The more we can shift from the mind's stories, where the self is habitually the star, into the physicality of our senses, the more we are grounded in ultimate reality, which is empty of self. Charlotte Joko Beck, a highly respected Zen teacher, explains, "When we meditate, basically we just sit there and notice what's going on. We might observe a tiny twitch in the eye, an ache in the back, the feeling of dryness in the mouth, stuffiness in the nose, the feeling of the buttocks in contact with the cushion, the feeling of the breath coming and going. We just experience it as it is. If a car goes by we hear it. If a plane flies overhead, we hear that. Usually, after about a minute or so, we begin to think because our interest in actual reality is very low. We want *to think*. We want to worry. We want to figure our life out. We are drawn to our dramas."[49] Off we go into our stories and the self emerges again as the central character.

Our practice task is to discern how the mind repeatedly creates a "me," and then choose to let it go. As Christina Feldman once explained to me, "The self arises and disappears into no-self and back again, like bubbles forming and then popping, over and over."[50] By observing the self arising and disappearing repeatedly in practice, we loosen our grip on our ideas of who and how we're supposed to be and find more reliable freedom.

Formal Meditation

When we're meditating, we're resting our attention in open awareness, the temporary weather of our conditioned mind simply appears and disappears. We can view the appearances of self as clouds that form and obstruct the blue sky. We don't try to stop the clouds from appearing because we know we can't stop the mind from thinking. The mind thinks — that's what it does. If we view the stories of self as clouds that temporarily arise, we can see

> We can view the appearances of self as clouds that form and obstruct the blue sky.

them clearly for what they are. There's a big difference between identifying with the clouds and identifying with the vast blue sky within which the clouds appear. By learning to rest in the presence of simply being nobody, the spaciousness of the blue sky, we realize the clouds are never as real or substantial as they seem from the inside or from below. We can let the me-cloud go and remain resting in open, spacious awareness.

We can bring clarity and precision to our awareness of the self when we meditate by using more detailed noting to clearly see the creation of self. Instead of just noting "thinking," "rehearsing," or "worrying," for example, change the noting to, "Having a thought about what *I'll* say to Vida about our conversation," or "Having a thought about how *I* screwed up that vacation plan with my daughter and now *I'm* afraid she's mad at *me*." This helps us see the "I" more accurately and makes it easier to let the story go completely. After you note the exact thought, return your attention to open awareness by connecting with sensations of the breath, the body sitting here, or the actual sounds the ears are hearing right now. Be sure to notice what you're experiencing without a story of self, being a "nobody" for a moment or two. Pause to sense if you feel some spaciousness, calm, or peacefulness. Be alert to when the feeling changes and the mind creates a story that has you being "somebody" again. Notice this with kindness, understanding that the more we can see these habits, the more freedom we create.

Informal Practice: Intentional Ego-Spotting

Because we get the most tangled up in our ideas of self off the cushion, in the midst of living our lives, develop the intention to spot ego as soon as it arises. Whenever you realize you're judging or comparing — either putting yourself down or up — simply note, "Oh there's ego. There's the self. There's a *me* again." Be happy you've seen it, and then choose to shift your attention to your senses and to what's real in the moment. Remember, whenever you're othering or upset — resentful, angry, anxious, or ashamed — a self is involved. A *me* is clinging to something *I* want or something *I* don't want. By recognizing the role of the self, we can choose to let it go and find our inner stability and wise, skillful response.

Rodney Smith offers this helpful suggestion. "When we're caught in ego, we could experience it like a temporary mist that we're simply walking through."[51] For example, you could recognize and move through the mind's ego story in the same way you pass through a gentle mist when you're walking in the woods. I've been using this mist image as I walk in the morning. First I recognize it: "Oh, here's a story about what's going to happen to me today." Next, I choose to let it go by focusing my attention on the sensations of walking or the sights I'm seeing as I walk.

In a few steps, I've walked out of the mist, leaving the story behind. Present and free again.

Betty, a woman who's been taking classes for several years, is intensely engaged in ego-spotting to help her leave a long-held job as director of a large nonprofit agency. Even though she knows she's highly respected for managing the organization skillfully, as a self-confessed expert otherer, her mind's negative views can have a painful hay day. Imagining people are judging her for leaving, blaming herself for not having done enough, and feeling responsible for not solving all of the community's problems can pull her into a swirl of anxiety and depression. By being aware of this and noting, "Oh there's ego," Betty can drop the story, return to her breath, and find her wisdom and inner stability again.

If we can notice the arising of self for what it is — a deeply conditioned habit at the root of suffering — then we can appreciate how truly fantastic it is we're seeing it. When we can observe the ego lightheartedly, and occasionally laugh at its antics, even better. The mind's stories can be really outrageous and funny. "There's ego again. Wow!" It's so liberating when we can see from our own direct experience that the Buddha's teachings are correct: the root cause of our suffering is clinging to an idea of self, and through mindfulness we can liberate ourselves on the spot.

Connection to Everything

Dogen Zen-ji, a wise and famous Zen teacher, once said, "To know yourself is to forget yourself....To forget yourself is to become enlightened by all things."[52] By understanding and accepting ourselves just as we are, we lose our self-consciousness and fears about not being enough, and instead reside in our authentic selves with care, respect, and trust. When we are not so self-involved, we can connect with everything, learn from everything, and belong with everything. We can be one with all that is. From this balanced and inclusive perspective, aware of our own experience, of what's happening for others, and of the conditions in this moment, we naturally respond more skillfully. We experience the circumstances of our life as they are, rather than clinging to how we think they should be. We simply are as we are with what is in the moment. Instead of avoiding pain, we can be with pain when it's necessary to do so. Instead of striving to make our life perfect, we can be with life's messiness as it happens. Instead of waiting for others to validate us, we can offer it sincerely to ourselves, understanding that we are the only one who can truly know the truth of our experience.

When we can rest in the validity of our present moment experience and be free from attachment to ideas of self, the sense of me versus other diminishes. Mindfully accepting our own present moment experience as our truth in the moment, there is no need to fear other's judgments or reactions to us. Gradually through practice the old othering groove dissolves and the sense of me versus you, self versus other transforms into abiding more and more in the inclusive sense of us and we. We truly understand we are all in the same boat, interconnected. Consequently we reside more and more in the stability and peacefulness of our natural open heart, blue sky mind.

As we practice spotting the stories of self, we might wonder, *who is observing this? Who* is recognizing that awareness is now here with the breath and the senses? *Who* is it that realizes when we are and aren't clinging to a self? This inquiry begs the age-old question of "Who am I?" The sages say it is awareness that knows. It is awareness, our Buddha nature, that is universal, enduring and deathless. Through letting go of the stories of being somebody and learning to abide in the awareness of being nobody, selfless, we relax into the innate freedom and unshakeable confidence of our true nature.

> Gradually through practice the othering groove dissolves and the sense of me versus you transforms into abiding more and more in the inclusive sense of us and we.

Ownwork Suggestions

Formal Meditation: Open Choiceless Awareness and Spotting the Arising of Self

Decide how long your practice will be and guide yourself into your body and the sensations of your body breathing.... Practice resting attention in open choiceless awareness, concentrating on whatever is predominant in the moment: sensations of breathing, other body sensations, sounds you're hearing, thoughts and stories arising, emotions appearing, the spaces between these phenomena appearing....

After you feel stable and present, encourage yourself to spot the arising of self. You might begin by asking what your mind-state is like. If it's anything other than calm and spacious, you are likely caught in some kind of self-activity.... Please take the attitude of kind curiosity. Remember this is all about your own freedom, so let yourself see honestly and clearly what's actually here.... Sooner or later as you sit, stories will arise.... Notice what the self is doing in these stories and what feelings the stories create.... Then move attention from the cloud of the story to your physical senses — sensations of breathing, hearing, other sensations in the body — and then notice what your direct experience is like. Is a self here, or is the experience free of self? Notice when self appears again and softly note it: "Ah, here's self." Practice dropping into direct sensory experience again, letting the story and construction of self dissolve.... See if you can sense the difference between resting in spaciousness, blue-sky mind, and being absorbed into the me-cloud and losing the vastness of the blue sky....

Take a few minutes at the end of your sit to notice the effect of this practice.

Informal Practice

• Practice ego-spotting: notice the me-clouds and shift to the perspective of your blue-sky mind as often as you can. Softly note: "Ah, here's ego. Here's self," and choose to shift attention to the breath and body, popping out of the self story. Always do this with kindness and wise understanding.

• Whenever you feel upset or uncomfortable, self is operative. It's likely things aren't as you want them to be in the moment. Turn towards your experience and inquire: what do *I* want or not want right now? When you can spot the story, notice the self, the ego operating, and encourage yourself to leave it by dropping into your body, your breath, and into what you're experiencing with your senses right now. From this more open stable place, see if you can discover what *you, your ideas of yourself,* or the me-cloud stories are demanding right now. Then access your blue-sky mind by asking: what's a wise and kind way to respond to myself right now? Notice the effect of this practice.

• Continue with the Dropping In practice throughout your day.

20

Where From Here?
Watering the Seeds of
Unshakeable Confidence

The privilege of a lifetime
is to become who you
truly are.

C. G. Jung

Being a Spiritual Warrior

Ultimately it's the habits of our mind reacting to the circumstances of our lives that create our misery, not the circumstances themselves. For that reason, if we want to live our lives with true happiness and freedom, we are wise to take on the challenge of becoming spiritual warriors. Clearly, as we've been exploring, due to our gender's position in the patriarchy, the habit of othering is deeply conditioned in us. The good news is that our subordinate reaction is not sustainable if we want the freedom to be true to ourselves and live authentically. Simply put, subordination and authenticity are incompatible.

Freeing ourselves is a gradual process of awakening. Each time we can turn towards our difficult experience with curiosity and kindness, plunk our anchor in the reality of the present moment, inquire more deeply into exactly what's happening, accept that completely, and then query to find a *wise* and *kind* way to respond, we're poking a hole in the cloud cover of our conditioning. To use a different image, we're chipping away some of the dried clay masking our inner gold. As we practice, we become less caught in these habits, their power gradually diminishes, and we find ourselves more stable, more relaxed, and free to be who we authentically are in the moment.

If you've been practicing as you've been reading this book, then you're already cultivating your ability to be a spiritual warrior and growing unshakeable confidence. I hope you're sensing your inner strength and stability deepening. As you now know, this is not a practice of transcending, or of distracting ourselves and running away from what's difficult. Rather, it's a radical practice of turning right towards what is painful and uncomfortable, and by relating to it with the skills of mindfulness we find our way through it, learning more about our conditioned patterns and innate wisdom all along the way. This approach is what makes the practice so transformative and healing. It's just as the wise Zen proverb instructs: The obstacle is the path. The way out is through.

Checking in

- I hope you've had some meditation practice spotting self and seeing how quickly and often the mind constructs a self over and over. Have you also had some moments of experiencing the freedom from attachment to an idea of self? Isn't this amazing?

- In life off the cushion — our most important practice moments — I hope you've seen how automatically stories of self arise and how the stories hook us. When we can spot this and drop out of the story back to the body, we can free ourselves for the moment.

- I encourage you to study all the ways *me*, ego, or self operates. For example, notice how quickly the mind forms a possessive relationship to experience by creating "me" and "mine." Mindful awareness of ego is the quickest route to freedom and ease.

- Even if you haven't clearly spotted the mind repeatedly constructing the self yet, I hope your curiosity is piqued. Please keep watching for the construction of self.

In this last chapter, I"ll highlight the most important aspects of the practice that I hope you will carry with you. I"ll also suggest ways to continue deepening your practice, and share experiences other women have had learning mindfulness.

The Key Elements and Principles

• The three basic mindfulness questions: (1) What am I actually experiencing in this moment? (2) How am I relating to that? (3) Given this, what's a wise and kind way to respond to myself?

• This moment is all we have — we are only alive *now*, in this present moment. The present moment is the power moment.

• Whatever we're experiencing in the moment is always valid and worthy of our attention. There is nothing else that we should be experiencing.

• Curiosity, or "beginner's mind," opens the mind to what is real in this moment, creates inner spaciousness, and is the natural antidote to reactive habits.

• We practice relating to all that we experience with kindness, gentleness, and unlimited friendliness — no matter what.

• We practice disidentifying with direct experience. "We" are not our habit and patterns — nor are we our emotions, thoughts, judgments, or stories.

• Our true nature, our unconditioned mind, is who we really are: wise, kind, stable, accepting, compassionate, loving, joyful, free, intelligent, and generous. Our true nature is always here, like the blue sky, regardless of the temporary personal weather. Our true nature is awareness.

• The mind perceives, thinks, and continuously creates stories. Some thoughts are accurate, true, and beneficial. Most thoughts are not. We are developing discernment regarding which thoughts are useful, and which are not. *Don't believe everything you think.*

• Clinging to what we want and resisting what we don't want creates suffering.

• Resisting our direct experience always makes whatever we don't want to be happening last longer — it's a second arrow.

• It's possible to experience pain without suffering. Avoid "second arrows," those reactive add-ons, by bringing curiosity and acceptance to the actual sensations, just as they are.

• By accepting our direct experience just as it is in this moment, we create the internal conditions and spaciousness for it to shift and change naturally.

• Impermanence is the only constant in nature. Everything, on every dimension, is in the continual process of change.

• There's no limit to how much inner spaciousness we can bring to our experience when it's difficult. "Can I relax around this? Can I give this a little more space or room?"

• When we're caught in a painful emotion, it's an opportunity for healing. We're the crying baby in our living room and mindfulness is our mother.

• The root of all suffering is attaching to an idea of a separate, independent, fixed, permanent *me*, or self.

• Loving Kindness, Metta, is a spiritual balm for the mind-heart caught in suffering. Apply liberal doses to yourself and others as much as possible.

• Compassion is essential for healing because it opens the heart, allowing us to remain stable, steady, kind, and loving with the pain and suffering that's here.

A Path With Heart

One aspect I love so much about mindfulness is that it involves learning to relate to whatever we experience with unconditional friendliness: with love, curiosity, kindness, and compassion. It is a path with heart. This way of relating applies to everything, without exception — the habits of othering, aspects of yourself you've learned to judge and abhor, the scariest emotions, and the most difficult physical sensations. Contrary to our habits of criticizing, condemning, and turning against ourselves when we aren't experiencing what we'd like, it's love and kindness that heals. As the Buddha, along with many other wise teachers, said, "Hatred never ceases by hatred, but by love alone is healed. This is an ancient and eternal law."

In many ways this practice embodies the intention to become our own wise and loving parent. Perhaps we are becoming the parent we never had but always longed for. We are learning to guide ourselves skillfully and compassionately through the often treacherous landscapes of our painful patterns. We practice staying and not abandoning ourselves. We learn to not turn against ourselves. We are learning to be loyal to ourselves, having our own backs — no matter what. When we're hurt and feeling far away from our stable inner home, we can offer ourselves Loving Kindness, or simply the compassionate heartfelt wish, "May I find ease with this pain." The inherent gentleness of mindfulness and Metta create a safe container for our difficult feelings.

> It's love and kindness that heals.

Relating to Ourselves More Wisely and Kindly

Essentially, mindfulness brings awareness to how we're *relating* to our immediate experience, which allows us to *choose* a more prudent and skillful response. Over time, as we practice both formally and informally, we gently transform the old dysfunctional habits caused by othering. Hopefully, you're beginning to see aspects of this emerging in yourself.

Relating to Our Bodies

Instead of ignoring, abusing, and abandoning our bodies, we are listening to, accepting, and appreciating them. By becoming more sensitive to the physical sensations that are continuously arising and passing away, mindfulness helps us respect and learn from our bodies. Through learning to companion pain without suffering, we develop the freedom of not fearing pain. As we practice disidentifying with the body and understand that "*I am not my body*," we effortlessly become better caretakers of our physical selves.

After learning and practicing mindfulness in the nine-week class, most women describe being more attentive and kind to their bodies. Many say they are sleeping better, especially those challenged with waking in the middle of the night. Many report less suffering with chronic pain. In a recent class, a woman who had daily migraines for years said she hadn't suffered a headache since her third week of practicing. Others tell of changing their relationship to food through eating mindfully and curbing the habit of trashing their bodies. Among many who have declared, "Mindfulness has saved my life!" a woman dealing with advanced cancer said she was convinced it brought her body into remission.

> Mindfulness helps us respect and learn from our bodies.

Respecting Our Emotions

Rather than judging, trying to diminish, or becoming swept up and overwhelmed by our difficult emotions, we're learning to respect them when they arise. Viewing them as "good news" because they are opportunities for healing and deeper understanding, we're making friends with our difficult "visitors." We see how, like everything else, emotions are impermanent. The power of accepting what's painful, yet true in the moment, generates a vulnerability that's empowering and invincible. By embracing our difficult emotions with open hearts and mind, we can also enjoy the lovely and sweet emotions more fully.

In general, by the end of the class, women report feeling less stressed and anxious, less depressed, and more calm. The monkey mind is generally quieter. One woman who has lived with depression for many years said through mindfulness she realized she spent a lot of energy resisting that "I don't feel good" state. She was always trying to make herself feel better, urging herself to be more cheerful, and fighting the heaviness of depression. She discovered that when she can accept that she doesn't feel good, opens to it, investigates it and lets it be, she actually feels better and has more energy. Another woman dealing with grief said that now she's not afraid of the painful feelings. She knows they won't last forever. She also learned she can quickly find relief from anxiety by offering Metta to herself.

> Difficult emotions are opportunities for healing and deeper understanding.

Assuming Wise and Appropriate Responsibility

Instead of assuming we are always responsible for *everything*, and especially responsible for what goes "wrong" with others, jumping in to do and fix, while ignoring and exhausting ourselves, we're learning to take correct and wise responsibility for ourselves and others. We're learning to be aware of our own needs, knowing they matter too, and balance tending to them as we're aware of the other's needs. This leads to wiser choices about what is truly helpful and life-enhancing for both ourselves and others.

Correcting the balance of responsibility has a direct impact on everybody. In general, women report more time and space for themselves, and feeling less habitually driven to do for others. Jackie, whose college-aged son suffers from anxiety, discovered that by curbing her over-responsibility habit, both she and her son are happier. She had habitually hovered over him, trying to make sure he was doing everything he was suppoed to. Now that she is mindful of this habit and no longer hovers, he is taking on more responsibility

> Being aware of our own needs, knowing they matter too, we balance tending to them as we're aware of the other's needs.

for himself, feels more empowered and less anxious. Their relationship is more relaxed and they are having more fun together.

Sometimes, however, others don't appreciate these corrections in responsibility. Doris, an oldest daughter, was always the go-to person in her family, the one who would organize family events and play the role of the harmonizer in conflicts. The family relied on her to maintain these roles, but her othering exhausted her and she carried a lot of resentment. After taking the class, she said the more self-responsible she became, tending to her own thoughts and emotions and responding wisely to her own needs, the more her family complained. They preferred her the old way, doing it all.

Squaring Up to Conflict

Rather than avoiding conflict with others, being afraid to rock the boat, when we're respecting and trusting our authentic experience, we learn to hold our own with disagreements and differing needs, feelings, and ideas. By accepting our own experience and view, understanding it is just as valid as the other's, we empower ourselves to find our voice and express what's true. Understanding that expressing our view is our responsibility, we encourage ourselves to be steady, forthright, assertive, and open in handling conflict. Most women say they feel less intimidated with conflict after learning mindfulness, more willing to hold their own and stay on their own side, and can remain more centered and mindfully present in the midst of disagreement.

Tina told the story of her six-year-old daughter, Sofia, who came home crying one afternoon because the neighbor had frightened her by yelling, "When you see a dead bird on the ground next winter it will be your fault!" Tina thought Sofia must have misunderstood, so she went over to ask the neighbor what had happened. The neighbor was livid, saying that Sofia and her friends had been picking berries from a bush in her yard. The neighbor, who passionately loves birds, said, "Your irresponsible kids don't know anything about nature! They stole all the berries and now there will be nothing left for the birds to eat this winter." To this remark, Tina responded calmly with, "I'm sorry Sofia and her friends were picking berries from your yard, but I don't want you to yell at them. There's no reason to scare them." Tina said she practically skipped back home, feeling so proud of herself for staying so mindfully steady in the midst of this conflict. She had remained present and calm, yet authentic and forthright in expressing herself during this challenging interaction with her unstable neighbor.

Understanding that expressing our view is our responsibility, we encourage ourselves to be steady, forthright, and open in handling conflict.

Presenting Ourselves Authentically

Othering has taught us to be vigilant about managing the impressions we're making on others. As we come to truly accept and respect ourselves, our concern and need for impressing others dramatically falls away. Self-acceptance allows us to drop our self-consciousness and relax with ourselves just as we are. With the freedom of being honest and transparent, we can release the need to make a certain impression on the other. As we accept ourselves and let go of attachment to ego and conditioned ideas of self, we naturally have more trust that however we are in the moment is enough.

Self-acceptance allows us to drop our self-consciousness and relax with ourselves just as we are.

Tina's experience of being true to herself as she dealt with her upset neighbor is a good example of being free from impression management. She was authentic, present, and firm in the exchange. Less dramatically, many women say they have more ease in showing themselves authentically without the automatic habit of a smile, or the typical "I'm fine" response when someone asks how they are. They have a growing desire to be honest and clear. They realize that the burden of hiding and pretending to feel different is tiring and prevents real connection with others. The poem by Elizabeth Appell is apt, "And the day came when the risk to remain tight in a bud was more painful than the risk it took to blossom."[53] It can be a relief to simply be ourselves as we are. Yet, because being authentic isn't the norm in much of our culture, some people are taken aback and don't know how to respond to this brave honesty. This gap can feel unsettling, yet it's part of our practice as spiritual warriors to stay steady and open with that, too.

Accepting Ourselves with Compassion

Through mindfulness we learn to accept, trust, and respect our present moment experiences, and consequently the painful habits of judging and attaching to rigid ideas about how we're supposed be ease and soften. We let go of our conditioned ideas of self, and accept ourselves just as we are in the moment. As a result, we can be truly compassionate with ourselves when we experience pain and suffering. We stay loyal and steady with ourselves. In turn, we are authentically more accepting and compassionate of others.

Over and over, women report how mindfulness helps them become more accepting of themselves. Many say they are being more patient, kind, and gentle with themselves. They realize they are not crazy or flawed and are becoming real friends to themselves. Many say they are more tender with themselves when they're feeling difficult emotions, and see how this compassion spills over into their relationships with others. Instead of fearing painful feelings, they have more capacity to stay steady and centered while their loved one feels sad or upset.

One woman said learning this practice helped her treat long-standing anxiety. She was always "willing herself" to do things, to take care of others, to be how she thought she was supposed to be, despite the distress she felt. In this way, she was always fighting with herself, trying to make herself be different, and it was exhausting. Now, as she experiences the acceptance inherent in mindfulness, she waits until she feels her own willingness, her authentic desire to do something or take action, and as a result her energy is returning.

Another woman, a physician going through her obstetrics/gynecology residency, said that before learning mindfulness, whenever she completed a surgery, she would worry fitfully for the next twenty-four hours about her patient, fearing she had done something wrong. Her mind created scary stories, which sometimes led to panic attacks. Now she practices mindfulness during surgery, making the surgery itself a meditation: she's present in each moment with each action, each cut, each stitch. When the surgery is over, she feels relaxed, peaceful, and confident. She's free of othering, self-doubt, and worries about the patient.

> We let go of our conditioned ideas of self, and accept ourselves just as we are in the moment.

Letting Go of the Need to Control

Othering creates a tremendous need for control. When we're centered and grounded in self-acceptance, aware of our experience *as* we're aware of the other, we don't need to be exerting control over anyone. We trust and respect ourselves as we accept and relate to the other. We understand that we can actually control very little in life, other than choosing how we relate to our immediate experience.

Mattie described herself as hyperactive and controlling, always busy and needing to be perfect. She felt anxious and tense, frequently harping on her kids to do things differently and better. A self-admitted "helicopter parent," she habitually scurried around making sure her kids were always doing their best, and then worried, intervened, and corrected when they weren't. After learning mindfulness, she said she felt much less judgmental and controlling of herself and others, more slowed down, remarkably less tense, and happier. She said both her kids and friends were now commenting about how calm she has become. "It has been a huge shift," she said. "And I'm liking myself much more, too."

Setting Clear Personal Boundaries

Instead of habitually giving ourselves away, placing our center in the other and having few if any boundaries, being mindfully aware of our authentic experience empowers us to find our personal boundary. We can say "No" when we need to and be okay. The world doesn't fall apart. In fact, as we understand what we are actually responsible for, it's likely that everyone else is better off, too. By being honest with the other and ourselves, we avoid the potential pain and confusion born from the desire to be pleasing. We become more trustworthy to ourselves and to others.

Although Robin is devoted to taking care of her 85-year-old widowed mother, her relationship with her mother has always been difficult. Regardless of the effect on her own life, Robin always complied with her mother's demands, even though her mother has been stubborn, disapproving, controlling, and sometimes outright mean to her. At the beginning of the class, Robin confessed that she was waiting for her mother to die so she could begin to live her own life. After nine weeks of practice, she is building more space for her own life by employing some boundaries with her mother. Instead of instantly jumping to her mother's demands, she *chooses* when *she* wants to do the errands. Instead of tolerating cruel remarks, she now refuses to listen by leaving or ending a phone call, stating, "Ouch. That hurts Mom. Gotta go." The boundary she has now created by this clean interruption seems effective and less painful for both of them.

Another woman, Judy, always played the role of the good daughter in her family of origin, rearranging her life around everyone else's to

> Being mindfully aware of our authentic experience empowers us to find our personal boundary. We can say "No" when we need to and be okay.

accommodate their needs. Consequently, she had little opportunity to follow her own desires. After a lifetime of accommodation, mindfulness helped Judy wake up to her painful and long-standing bitterness, as well as to the guilt she felt whenever she'd attempt to create a boundary for herself. Now, understanding her conditioned habits, she accepts and companions her painful feelings, has the clarity that her needs are important, and is beginning to assert herself and say "No." By putting limits on how much she is willing to rearrange her life for others, she is feeling lighter and finding new zest for life as she makes room for her own interests and desires.

Appreciating and Trusting Ourselves

Ultimately, applying mindfulness to the habits of othering transforms the habits of self-doubt, self-loathing, and deep insecurity. We come to realize we can rely and depend upon our own agency and authority, which over time deepens our sense of unshakeable confidence. We come to trust and believe in ourselves.

With deepening awareness and self-acceptance, women describe their minds becoming quieter, feeling more relaxed with themselves, and having more clarity and confidence about what they want and the decisions they need to make. Marsha, who began the class on the verge of an emotional breakdown and trapped in an unhappy marriage, said the practice had been truly transformative. "By taking my monkey mind less personally, I now enjoy being with myself. I've turned off the radio and TV. I'm listening to myself deeply, and I'm now finally able to make a life-changing decision that I know is right for me."

> We can rely and depend upon our own agency and authority.

Elizabeth, claiming to be an expert otherer, always left social gatherings feeling like she stood out as the odd and stupid one, and would spend days beating up on herself for the ridiculous things she thought she said. Now she is different. Rarely does she have an "othering hang-over" after a social event. Instead, she goes to the event with the intention to mindfully stay with herself, and the effect is remarkable. She enjoys herself and the others, trusts that whatever she said is "good enough," and when she's caught in the old patterns of self-criticism and doubt, she names them for what they are, forgives herself, and lets them go. She says, "I've lightened up on myself so much. I trust myself way more, and I'm having a lot more fun."

Another woman who teaches courses in women's studies at the university said, "I'm a feminist. I teach about subordination and domination. I thought I had worked through all my internalized oppression, but I realize there's been a gap between my intellect and my conditioning. Mindfulness is the experience of being with and transforming the oppression that's still in my brain's patterns. Through this practice, I'm building a healthy relationship with myself. Finally, I feel like I'm truly rooting out the remaining dregs of internalized oppression. I'm connecting with the power in me, and it's freeing."

So Now What? Get to the Gym for Regular Exercise

Sitting meditation, the intensive work out for the mind, is our formal support for developing the skills of mindfulness and learning to stay with our authentic experience. Establish a daily sitting practice to build your mindfulness muscles. Doing so is a radical act of self-care and flies in the face of othering. Most of the women who take class with me initially find it difficult to make room for daily practice. The common complaint that "I just don't have the time" reflects the conditioned urge "to do," and especially to do for others, along with the deep belief that our own self-care needs and time don't matter as much. I encourage you to summon your power and make the choice to sit and meditate every day. It's an act of empowerment, and it's all up to you.

It may help to remember that our brains have neuroplasticity, meaning they are flexible and change in response to practice. We're wise to practice what inclines us towards less suffering and more happiness. Solid science shows meditating daily brings about beneficial and measurable changes in the brain. Good evidence also indicates that the area called the default mode network, the aspect of the brain that generates personal narratives — those habitual stories of me — grows smaller, and the insula, where body and subjective awareness reside, grows bigger. Daily meditation helps us move out of the mind's stories and connect with our actual lived experiences. Connected with our authenticity we feel more alive, whole, empowered, and free to be however we are in the moment.

Sitting meditation is a radical act of self-care and flies in the face of othering.

It's best, then, to sit *every day* for whatever amount of time you can manage. The daily practice and the repetition are what matters, not so much the length of time you sit. Just like building physical strength, we see gains more quickly if we exercise daily rather than once a week. Find an amount of time you can manage, and then sit and practice every day. *You can do this.* Truly, there is no reason you can't find even five minutes a day that's just yours for meditation practice.

Bring It Into Our Lives: The Power of Informal Practice

Given the whole point of formal meditation is to train us be awake as we live our lives, it's smart to extend our practice intentionally into daily activities. By now I'm sure you've realized that one of the biggest challenges is *remembering* to be mindful. Those neural grooves pull us back into our dream silently and swiftly. It takes clear intention and sometimes herculean effort to bring ourselves back to mindfulness again and again.

The Dropping In practice is invaluable to use throughout the day. As often as possible, intentionally shift awareness inward to breathe several breaths mindfully and then ask the three core questions: "What am I experiencing right now, exactly? How am I relating to this? Given this, what's a wise and kind way to respond to myself right now?" This simple practice builds presence and helps us sustain mindfulness throughout the day.

As you know by now, every time we can be 100 percent present as we listen to our friend or snuggle with our child or sweetie, it's profoundly beneficial. It's a moment of authentic loving connection, and real connection is a core human need. We're all hungry for it. Every time we choose to mindfully enjoy a meal, our morning coffee, or a fine piece of chocolate, we experience the pure deliciousness and the sense pleasures of living in this body. Likewise, doing ordinary or even tedious activities mindfully, like folding laundry or shoveling snow, makes them more interesting. By concentrating solely on the activity, we give our busy discursive story-making mind a much needed rest.

We can trust that as we practice, change is happening, even if it isn't yet apparent. A woman taking the class for the second time said she was really "bad" at practicing because she just couldn't remember to do it. Yet, she reported this experience: "I awoke in the middle of the night feeling completely caught up in anger — older anger at my family. My mind was spewing the old stories rapidly, one after another. Then suddenly, as if out of nowhere it occurred to me, 'Oh, this is anger.' And then a moment later I thought, 'And I can let it go.' A moment later the anger simply disappeared and I went right back to sleep. When I woke up in the morning and recalled this, I was amazed at the power of mindfulness and wondered, 'Where did this thought or awareness come from? How did I manage to remember to be mindful?'" The effect of practicing does sink in.

Set the Intention to Practice

Because it's not our habit to be mindful, it can be a great help to create specific intentions for practice. Establishing intention is like setting

367

our compass in the direction we want to go. The intention becomes our North Star guiding us in the right direction. "Wise Intention" is one of the aspects of the Eightfold Noble Path, the map for the journey to freedom from suffering in the Buddha's teachings of the Four Noble Truths. Clear and beneficial intention is necessary to help us travel towards more ease and freedom.

You might create the intention to meditate every day for a certain number of minutes, as well as set intentions to practice informally. If a particular habit is clearly causing you suffering, you might work to intentionally spot it and interrupt it. You might set your intention to be aware of some aspect of othering, like being overly responsible, or operating out of the conditioned belief that you're not enough. Or, if you have the habit of zooming off in your to-do list whenever you take a shower, and find yourself tense and stressed as you dry off, then intending to shower mindfully could be a kind and wise practice.

With intentions set, we have to follow through and embark on our plan or nothing will change. Many of us set the bar of achievement so high that we disappoint ourselves, which only adds more suffering. Please be kind and wise with yourself. Be sure to appreciate any efforts to follow your intention. Keeping a practice journal can be a gentle and effective way to create accountability for yourself.

Practice With Others

It's generally easier to meditate in a group than solo. People practicing together is energetically helpful. Perhaps it's because intentions are aligned, or values of the group members are likely congruent, or because we're all intending to be present, stable, and mindful at exactly the same time. Regardless, a practice community, or sangha, is a wonderful and rich support for practice.

One way to find a sangha and deepen your practice is to take a class in mindfulness. Meditation classes offer a rich learning environment because you're not only benefiting from the teacher's experience and instructions on the practice, but you also benefit from the rich sharing of experiences from the other students. It's affirming to realize your mind isn't the only one that does such goofy, bizarre, or trying things. The women in my classes are always deeply appreciative of all they learn from each other as they practice learning the method together.

Go on Retreats

The best way to intensively deepen your practice is to attend a silent mindfulness meditation retreat. I have found intensive retreats to be profoundly healing and transformative. A one-day retreat is a gentle way to begin. Later, you might feel comfortable expanding to a weekend retreat, and perhaps then to seven days or more. Centers in the U.S. and around the world regularly offer retreats throughout the year, ranging from three days to three months, all supported and guided by amazing teachers.

In the retreat context, we unplug from regular life, and with the aid of Noble Silence, we practice sustaining mindfulness from the time we wake up to when we go to bed at night. Seamlessness of attention, as it's called, serves to powerfully focus awareness. In my own experience, it is possible to observe and work with the mind with much more depth, clarity, and understanding than is possible in a daily sitting practice at home. Retreats are often life-changing experiences.

The Willingness to Begin Again

Healing from the oppression of othering and helping our minds become free, open, and less caught up in the debris of conditioned habits takes courage, commitment, effort, and patience. It's all practice. When we   It's all practice! forget and find ourselves swamped in the old painful patterns again — second-guessing ourselves, caught up in believing we're the worst, or stuck in trying to assure perfection

369

— at whatever moment we wake up to the mind's stories, we're already back. We can be happy that we woke up, and begin again. In many ways, mindfulness is the willingness to wholeheartedly return to the present moment and begin again.

Each time we practice matters: we turn towards our habitual reactions with kindness and compassion and recognize them for what they are. We see they are conditioned beliefs and habits, not true and no longer serving us. We let go of the content, shift attention to the breath and body, and discover what is true and real in the moment. We are loving ourselves just as we are, building trust in our ability to be present and stable, and resting, even if briefly, in the wisdom and spaciousness of our true nature. Every time we practice, we're training and inclining our mind towards becoming our own best parent and best friend. Just as a bucket becomes filled with water one drop at a time, so too does the mind through practice gradually become more clear, stable, and reliable. Steadily as we practice, we are cultivating our appetite for living authentically in the present and building trust in our capacity to handle and respond wisely to all that arises in life: the ten thousand joys and the ten thousand sorrows.

> Mindfulness is the willingness to wholeheartedly return to the present moment and begin again.

The World Needs Us to Be Authentic and Strong

To free ourselves from othering, we let go of believing in a "not good enough me." We accept and trust ourselves just as we are, knowing we are enough and have always been enough. Centered in our authentic present-moment experience, rather than other-centered, we establish wise balance in our attention between self and other. We know and accept our genuine experiences as we relate to the other. As we inhabit this way of being, we let go of the conditioned ideas of self and how we're supposed to be and increasingly reside in the stable spaciousness of our true nature, our blue sky mind. From this place of connection and balance, we naturally respond skillfully to whatever is here in this moment with kindness, wisdom, compassion.

We know this takes courage. We are being spiritual warriors as we explore the unknown, moment by moment, staying with our direct experience and encouraging ourselves to let go of those familiar patterns and their underlying beliefs. We are building faith and trust in ourselves each time we can mindfully open to what's difficult, even though it's scary or painful and we feel vulnerable. As we stay steady through the difficulty and realize we're actually okay, we come to understand ourselves more deeply. We realize we have the answers within ourselves, and can access tremendous wisdom. We're cultivating our own inner strength and stability. No one has the key to cultivating strength and stability but ourselves. We're learning that we can handle what arises. We're cultivating unshakeable confidence.

> By understanding that we are each 100 percent responsible for our own experience, we become our own source of power, acceptance, and validation.

The way I see it, freeing ourselves from the habits of othering is our personal responsibility. No one else can be responsible for what we're thinking, feeling, hoping, and fearing but ourselves. It is our responsibility to empower ourselves. By understanding and accepting that in the end we are each are 100 percent responsible for our own experience, we become our own source of power, acceptance, and validation.

Because everything in life is interdependent, doing this transformative work is our spiritual responsibility as well. How we are, how we feel about ourselves, and how we act and behave affects every person we have contact with, and therefore affects the world. The more we can live our moments present, centered, authentic, and accessing the wisdom and kindness of our true nature, the more everyone benefits. The more we accept, respect, and trust ourselves, the more we relate to others in the same healing and loving way. This is how we change the world, beginning with the one person whose life we actually can save: our own. In these challenging and uncertain times, the world desperately needs us all to be our authentic, powerful, and amazing womanly selves.

Every time you meditate, every time you recognize you're othering and mindfully pause to breathe and find your authentic self and wise response, you are making a difference, not only for yourself and your life, but for all beings. Because everything is interconnected and nothing and no one exists independently, each time you liberate yourself from your conditioned habits and internalized oppression, you are helping the world. Each moment of your growing freedom truly matters.

> Each time you liberate yourself from your conditioned habits and internalized oppression, you are helping the world.

The Quest

We must encourage ourselves to be brave and curious, to be our own wise and loving loyal friend, and invite ourselves to stay when we experience discomfort. We coach ourselves to come back with gentleness, tenderness, and patience when we realize we've turned against ourselves again. We commit to accepting ourselves and staying on our own side, no matter what we are experiencing, out of respect and care for ourselves. At whatever moment we wake up and realize we've been gone again, we companion ourselves back to this moment gently and kindly, and then begin again, understanding we are spiritual warriors in training. This is the essential practice for living our lives with *unshakeable confidence.*

May you accept yourself completely.
May you know that you are enough.
May you be your own best friend.
May you be happy and free from fear.
May you live with unshakeable confidence.
May all beings be free.

Acknowledgements

This book has been a true labor of love and is the result of so many amazing women sharing their hearts, minds, talents and wisdom. I am forever grateful to the first twenty-five women in the pilot study, and to all who have since taken class with me. You have taught me so much. I bow to your willingness to bring mindfulness to these conditioned patterns and your courage to live authentically.

To my book team, my heartfelt gratitude for devoting your time and vast expertise to this project. For Lisa Ruffolo's kind and painstaking editing, for Lillian Sizemore's capable and creative talents to bring the project into this form, and for Kate Peyton's continual encouragement, feminist spirit and dedication to the practice. And for Pam Porter, my best friend, spouse and partner in aiming to make the world healthier, more loving and just. I could not have completed this project without her consistent encouragement, tireless efforts, and amazing talents.

A very special thanks to Sharon Salzberg and Tara Brach for their profound teachings and generous support. My deep appreciation to Dale Kushner for her dear friendship, faithful encouragement, and professional guidance. And whole-hearted gratitude to Roseanne Clark for her generous contribution and unending support.

My everlasting gratitude also goes to my dear friends and dharma sisters Mary Bennett, Cheri Maples, Jackie Beaudet, Kalleen Mortensen, Maureen Brady, Kiva Adler, and Mary Carson Bumann. Their love, guidance, kindness, deep conversation and support has helped me stay steady through this process.

Finally, I am enormously grateful to my family. To my parents, Lois and Lloyd, who raised me to value service and equality. To my grandfather, Henry De Pree, who advised me to be a big as I could be. And to my beautiful children, Dave and Wendy, and my grandchildren Josh, Evan, Addie and Henry Toki, who are my greatest teachers and continual source of inspiration.

About the Author

Mare Chapman. M.A., is a psychotherapist and mindfulness teacher in private practice since 1983. An insight meditation (vipassana) practitioner for 30 years, she finds mindfulness to be the most transformative tool for working with the mind, healing deeply conditioned habits, and handling the gamut of life's challenges with greater ease and stability. Also trained in interactive guided imagery, a method for using the imagination to heal challenges in the body and mind, Mare brings a truly holistic approach to her work.

Mare began her work at Lafayette Clinic, a psychiatric hospital in Detroit, Michigan, and taught undergraduate classes at Wayne State University and the University of Wisconsin, Madison. In 1976 she founded and directed the Yahara House, the first non-profit in Wisconsin to offer day treatment services for adults with chronic mental illness. Mare teaches a popular nine-week "Mindfulness for Women" class, on which this book is based. She has mentored more than 5000 students through mindfulness classes on a range of other applications including self-acceptance, compassion, befriending fear, chronic pain and life-threatening illness, eating disorders, Loving Kindness, LGBTQ issues, and teen challenges. She leads day-long and three-day meditation retreats.

Additionally, Mare gives presentations, conducts trainings, and consults with companies and non-profits on mindfulness. She teaches mindfulness to clinicians through the Department of Psychiatry, and Continuing Education at the University of Wisconsin, Madison. She is the author of five journal articles and two audio podcasts, *Cultivating Mindfulness Through Insight Meditation*, and *Cultivating Mindfulness: Physical Pain and Difficult Emotions*. These are available at marechapman.com.

An avid bicyclist, track racing champion, and nature lover, Mare has two children and four grandchildren, and lives in Madison, Wisconsin with her spouse Pam, their dog Gracie and cat Smokie Joe.

Notes

[1] Chapman, M. (1995). *Using Mindfulness to Create a Healthier Connection to Self in Women*, Norwich University. Montpelier, Vermont.

[2] Miller, J. B. (1986). *Toward a New Psychology of Women*, Beacon Press, Boston.

[3] Brown, L. & Gilligan, C. (1992). *Meeting at the Crossroads: Women's Psychology and Girls Development*, Harvard University Press, Boston.

[4] Bayda, E. (2004). *At Home in the Muddy Water: A Guide to Finding Peace within Everyday Chaos*, Shambhala, Boston.

[5] Brown, B. (2010). *The Gifts of Imperfection: Let Go of Who You Think You're Supposed to Be and Embrace Who You Are*, Hazelden, Center City, Minnesota.

[6] Spar, D. (2013). *Wonder Women: Women, Sex, Power, and the Quest for Perfection*, Sarah Crichton Books, New York.

[7] Brown, L. & Gilligan, C. (1992). *Meeting at the Crossroads: Women's Psychology and Girls Development*, Harvard University Press, Boston.

[8] *Research agenda for psychosocial and behavioral factors in women's health.* (1996, February). Washington, DC: Women's Programs Office, American Psychological Association.

[9] Glied, S. & Kofman, S. (1995, March). *Women and mental health: Issues for health reform background paper.* New York: The Commonwealth Fund, Commission on Women's Health.

[10] National Alliance on Mental Illness. (2016). *Facts for Policymakers: Treatable Causes of Disability.* Retrieved from nami.org: http://www2.nami.org/walkTemplate.cfm?Section=NAMIWALKS&template=/ContentManagement/ContentDisplay.cfm&ContentID=42745.

[11] hooks, b. (2001). *All About Love: New Visions*, Harper Collins Publishers, New York.

[12] Chödrön, P. (1997). *When Things Fall Apart: Heart Advice for Difficult Times*, Shambhala, Boston.

[13] Boorstein, S. (1997). *It's Easier Than You Think: The Buddhist Way to Happiness*, HarperOne, San Francisco.

[14] Kabat-Zinn, J. (1990). *Full Catastrophe Living: Using the Wisdom of Your Body and Mind to Face Stress, Pain and Illness*, Delacorte Press, New York.

[15] Hanson, R. (2009). *Buddha's Brain: The Practical Neuroscience of Happiness, Love and Wisdom*, New Harbinger Publications, Oakland.

[16] Suzuki, S. (2006). *Zen Mind, Beginner's Mind*, Shambhala, San Francisco.

[17] Hanson, R. (2009). *Buddha's Brain: The Practical Neuroscience of Happiness, Love and Wisdom*, New Harbinger Publications, Oakland.

[18] Salzberg, S. Loving Kindness Retreat, (2010, July). Madison, Wisconsin.

[19] Rimer, S. (2007, April 1). For Girls, It's Be Yourself, and Be Perfect, Too. *The New York Times*, p. A1.

[20] Begley, S. (2007). *Train Your Mind, Change Your Brain.* Ballantine Books, New York.

[21] Salzberg, S. (2014). *Real Happiness.* Workman Publishing, New York.

[22] Nhat Hanh, T. (2012). *Fear: Essential Wisdom for Getting Through the Storm*, Harper Collins, New York.

[23] Brown, L. & Gilligan, C. (1992). *Meeting at the Crossroads: Women's Psychology and Girls Development*, Harvard University Press, Boston.

[24] Tolle, E. (1999). *The Power of Now*, New World Library, San Francisco.

[25] Taylor, J.B. (2008). *My Stroke of Insight: A Brain Scientist's Personal Journey*, Viking. New York.

[26] Pert, C. (1999). *Molecules of Emotion: The Science Between Mind-Body Medicine*, Scribner, New York.

[27] Greenspan, M. (2003). *Healing Through the Dark Emotions*, Shambhala, Boston.

[28] Davidson, R. & Begley, S. (2012). *The Emotional Life of Your Brain: How its Unique Patterns Affect the Way You Think, Feel and Live – and How You Can Change Them.* Penguin Books. London.

[29] Brach, T. (2003). *Radical Acceptance: Embracing Your Life with The Heart of a Buddha*, Random Dell, New York.

[30] Nhat Hanh, T. (1991). *Peace is Every Step*, Bantam Books, New York.

[31] Gilligan, C. (1982). *In a Different Voice: Psychological Theory and Women's Development*, Harvard University Press, Cambridge.

[32] Miller, J.B. (1986). *Toward a New Psychology of Women*, Beacon Press, Boston.

[33] Bepko, C. and Krestan, J. (1991). *Too Good for Her Own Good*, HarperCollins, New York.

[34] Spar, D. (2013). *Wonder Woman: Sex, Power, and the Quest for Perfection*, Sarah Crichton Books, New York.

[35] Goldstein, J. (2003). *Insight Meditation: The Practice of Freedom*, Shambhala, Boston.

[36] De Beauvoir, S. (1952). *The Second Sex*, Alfred A. Knopf, New York.

[37] National Coalition Against Domestic Violence, *www.ncadv.org/learn/statistics.*

[38] Brown, B. (2010). *The Gifts of Imperfection: Let Go of Who You Think You're Supposed to Be and Embrace Who You Are*, Hazelden, Center City, Minnesota.

[39] Brown, L. & Gilligan, C. (1992). *Meeting at the Crossroads: Women's Psychology and Girls Development*, Harvard University Press, Boston.

[40] Pipher, M. (1994). *Reviving Ophelia: Saving the Lives of Adolescent Girls*, Ballantine Books, New York.

[41] Hinshaw, S. (2009). *The Triple Bind: Saving our Teenage Girls from Today's Pressures.* Ballantine, New York.

[42] Feldman, C. (1990). *Woman Awake*, Penguin, London.

[43] Hanson, R. (2009). *The Practical Neuroscience of Buddha's Brain*, New Harbinger Publications, Oakland.

[44] Salzberg, S. (1995). *Loving Kindness*, Shambhala, Boston.

[45] Neff, K. (2011). *Self-Compassion: Stop Beating Yourself Up and Leave Insecurity Behind*, Harper Collins, New York.

[46] Richo, D. (2015). *You Are Not What You Think*, Shambhala, Boston.

[47] Smith, R. (2010). *Stepping Out of Self-Deception. The Buddha's Liberating Teaching of No-Self*, Shambhala, Boston.

[48] Khema, A. (1999). *Be an Island. The Buddhist Practice of Inner Peace*, Wisdom Publications, Boston.

[49] Joko Beck, C. (1989). *Everyday Zen. Love and Work*, Harper, San Francisco.

[50] Feldman, C. (2014). Women's Retreat, Spirit Rock Meditation Center. Woodacre, California.

[51] Smith, R. (2010). *Stepping Out of Self-Deception. The Buddha's Liberating Teaching of No-Self*, Shambhala, Boston.

[52] Chödrön, P. (2001). "Pema Chodron: To Know Yourself is to Forget Yourself" *Shambhala Sun*.

[53] Records show that this quote was written by Elizabeth Appell while she was working at the John Kennedy University in Orinda, California. However, it is commonly attributed to Anais Nin. See http://anaisninblog.skybluepress.com/2013/03/who-wrote-risk-is-the-mystery-solved.

44277703R00217

Made in the USA
San Bernardino, CA
11 January 2017